RAJA DHANDAPANI

Java & BAPI Technology for

SAP®

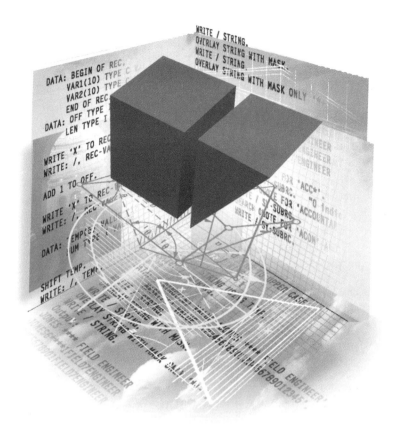

Java & BAPI Technology for
SAP®

Ken Kroes
with
Anil Thakur

A Division of Prima Publishing

A Division of Prima Publishing

Prima Publishing and colophon are registered trademarks of Prima Communications, Inc. PRIMA TECH is a trademark of Prima Communications, Inc., Roseville, California 95661.

SAP, R/3, and BAPI are either registered trademarks or trademarks of SAP Aktiengesellschaft, Systems, Applications and Products in Data Processing, Neurottstrasse 16, 69190 Walldorf, Germany. SAP is not the publisher of this book and is not responsible for it under any aspect of press law.

Java and JavaBeans are trademarks of Sun Microsystems, Inc.

Microsoft, Windows, Windows NT, ActiveX, and Visual Basic are registered trademarks of Microsoft Corporation.

Important: Prima Publishing cannot provide software support. Please contact the appropriate software manufacturer's technical support line or Web site for assistance.

Prima Publishing and the author have attempted throughout this book to distinguish proprietary trademarks from descriptive terms by following the capitalization style used by the manufacturer.

Information contained in this book has been obtained by Prima Publishing from sources believed to be reliable. However, because of the possibility of human or mechanical error by our sources, Prima Publishing, or others, the Publisher does not guarantee the accuracy, adequacy, or completeness of any information and is not responsible for any errors or omissions or the results obtained from use of such information. Readers should be particularly aware of the fact that the Internet is an ever-changing entity. Some facts may have changed since this book went to press.

ISBN: 0-7615-2305-7
Library of Congress Catalog Card Number: 99-64788
Printed in the United States of America

00 01 02 03 04 DD 10 9 8 7 6 5 4 3 2 1

Publisher:
Stacy L. Hiquet

Marketing Manager:
Judi Taylor

Associate Marketing Manager:
Heather Buzzingham

Managing Editor:
Sandy Doell

Acquisitions Editor:
Jawahara Saidullah

Senior Editor:
Kim V. Benbow

Project Editor:
Estelle Manticas

Editorial Assistant:
Cathleen D. Snyder

Technical Reviewer:
Anil Thakur

Copy Editor:
June Waldman

Interior Layout:
Marian Hartsough

Cover Design:
Prima Design Team

Indexer:
Johnna VanHoose

To my wife Donna and children Megan and Jarid;
thanks for your support over the past several months.

—KK

Acknowledgments

The authors wish to acknowledge and thank Matt Carleson and Stacy Hiquet for their continued support and vision throughout the development of this book and the entire SAP series, and Jawahara Saidullah, Estelle Manticas, and Cathleen Snyder, for their patience and moral support throughout the writing process.

Finally, the authors wish to thank SAP America.

About the Authors

Ken Kroes has over 17 years of programming and consulting experience and has worked as an independent SAP consultant in both R/2 and R/3 for many large clients. Since completing his engineering degree at the University of Calgary, Canada, Ken has worked in a variety of business areas and is currently specializing in implementing SAP for clients with build-to-order (configurable) products and Internet applications. Contact Ken at kenkroes@bigfoot.com.

Anil Thakur operates a boutique consulting firm specializing in Web-enabling ERP Implementation. He has worked as a senior consultant offering ERP and E-commerce expertise to Fortune 500 companies such as Kodak and Hewlett-Packard. In addition, he performs independent code reviews, writes white papers on integrating SAP to E-commerce environments, and makes technical presentations at various client sites.

Contents at a Glance

Contents

Chapter 3 VisualAge for Java. 25

PART III   **DETAILS ON JAVA RFC AND
BAPI CONNECTIONS. 301**

Chapter 19 **The COM.SAP.RFC Package 303**

Appendix B Basic HTML Reference............ 377

Introduction

This book is the bridge between what has been up until now two different areas of application development. The first area is development within the SAP environment, where the code is written in SAP's programming language, ABAP; the second area is development with two of the primary Internet development tools, Java programming and HTML (*Hypertext Markup Language*). In my experience, most programmers handle and stay current in only one of these areas, resulting in cumbersome solutions that could be performed simply if the two areas were melded.

In addition to covering the technical details of programming in Java, BAPIs (*Business Application Programming Interfaces*), and their integration within SAP, this book also covers the methodology that you can use to determine which development approach is best for solving a specific problem. The integration of the various modules within SAP—such as the employee or sales module—to other applications, and the ability to access SAP data are becoming more and more important as e-commerce within and between corporations increases.

Until about release 4.0 of SAP, integrating the ERP (*Enterprise Resource Planning*) systems with other solutions was not easy. Even development within SAP itself has been difficult, requiring thorough knowledge of how the different tables are related to one another in order to accomplish a specific business transaction or report. For example, consider a report that is supposed to display a list of materials. In addition to reading directly from the main table that contains materials (MARA), in earlier releases of SAP you must also access other tables for descriptions (MAKT), plant-specific information (MARC), and perhaps sales information (MVKE). You may also have to filter materials or views that are marked for deletion.

SAP has now cleared most of these hurdles with the introduction of the SAP Automation toolkit and the concept of BAPIs. Now, to get a list of materials, you simply perform one function module call, and the logic for the different tables, delete indicators, and so on is taken care of automatically.

SAP and other software manufacturers are beginning to develop the tools that allow users to access ERP systems with other development languages, such as Java, Visual Basic, and C++. While all of these languages can be used with SAP Automation software, this book concentrates on Java because it is currently the most popular programming language for Web development, and because it allows you to develop truly platform-independent code.

If you believe that an ERP system should provide all of the software needed to run a large corporation, you may wonder why anyone would want to use Java to access an SAP or other system. The answer goes back to the fundamentals of installing an ERP solution. The simple installation of a system such as SAP is not the end of system integration within a corporation, but merely the beginning. An SAP installation can be thought of as the primary building block in a complete data solution. After the ERP system is up and running, all primary business transactions are performed and all data is stored in one central location. Then the real synergy begins, with the ability to create reports and applications that will streamline business processes. Data that used to be stored in multiple databases can now be accessed through a single database.

Many clients that I have worked with have misunderstood this concept of developing and streamlining business software after the ERP solution has been installed. They believe that they will see instant cost savings and faster throughput times as soon as the ERP system is installed. What usually happens, however, is just the opposite. During the first year after a major ERP solution is introduced, costs for both support and training generally increase as people become familiar with the new environment. It's in the second year that clients begin to see ways to make their business methods more efficient; that's when the development really pays off and the cost savings are realized.

The SAP ERP system can be accessed through the standard SAP GUI (*Graphical User Interface*), through the Internet Transaction Server, or through custom applications. The last method is the main focus of this book. Through the use of BAPIs and Java, data and even entire business processes are accessible from this core data system. You can take information to a Web page directly from the SAP system, and because of the fundamentals of Java, the Web page or application can be run on any computer in the company. Java is platform independent, which reduces both development and ongoing maintenance costs for custom software.

This book also introduces other topics and technologies that are related to ERP software integration and Web development. Though the primary tool used in this book is the SAP Automation toolkit, one chapter covers tools such as IBM's VisualAge, and another is devoted to the ITS (*Internet Transaction Server*) technology from SAP. Other topics, such as ActiveX controls and COM (*Component Object Model*) compliant programming, are also discussed, in order to broaden your understanding of how the software development universe is evolving. This book also contains sections on HTML developments, along with many Internet URLs (*Uniform Resource Locators*) that will lead you to more current or more detailed information.

The basics of Java language make up the first part of the book. If you have never programmed in Java before, these chapters will teach you enough to develop fairly complex applications, and will give you a foundation for learning more about the Java language and its various classes. Readers who are familiar with Java may want to browse through this section as well. Java 2.0 introduces many new commands; for example, the first section of the book shows how to properly handle listening for events, such as buttons or field I/O (*Input/Output*) in Java 2.0. I spend a fair bit of time on the fundamentals of Java and object-oriented programming in general; with a good understanding of the fundamentals of Java, figuring out the more advanced concepts is relatively easy. The background material on object-oriented programming is also a good base for ABAP (*Advanced Business Application Programming*) programmers, as SAP is working to develop ABAP into a true object-oriented programming language.

The second section of this book focuses on how to integrate Java with SAP. This section covers the basics of integrating the SAP Automation toolkit so that you can develop applets or Java applications and access data within SAP. The examples start with step-by-step instructions for building simple projects, and then evolve into practical examples that allow you to see how the two areas, Java and SAP, can be used together. The Java classes that are used to integrate into SAP are discussed in detail so that even demanding applications can be written. Topics include connectivity through intranets, security, and exception handling.

SAP BAPIs

The final section of the book concerns SAP BAPIs, which are the main function blocks used in the integration of Java and other applications. BAPIs enable programmers who are not fully fluent in how the SAP database is set up to write programs that perform SAP business transactions or generate reports. This section also covers what BAPIs are, how to find them within SAP, and how to build your own custom BAPIs.

Finally, this book is meant to be an introduction to Java programming within the SAP environment. Many step-by-step examples help you fully reproduce and understand the concepts that are introduced. For example, an entire chapter is devoted to the installation and setup of the development environment. Usually, too much haste is made when getting started in new development areas, and counterproductive habits are learned early on. It is my philosophy that if people take the time to understand the basics well, then the advanced topics will come naturally.

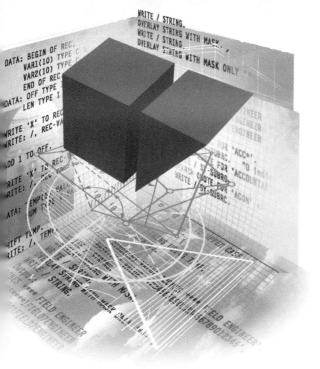

PART

I

The Basics

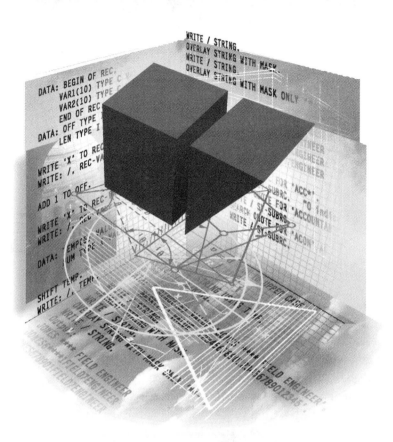

Chapter 1

The Roles of Java in the ERP Industry

In This Chapter

- Why Use Java?
- Advantages and Disadvantages of Java
- Java with SAP
- Other ERP Providers
- The Future of Java

The Java programming language is a young computer programming language that is becoming accepted as a stable, platform-independent tool that speeds up and reduces the cost of development and support. Java now ranks third as the preferred programming language, behind Visual Basic and C/C++. Such a standing isn't bad for a programming language that has been around for less than a decade. Java's increase in popularity is due to several factors, including solid product support, a growing need to develop software that will run on a variety of platforms, and the need to find an efficient and secure way to execute client/server applications.

The acceptance of Java does not mean that Java will replace ABAP, C/C++, Visual Basic, and other software programming languages. Instead, many ERP (*Enterprise Resource Planning*) environments use Java as a tool in several unique areas, usually related to Internet applications and other interactions between ERP systems and complementary third-party software.

Why Use Java?

To begin to understand why Java is becoming popular, you need to understand the development requirements that companies face in today's environment. Technology on both a hardware and software level is moving very quickly. The Internet and the e-commerce revolution that are currently underway are putting huge strains on IT (*Information Technology*) departments to come up with solutions at "Internet speed." Developing and supporting the same software across multiple platforms and operating systems is a very costly and time-consuming endeavor for software development shops. In the case of C/C++, you need to move the code to each hardware/OS platform and perform a compilation of the program. The code usually also needs to be modified to accommodate special features of the platform. If a problem is found in the software, the same code needs to be fixed on all the platforms and then recompiled and tested. Java eliminates these problems because there is only one version of the code, and it will behave the same way on all systems (with just a few exceptions). If a new operating system appears, as Linux did, software that was developed in Java can be executed immediately, whereas with C/C++ the code needs to be recompiled and then shipped to the customer.

Corporate IT departments also like to keep things simple. Finding qualified IT specialists is hard enough these days; finding specialists for a variety of languages is even harder. Therefore, when installing new applications, companies like to find applications that can be supported by their current IT infrastructure. With Java, these corporations do not have to invest in training or hiring people to support various languages.

Another challenge that IT departments face comes when the realization dawns that the installation of an ERP is only the beginning of a complete information solution. Data warehouses, production-planning optimizers, front-end sales CRM (*Customer Relationship Management*) packages, and other applications integrate into the ERP systems and make use of the centralized data and support services. Depending on the ERP system and the customizations that were made to it, a fair bit of development work is usually involved in integrating these systems.

Also, keep in mind that one reason for installing ERP systems in the first place is to reduce the overall long-term IT budget (for example, companies will not have to maintain skill sets to support numerous systems and programming languages.) Companies are more inclined to purchase third-party software to integrate into their own solution if the proposed package will save them exorbitant staffing costs.

Advantages and Disadvantages of Java

Java is best known for its ability to execute programs on computers over the Internet. Through the World Wide Web, programs can be downloaded to a user's computer; these programs, known as *applets*, can be used to create animation, figures, forms, and other functions that make a Web page more functional. Though enhancing user interfaces is an important area for Java, the language is also used to develop entire applications and is also now becoming a common gateway or portal tool for systems integration.

By design, Java is platform independent; this is one of Java's strongest advantages over other languages. If you program something in C or in most other languages, the compiler translates your source file into assembly instructions that can be read and executed only for the processor on which your computer is running. Java gets around this problem by compiling your source code into instructions that can be read and executed by a program commonly referred to as the *Java interpreter*, *Java Runtime*, or the *Java virtual machine*. Therefore, as long as a hardware platform has a Java interpreter, it can execute any Java program. As more Internet technology is developed, the use of Java will no doubt increase. Consider the emerging technology of Web appliances, which will rely on many different processor chips. Anyone who wants to write software to execute on these platforms will undoubtedly use Java, because it is becoming the standard. Every processor/operating system in this new arena is sure to include a Java interpreter.

Another key advantage of Java is that it is built with security in mind. This feature is not necessarily true for other programming languages. If you execute a Java program from the Internet (an applet), the program can neither write to files on your computer nor connect to Web servers other than the one on which it has been stored. In addition, restrictions prevent applets from executing other programs on the computer on which they are executing, and applets cannot define native methods.

Because Java is an OOP (*Object-Oriented Programming*) language, learning it is relatively easy for programmers who are used to other OOP languages, such as C++. This feature is important because C++ is currently the second most popular programming language, and experienced programmers need an easy migration path to move from C++ to Java.

Java, however, does have some disadvantages that hinder its acceptance in some application development areas. The first drawback, or perceived drawback, is Java's relative slowness of execution. Remember that Java programs are platform independent; therefore, the interpretation of the Java programs by the Java interpreter is a step that programs compiled with C and other languages do not require. Better Java interpreters, just-in-time compilation of Java programs, and overall better hardware and communication software have made execution speed much less of an issue than it has been in the past.

Another potential problem is version control. When new major releases of Java are introduced (such as Version 2 recently), not all machines are immediately ready to run the newer features of the language. If you want your program to run on all platforms, you must stick to using the older version of the language until the newer version is widely accepted. However, this issue is relatively minor: New versions of Java do not come out that often; in addition, developers of the Java interpreters are now getting their new releases out faster.

Java versus Visual Basic

Visual Basic is currently the preferred programming language for global applications. Visual Basic is an object-based language; Java, as you've learned, is an object-oriented language. As you will see later in the book, an *object-oriented* approach allows you to create an object and then use that object in multiple places. With Visual Basic, programmers are severely limited in their ability to use a precreated object in other areas of their programs.

Visual Basic does not support other features that make for a truly robust programming language. Some of these features include threads, full network capabilities (such as HTTP and sockets), and true exception handling. Another drawback to Visual Basic, in my opinion, is that it ties you to a sole supplier, Microsoft. Though Microsoft's products are good, Visual Basic applications must run on a Microsoft operating system. At a large corporation, this restriction limits your future choices and increases your development time if you should want to expand to other systems, such as Linux.

Java versus C/C++

For convenience I am going to combine the C and C++ worlds, even though C is not an object-oriented language. When you compare Java to C/C++, you will see that Java does not support some of the features that C/++ does. One of these features is the concept of *pointers*, which means referencing one memory location in a program through another memory location. C/C++ programmers love this concept. It allows them to write very powerful programs with few lines of programming; however, it also opens a large security hole, which is one of the fundamental concepts that Java addresses. Another disadvantage of pointers is that their use makes it very easy to introduce subtle bugs into a program. In my opinion, the lack of pointers in Java generally results in programs with far fewer bugs than similar C/C++ programs have.

Another feature that Java does not support is multiple inheritance. This feature of C++ is useful, but it also introduces many complexities. The designers of the Java languages chose to avoid this added complexity by using the concept of interfaces. The interface approach may not be quite as easy or elegant as multiple inheritance, but it does make code less complicated.

C/C++ has several other features that are not included in Java (such as operator overloading), but in general Java has all the commands and features that are necessary to write any standard business application. Because Java does not include every C/C++ feature, Java code is relatively simple to read, which from a pure business standpoint is good news. Simpler code should reduce overall code development and maintenance costs. You should also realize that a significant amount of IT cost is devoted to supporting existing applications. Code that is simple to read and that avoids complexity will ultimately be less expensive to support.

Java with SAP

A few years ago, SAP decided to decentralize its software and allow modules to stand alone. The company promotes the openness of its products through a program that SAP calls the CSP (*Complementary Software Program*). The Java programming language is particularly suited for this type of integration; SAP and other software providers merely provide a gateway into the core SAP system and then allow third-party applications to work from there. Using Java reduces the amount of development time SAP must do to support a wide range of platforms, so you can have a third-party application now running on Linux on, a Sun server, say, and have this application access an SAP system through Java (see Figure 1.1).

SAP has developed several tools to enable this type of integration. Though this book covers these tools in later chapters, the main package here is called the SAP Automation package, which includes the SAP JRFC (*Java Remote Function Calls*, also called the *Java Class Library*). This tool set enables programmers to access the entire SAP ERP system from a Java environment.

Other ERP Providers

SAP is the market leader when it comes to providing ERP systems. There are, however, other ERP providers, and understanding where they are going with

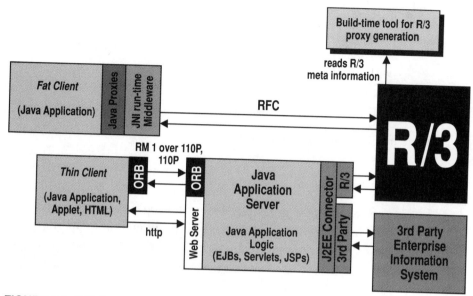

FIGURE 1.1 *Third party applications accessing SAP through Java*

respect to Java will help you to understand the importance of the language. One of the main goals of the ERP industry is to allow third-party software to integrate into the main ERP system. Integration through Java seems to be picking up momentum in this area.

IBM has introduced a package called *VisualAge* that allows Java programs to tie into ERP systems with relative ease. VisualAge for Java is an integrated development environment for creating Web-enabled enterprise applications. This tool provides support for building, testing, and integrating 100 percent pure Java applications and components like applets.

Oracle

Oracle has embraced the Java language with a full suite of Java products that provide comprehensive support for the new Java 2 Enterprise Edition standards. Oracle's Java tool set includes the following items.

♦ Oracle Business Component for Java with Oracle JDeveloper 3.0 delivers a 100 percent Java- and XML-driven framework that simplifies component design, application deployment, and business rules.

◆ JSP (*Java Server Page*) Support is a tool for developing and debugging dynamic HTML clients for Enterprise JavaBeans and CORBA (*Common Object Request Broker Architecture*) applications, and is integrated with the JDeveloper application.

◆ Oracle Application Server supports Business Components for Java, such as Enterprise JavaBeans, Java Servlets, and JavaServer Pages.

More information is available at www.oracle.com/java.

PeopleSoft

Java is tightly integrated in PeopleSoft's new People Tools Internet Architecture. This new release includes a full suite of powerful enterprise application integration tools such as Application Messaging, Business Components, and Business Interlink, all of which are based on—or are fully capable of being integrated with—Java.

Intentia International

Intentia International is a Swedish firm that has converted its existing ERP software, Movex, which was written in RPG, to Java. Though this vendor is a relatively small player in the ERP world, the fact that the company converted its entire ERP suite to Java is significant.

J.D. Edwards

J.D. Edwards views Java as a critical language for the future of ERP and as a crucial component to an effective e-commerce strategy for OneWorld, J.D. Edwards's ERP solution. The company has implemented Java for both the client side and the server side of the OneWorld Enterprise computing model. This strategy takes the form of the OneWorld Java Server and is designed to conform to Sun Microsystems specifications for 100 percent pure Java compatibility. Currently, the OneWorld Java Server uses Java 2 and Enterprise Java Beans version 2.0.

For more information, visit www.jdedwards.com/technology.

Baan

Baan has announced that as a part of a three-pronged Internet strategy it will develop a new Java-based Web user interface for all Baan applications. However, at the time of this writing, no concrete Java-based interfaces are available.

The Future of Java

The future of Java is not only in the business application programming area but also in the new and growing networked-consumer-device area. Indeed, this category is expected to grow so much in the next decade that Java may be the only viable development platform. As mentioned earlier, Web appliances will run a wide variety of hardware and operating systems. It is simply not realistic to imagine a third-party software vendor writing an application, say, for a cell phone, and then compiling that application for every cell phone processor. The cost-effective and quicker way to develop these products will be to write them in Java and then let the manufacturers of the phones and hardware worry about getting a Java interpreter of some type to work on their system.

Another example of a consumer device is the digital interactive TV. The Java platform has become a preferred solution for the development and deployment of interactive digital television content. Java and HTML are the only technologies that are currently available for developing complex interactive applications, and Java TV is being pushed by the likes of Motorola, Phillips, Sony, Toshiba, and Matsushita.

All is not completely golden for Java, though. Competition in the form of Windows CE exists in the Web appliance arena. Windows CE is a version of Microsoft Windows that enables these small devices to run on software that has been developed with Microsoft's C++ or Visual Basic. Within the next two to three years, we should know whether Windows CE or Java will be the dominant operating system and programming language in the consumer-devices arena.

Summary

Java's use is becoming more widespread and will continue to do so as the Internet and e-commerce applications mature. The language is designed with security, platform independence, and reduced development and maintenance costs as core features that will enable it to handle the hardware and operating system changes that are currently happening at Internet speed.

ERP systems are becoming commonplace among successful corporations. Thus, the ability to integrate with these large and complex pieces of software is mandatory for both third-party developers and the corporations themselves. Java allows this integration to be as cost-efficient and timely as possible. The cost savings are mainly derived through a write-once philosophy because Java code is truly platform independent. Another cost saver is in the way that the language was developed. Though Java is not as robust as C++, Java code can get the job done with the final version of the code usually being easier to read and less complicated than a similar program written in C++. Finally, Java was designed for the Web and includes threads, security, sockets, and more. Java is a revolution in computing because it represents a shift in the corporate viewpoint of computing from a desktop-centric to a network-centric model. This approach moves a great deal of application complexity away from the desktops and onto the network and servers, where it can be centrally and professionally managed.

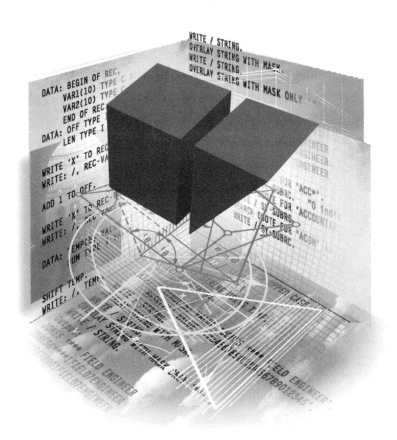

Chapter 2

**SAP Automation
Architecture**

In This Chapter

◆ Overview of SAP Automation

◆ Automation Component Description

◆ Integration of Components

SAP Automation is a collection of tools provided by SAP to assist you, the programmer, in integrating your applications with SAP. You may want to implement a process as simple as getting a piece of data out of SAP through a Java applet, or as complicated as replacing the entire SAP GUI (Graphical User Interface) with a new stand-alone application. Tools for doing both, and much more, are available in SAP Automation; some of them support all programming languages, whereas others support only certain coding environments. You can use some of these tools online to get information about the SAP system with which you are working. This chapter presents a broad overview of these tools, including the ones that do not support Java. Knowing which tools are available will enable you to make informed decisions about how to integrate your application with SAP.

Overview of SAP Automation

The SAP Automation tools enable you to do the following from outside of the R/3 environment:

◆ Read, write, and execute access BAPIs (*Business Application Programming Interfaces*) and their contents or metadata.

◆ Read, write, and execute R/3 RFC (*Remote Function Call*) function modules and their contents or metadata.

◆ Input data into R/3 in a batch mode through R/3 transactions.

◆ Access and change R/3 application screen data.

◆ Trap the interaction between an end user and SAP GUI screens.

◆ Provide an interface other than the standard SAP GUI to the SAP screens.

◆ Transmit inbound and/or outbound IDocs (*Intermediate Documents*) to SAP.

Automation Component Description

SAP Automation can be broken down into two broad categories: GUIs and RFCs. The GUIs require only a small amount of knowledge of the business logic within R/3 and require no logic of ABAP (*Advanced Business Application Programming*), because the GUI method just simulates actual SAP screens which already have the business logic built in. The RFC interface can be implemented in many different ways, including directly, through BAPIs, and through IDocs.

GUIs

In a standard SAP environment, the Application Server communicates with a program called the *SAP GUI* on the user's workstation. The SAP GUI has a link with each session that the user has open on his or her PC or workstation (the program name is usually FRONT.EXE). When using the GUI tool, you are really intercepting the communication between the SAP GUI software and the Application Server, which allows you to handle two major functions.

The Fine Print

The set of GUI tools works with release 2.1 and later of the R/3 Application Servers. Starting with 3.1H, the SAP Automation GUI software also works with R/2 systems via the CUA gateway. The SAP Automation GUI software provided with R/3 4.5A is for Win32 platforms only (32-bit Windows 95 and Windows NT 4.0 and later). On Windows NT 4.0 systems, Service Pack 3 is strongly recommended.

The first set of functions allows you to replace the screen the user sees with something that may be better suited for the user environment, or to send output to a scrolling display instead of a computer screen.

The second set of functions allows you to record user events or data that SAP is sending to the user. For example, you could fire off an application on the user's PC in response to a certain command code. Or, you could display a picture of a product when the material master transaction is brought up for that product.

Figure 2.1 shows the SAP Automation GUI main screen.

The GUI toolbox can be broken down into three areas: the low-level GUI calls, the GUI Component, and the GUI Code generator. Each level has different capabilities, complexities, and restrictions.

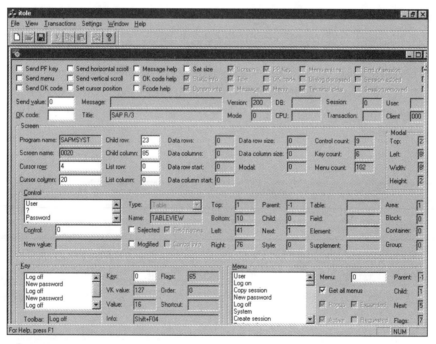

FIGURE 2.1 *An example of the SAP Automation GUI main screen. From this screen you can view all the data that is contained on the GUI.*

GUI Library

The GUI library is a series of relatively low-level calls that you can access from a C program (sorry, no Java here!). These calls allow you to both read and write to the data stream between the Application Server and SAP GUI software. This type of GUI interface gives you by far the most functionality of any interface, as you have access to all the features that are on a regular SAP screen. These features allow you to log on to an R/3 system, call up a transaction, query the results returned from SAP, and then send data back or execute any function available from the normal SAP GUI screen. The heart of the GUI library tool is the GUILIB.DLL, which contains the API functions. SAP uses the same DLL file for the development of its own GUI and associated recorder.

GUI Component

The GUI Component is a layered application that communicates with the SAP Automation library and any COM-compliant (*Component Object Model*) software through OLE (Object Linking and Embedding). The GUI Component allows nearly all the same functions as the GUI library but with greater error checking, and it is available as an out-of-process EXE server or as an OLE control. The GUI Component can also be used with any COM-compliant application, such as Office 97 or Lotus Notes.

GUI Code Generator

The GUI Code generator provides yet another layer of software and sits on top of the SAP Component. The purpose of the Code generator is to help the user write code in Visual Basic, HAHTtalk Basic, or Delphi's Object Pascal language. This tool enables you to step through a series of actions in SAP; then, the generator builds up the code in the desired language for you to use as is or incorporate into a larger application.

Remote Function Calls

RFCs, in terms of the SAP world, are simply pieces of code-named function modules that can be called on one system from another system. The two systems can be two different SAP systems or an SAP system and a non-SAP system.

Compared with using the GUI interface methods discussed in the preceding section, using RFCs requires a bit more knowledge of the technical SAP architecture and business logic. Using RFCs, however, gives you a wide range of flexible programming alternatives, including working from non-Windows systems.

Closely related to RFCs are BAPIs. A BAPI is a business object; it could be a purchase order, an employee, or a customer. The reason for the close relationship between RFCs and BAPIs is that currently BAPIs in SAP are implemented through RFCs. Though this situation will probably continue for some time, there is no guarantee that SAP will stick with this practice over the long haul. You should, therefore, clearly understand the difference between an RFC and a BAPI. An RFC is simply a piece of code, whereas a BAPI is an interface to a business object. Thus, when you want to create a business object such as a purchase order, you are really calling a remote function module. You do not need to know ABAP or the name of the function module when using BAPIs. All you do (through the Java BAPI class) is call for a new instance of the purchase order, for example.

The tools from the SAP Automation suite that use RFCs can be broken out into 10 areas. These areas provide varying degrees of support; some can be executed in any environment, but others work only under Windows. Also, like the GUIs, some RFC tools support Java and some do not. In Chapter 16, "Deciding Which Technology to Use for a New Application," we compare the various tools and build up a logic flow so that you can decide what to use for your particular application programming needs.

Logon Control

The Logon control is implemented through an ActiveX control and allows any COM-compliant application to log on to an SAP system. The Logon control allows you to hide the SAP logon window if you want to determine the system or log on via a program. Though this control can be used through Java, a connection interface provided with the Java class is easier and quicker. The Java class is discussed later in this section.

You can use the Logon control to build a button on your application that allows the user to log on to SAP. The Logon control was specifically designed for Visual Basic (VB) and C++.

RFC API

The RFC API routines allow access to an SAP system through RFCs. This process includes two-way communication so that a C program can call an ABAP RFC and an ABAP program can call a C program. The required files and documentation can be found in the RFC Software Development Kit (RFC SDK) and are part of the standard SAP Automation installation under the . . ./rfcsdk/include/ directory. In addition, examples and help documentation are under the . . ./rfcsdk/text/ directory. From within SAP you have the ability to create C program stubs, as shown in Figure 2.2. A *stub* is a shell of a C program with the calling parameters already set up.

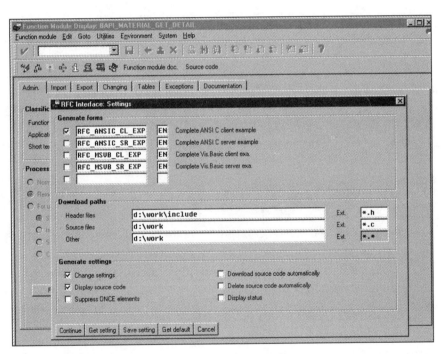

FIGURE 2.2 *An example of the creation of a stub in SAP*

RFC Component

The RFC component is an ActiveX component that exposes RFC functionality to COM-compliant applications. By automatically performing some of the preparation work that is usually required when using RFCs directly with C, the RFC Component makes using RFCs easier from within programs written in languages like Visual Basic. For example, when using RFCs directly, you need to declare and configure the desired RFC functions and their parameters. The RFC component eliminates the need to do so in the COM-compliant programs using it. The RFC component comprises two objects: Function components and Table components.

Transaction Component

The Transaction component is an OCX control that can be used either through the online Assistant or through a COM-compliant application program. Online users use the control when they select the Transactions tab. Application programs use the Transaction control to create Transaction objects. This process is very similar to generating BDC (*Batch Data Communications*) sessions in SAP. The data flow is only one-way, though—into SAP; the status of the current transaction is not communicated back to the calling program. The Transaction component can be executed only in a Windows operating environment.

RFC Java Class Library

The Java Class library provides Java programmers with an object-oriented view of RFCs within SAP and allows Java programs to use all the functionality of the RFCs. As you may already have guessed, RFC functionality is the primary focus of this book, because most of the application programs and applets use RFCs to get into an SAP System.

The Java Class library acts like a buffer between your Java program and the low-level C calls that are required to connect to the SAP system. The Java Class library has two components: the Java client and the Java server. Installation of these components, along with more technical information, is provided in Chapter 4, "Setting up the Development and Operating Environments."

Through the Java Class library, you have access to the SAP RFCs via the classes com.sap.rfc (see Chapters 19, "The COM.SAP.RFC Package," and 20, "The COM.SAP.RFC.EXCEPTION Package") and com.sap.bapi (see Appendix C, "ABAP/4 Data Types to Java Cross-Reference").

RFC C++ Class Library

The C++ Class library works in a similar fashion as the Java Class library, but for the C++ language.

IDoc C++ Class Library

IDocs, or Intermediate Documents, are structured data packets that are sent back and forth between two systems via RFCs.

The IDoc Class Library allows you to write C++ code that:

◆ Makes transactional RFC calls to send IDocs inbound to R/3.

◆ Acts as a transactional RFC server to receive outbound IDocs from R/3.

◆ Creates IDocs segment by segment.

◆ Navigates through the IDoc tree structure to access IDoc segments by name.

◆ Reads data from and writes data to fields in segments. Fields are accessed by name; data type conversions are done automatically.

As the name of the section suggests, this library can be used only to generate C++ programs.

Repository Services

The Repository Services tool retrieves information from SAP about business objects and RFCs, such as calling parameters and exceptions. This information can then be stored at the local server, which can be viewed offline or used to speed up access to the R/3 system for programs running online. The database that is used for local storage adheres to Microsoft Access format and allows the storage of several SAP systems on the same database (though you can only access one at a time). The Repository Services tool works with any COM-compliant application but runs only on Windows.

See Chapter 14, "SAP Assistant," for more details on the Repository Services tool.

Repository Browser

The Repository Browser opens up RFC and BAPI to the outside world. Through the Repository Browser tool you can view, search, and execute RFCs either online or through a COM-compliant application. The Repository Browser is implemented through an ActiveX control. The online functionality is achieved through the SAP Assistant, which is discussed in the next section.

SAP Assistant

The SAP Assistant is a multifunction tool that allows you to search, view, and call RFCs. Through the SAP Assistant, you can generate both C++ and Java classes based on existing SAP BAPI functions. The SAP Assistant is covered in detail in Chapter 14. The SAP Assistant screen is shown in Figure 2.3.

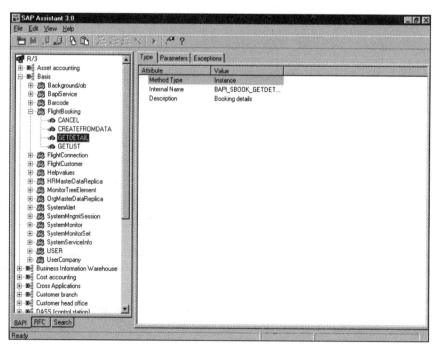

FIGURE 2.3 *An example of the SAP Assistant screen*

Integration of Components

The relationships among all the components discussed in this chapter are shown in Figure 2.4.

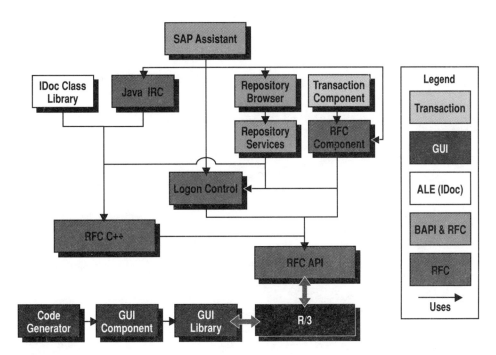

FIGURE 2.4 *A view of the relationships among the various components of the SAP Automation suite of tools*

Summary

There are many pieces to the SAP Automation toolkit, including tools that allow you to work in a variety of environments and languages. This chapter gave you an overall feel for what is available and what is relevant to Java. The two general types of SAP interfaces are the GUI and RFC modules. The specific areas that are important to the Java programmer are the GUI Component, the Java Class library, the Repository Services, and the SAP Assistant. Some of the other areas can be used with Java as well, but these are the most direct and efficient, and are best for an introduction to integrating Java with SAP. After you understand the Java Class library, integrating with the Logon control will not be difficult. This chapter concluded with an overview of how all these components work together.

Chapter 3

**VisualAge
for Java**

In This Chapter

- ◆ VisualAge Versions
- ◆ System Requirements
- ◆ Your First Applet
- ◆ Importing and Exporting Java Code
- ◆ JavaBeans
- ◆ Class Browser
- ◆ Visual Composition Editor
- ◆ Beans Palette
- ◆ Managing and Storing Your Code
- ◆ Relational Database
- ◆ Using JDBC in VisualAge for Java
- ◆ VisualAge for Java Scrapbook
- ◆ Servlets
- ◆ VisualAge for Java with the R/3 System

IBM's VisualAge for Java is an integrated development environment for creating Web-enabled enterprise applications; its visual environment supports the complete cycle of Java program development. With VisualAge you can build Java applications, applets, and JavaBean components.

VisualAge for Java reduces development time by helping developers create easy-to-use functions; in addition, it is the only Java development environment that supports the creation of Java applications that can scale from Windows NT to OS/390 enterprise servers.

VisualAge Versions

VisualAge for Java is available in three editions: Enterprise, Professional, and Entry. Each version is designed to meet a different level of developmental need.

VisualAge for Java, Entry Edition

The Entry edition is suitable for learning purposes and for building small projects of up to 500 classes. This edition is available as a free download from the VisualAge developer domain at www.ibm.com/software/vadd.

VisualAge for Java, Professional Edition

The Professional edition is a complete Java development environment that includes access to JDBC (*Java Database Connectivity*) for building full-function Java applications.

VisualAge for Java, Enterprise Edition

The Enterprise edition is designed for building enterprise Java applications. It has the same features as the Professional edition, as well as support for developers who work in large teams, develop high-performance or heterogeneous applications, or need to connect Java programs to existing enterprise systems.

System Requirements

To run VisualAge for Java on your PC, you must have the following:

- Windows NT 4.0, Windows 95, or Windows 98
- VisualAge 2.0 or 3.0

The Entry, Professional, and Enterprise editions run on OS/2 Warp 4.0. The Enterprise edition also runs on AIX 4.2 and 4.3.

Your First Applet

Before you can create an applet with VisualAge for Java, you must install the software on your computer. To launch VisualAge, double-click the VisualAge for Java icon, or select Start, Programs, VisualAge for Java. The Welcome to VisualAge dialog box, shown in Figure 3.1, appears.

Clicking Close not only closes the dialog box, but also opens the Workbench window, which is where you usually create and change classes. The layout of the

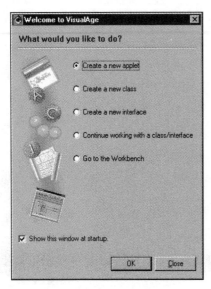

FIGURE 3.1 *The Welcome to VisualAge dialog box*

Workbench window depends on which tab is selected: Projects, Packages, Classes, Interfaces, or All. To switch to a different tab, click on it. The menu bar also changes as you switch from tab to tab.

To begin, select File, Quick Start from the Workbench menu bar. The Quick Start dialog box offers four options: Basic, Repository, Management, and Features. Select Basic, Create Applet, and then click OK. The SmartGuide dialog box, as seen in Figure 3.2, will help you create Java applets and applications.

Specify the project name as **Java Applet,** the package name as **JavaApplet,** and the applet name as **Hello.** Deselect the Browse applet when finished and the Compose the class visually check boxes, and click on the Finish button. At this point, SmartGuide creates the code needed for your new applet. To test your newly created applet, select the Hello applet, and then choose Selected, Run, In Applet Viewer from the Workbench menu bar, as seen in Figure 3.3.

The Applet Viewer runs the applet without having to use a Web browser. You can resize the window to see the complete message. To do so, you must change the properties of the applet by selecting the Hithere class in the Workbench and then

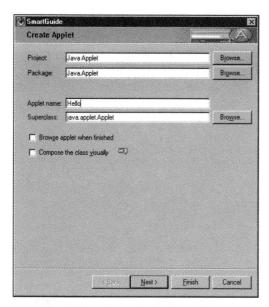

FIGURE 3.2 *The SmartGuide dialog box*

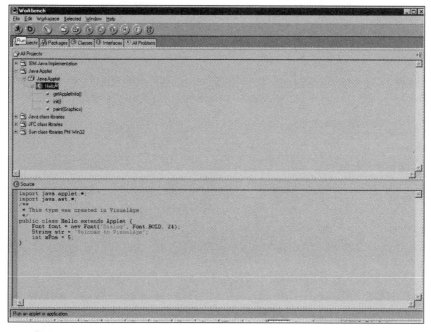

FIGURE 3.3 *Run the Hello applet through Workbench*

FIGURE 3.4 *An applet running in the Applet Viewer*

choosing Selected, Properties. Figure 3.4 shows the result of the applet we created and ran with VisualAge for Java.

You can also modify the applet to display different output by selecting your class in the Workbench. To change the text "Welcome to VisualAge" to "I am having fun with VisualAge," just type over the text and select Edit, Save from the menu bar. You can then test the result by compiling the code. To do this, choose Selected, Run, In Applet Viewer from the menu bar.

Importing and Exporting Java Code

VisualAge for Java stores projects in a repository, rather than directly in the file system. To allow developers to share the code, you must import and export Java classes. Many formats are available for importing and exporting Java classes and resources from VisualAge for Java.

Java Class Files

You can export Java class files when you are ready to test them outside the VisualAge for Java environment or deploy your program. Class files can also be imported into VisualAge for Java. However, the imported class cannot be changed, and the source code is not visible.

Java Source Code

Java source code can be compiled while it is being imported from the file system. It can also be exported when you want to share it with other developers.

Java Archive Files

Java archive files use the file type JAR and enable you to compress a Java applet and its resources (such as class files, images, and sounds) into a single file. Any VisualAge for Java project can be exported as a JAR file.

JavaBeans

JavaBeans is a component architecture for Java. It can be used in graphical programming environments, like VisualAge or Borland's Jbuilder. By using a graphical tool, you can connect a lot of Beans to make an application, without actually writing any Java code. In fact, no programming is required at all. To build an application or an applet with a Bean manipulator tool, such as VisualAge for Java Visual Composition Editor, you drag-and-drop the Beans into a working area, or connect them together.

The biggest users of JavaBeans are developers who need to stay current with the latest developments in programming technology. At a minimum, developing Beans means adopting several simple design patterns in your code. You can see the main advantage of the JavaBeans architecture when you need to understand how to write classes that are serializable. You should know when and how to provide BeanInfo classes that give graphical environments more information about your components, and when to use events for communication between classes.

Class Browser

The Class Browser is used to create and assemble Beans. It consists of five views, or *pages*.

- ◆ **Methods.** This page is used for coding Java methods in the class being browsed.
- ◆ **Hierarchy**. This page is used to edit Java code and the class declarations of superclasses.
- ◆ **Editions**. This page is used when you want to compare and replace different editions of the class and its method.
- ◆ **Visual Composition Editor**. This page is used to build user interfaces. Project developers spend most of their time with this page.

   ◆ **BeanInfo**. This page is used to create and view the events, methods, and properties of a Bean.

Figure 3.5 shows the five pages of the Class Browser.

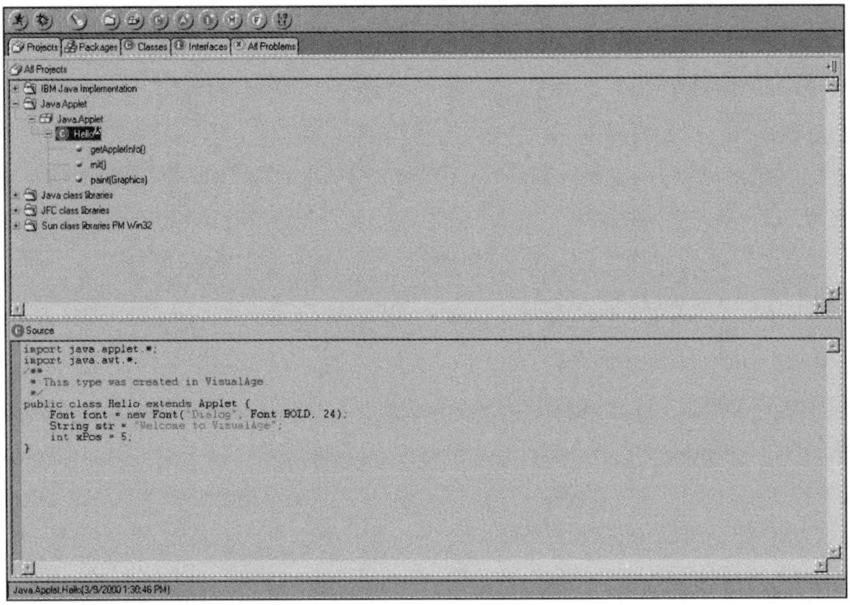

FIGURE 3.5 *The Class Browser window*

Visual Composition Editor

Visual Composition Editor, shown in Figure 3.6, is a powerful tool for building GUIs (*Graphical User Interfaces*). You can specify the logic of your application by connecting Visual or GUI Beans with nonvisual Beans. Visual Composition Editor consists of visual and nonvisual beans.

Visual Beans

Visual Beans are subclasses of the Abstract Window Toolkit (AWT) component class. This subclass has the same visual representation at design time that it does at run time.

FIGURE 3.6 *Visual Composition Editor*

Nonvisual Beans

This subclass, which doesn't appear at run time, usually represents a program's business logic. At design time, a nonvisual Bean appears as an icon.

Beans Palette

There are three categories of Beans on the Beans Palette: Swing, AWT, and Helper Beans. You can modify the palette by resizing it; by changing the icon size; or by adding or removing categories, separators, Beans you have constructed yourself, or Beans supplied by a vendor. Figure 3.7 shows a Beans Palette.

You select a Bean from the Beans Palette and then drop it on the free-form surface when you do your visual programming. The free form surface is like a blank sheet of paper or work area on which you can add Beans to create your component Bean. After you drop a Bean on the free form surface, you can customize it by double-clicking on it to open its property sheet. Figure 3.8 shows the property window.

FIGURE 3.7 *A Beans Palette*

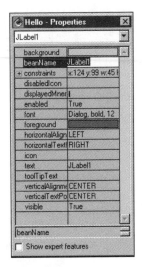

FIGURE 3.8 *The property window of a Bean*

Managing and Storing Your Code

To store all the program elements, such as projects, packages, classes, and methods, Workspace is automatically loaded. The Workspace is stored as a single file (IDE.icx). Your code is stored in a larger database called the *repository*, which contains other program elements in a defined state, or edition. You can add these program elements to the Workspace if you need to use them. The Workspace stores the byte codes of the programs with which you are working, and the repository stores the source code for the program elements in the Workspace, as well as all other elements not currently in the Workspace.

Relational Database

A relational database provides secure, scalable, and efficient ways of storing and accessing large amounts of data, and is used to store program data. To access a relational database, Java developers typically use JDBC. The JDBC API (*Application Programming Interface*) is a standard SQL (*Structured Query Language*) database access interface for Java. With JDBC, you can access most SQL databases and concentrate on business logic, rather than on maintaining the database and communications programming.

Using JDBC in VisualAge for Java

When using VisualAge for Java, you do not have to know too much about the JDBC interface to access the database. The following bits of code illustrate some key points.

To connect to the database:

```
java.sql.connection jc =
java.sql.DriverManager.getconnection("jdbc:db2:Matrix");
```

To create a statement object:

```
java.sql.statement obj = jc.createStatement();
```

To execute a query from the Customer table:

```
java.sql.ResultSet sql = obj.executeQuery("Select * from customer");
```

To try these examples, you must have DB2 running on your machine. Then, you can try the examples yourself in the VisualAge for Java Scrapbook.

VisualAge for Java Scrapbook

Scrapbook enables you to evaluate Java expressions. Just type in any expression, highlight it, and execute it. To enter and run Java code in the Scrapbook, select Window, Scrapbook from the Workbench menu.

Type some Java code and highlight the text, then select Edit, Run or click the Run button on the text bar. Figure 3.9 shows the Scrapbook screen.

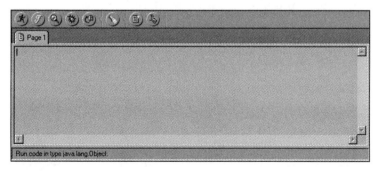

FIGURE 3.9 *The VisualAge for Java Scrapbook*

Servlets

Servlets are very powerful, and they can be faster than other server-side Web techniques. *Servlets* are Java programs that use the Java Servlet API and the associated classes and methods. In addition to the Java Servlet API, servlets can use Java class packages that extend the API. Servlets are similar to applets that run on a browser and extend the browser's capabilities. HTTP (*Hypertext Transfer Protocol*) servlets run on a Java-enabled Web server and extend the Web server's capabilities.

You can execute, run, and debug servlets within the VisualAge for Java environment; however, the Enterprise version of VisualAge has more powerful servlet support than the other two versions.

VisualAge for Java with the R/3 System

Companies that use SAP R/3 can use VisualAge for Java to become e-businesses. VisualAge for Java is the first Java integrated development environment to receive BAPI (*Business Application Programming Interface*) validation from SAP. VisualAge for Java fully supports the BAPI standard for Java, and can create business applications that access and integrate SAP R/3 into new, Web-based applications. For example, companies that use R/3 for sales orders can use Java applets to extend sales to the Internet. In this case, Java applets connect to R/3 and generate a sales order object that can be processed just like a normal sales order in R/3.

Summary

This chapter introduced the features of VisualAge for Java and showed you how to build applets and applications. It also described the VisualAge Composition Editor, which helps build GUIs by connecting visual or GUI Beans with nonvisual or invisible Beans. VisualAge for Java is an alternative tool that can be used to integrate with R/3 systems and access BAPIs. SAP's BOR (*Business Object Repository*) can also be used to obtain the same functionality as VisualAge for Java. As an SAP tool, BOR is more integrated with SAP than Visual Age for Java is, and it has other advantages as well. Chapter 12, "SAP's Business Object Repository," covers BOR in more detail.

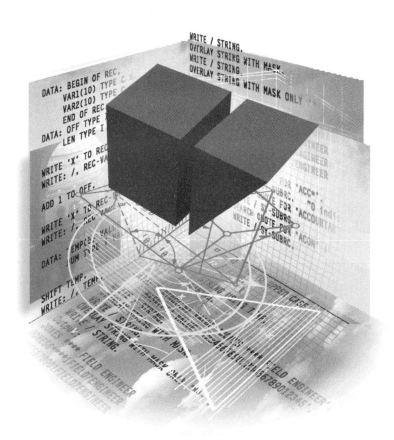

Chapter 4

**Setting up the
Development
and Operating
Environments**

In This Chapter

This chapter covers the installation of the SAP Automation toolkit, the client/server components for the RFC (*Remote Function Calls*), and other items that you must install and configure to set up the development and operating environments. For the most part the installation procedure is fairly straightforward, but some areas, particularly the server configuration, require an understanding of the overall architecture and how it relates to your business and development requirements.

SAP Automation Setup

As described in Chapter 2, "SAP Automation Architecture," the SAP Automation Suite has two basic ways of getting data to and from the SAP application servers. The first way is through RFCs, and the second is through the GUI (*Graphical User Interface*). When you install the Automation Suite, you need to know which access points you will be using. For instance, if you are only interested in the GUI side, then you do not need to create or install a server for the RFC calls. If you are using RFC calls (to access SAP's BAPI calls, for instance), you need to decide whether to have a separate machine running the server software or to install the client and server software on the same system.

Whichever configuration you choose, the server software must be installed on a system running the Windows NT operating system. In most installations you will eventually have a separate server machine and then install client software on each system that uses your Java software. However, the easiest setup for initial development is to locate both servers on the same system. Another consideration here is whether you are using Java applets in your solution. If you are, you need to install the server software on your Web server system because most Web browsers enforce restrictions on applet operations.

Obtaining the Automation Suite

The best place to obtain the SAP Automation Suite is from SAP Labs, Inc. The URL for the site is www.saplabs.com, and the latest version of the Automation Suite is located in the download area of the U.S. site. You can also get a description of the latest features. Figures 4.1 and 4.2 are from the SAP Labs Web site and show the kinds of information available there.

TIP

To learn about the SAP Labs site, go to www.saplabs.com and click on the U.S. location you want on the left side of the page. When you are on the U.S. page, look for a download area link (it is currently on the bottom of the page). This link takes you to the area where you can get the Automation software and other software, such as Internet Transaction Server and Help files.

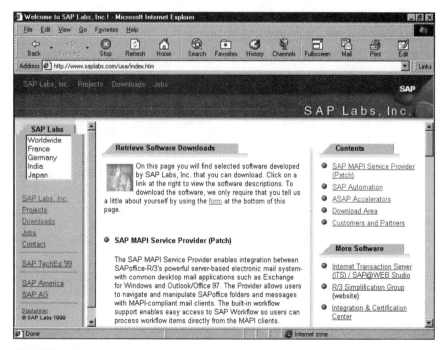

FIGURE 4.1 *SAP Labs, Inc., Web site for SAP Automation download*

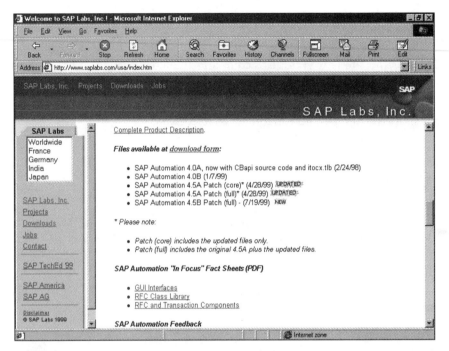

FIGURE 4.2 *The SAP Automation downloadable files*

From the SAP Labs site, you have two options. The first is to download the entire Automation Suite, which, as of release 4.5B, is about 27MB. This file allows you to install both the server and client software. The second option is to do a Web install; this only installs the client-side software but is much quicker than downloading the full Automation Suite. The InstallFromTheWeb software analyzes your system and transfers only the necessary software to your system.

The Automation software is also available on the SAP Presentation CD or through one of SAP's sapservX ftp sites; with the ftp sites, you must have an (Online Service System) login.

SAP Automation Installation

When you have the installation file for the SAP Automation Suite, you can start working through it by executing the setup.exe file. Figure 4.3 shows the first

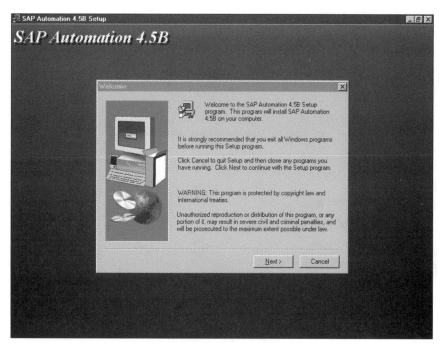

FIGURE 4.3 *Opening screen of SAP Automation setup*

screen of the setup procedure. Move through the screens until you get to the box that asks you to choose between a typical or a custom installation, as shown in Figure 4.4.

The Typical option installs some of the components of the Automation Suite. These include the SAP Assistant, GUI libraries, and RFC components, but not the Class or Help files.

If you select Custom, you can choose the components you want to install, as shown in Figure 4.5.

 CAUTION

A full installation takes about 50MB of disk space, so choose only the components that you require!

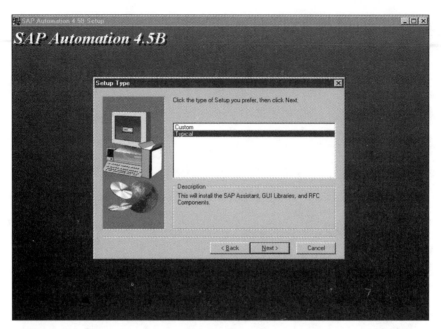

FIGURE 4.4 *The Setup Type screen asks you to choose between a typical and a custom installation.*

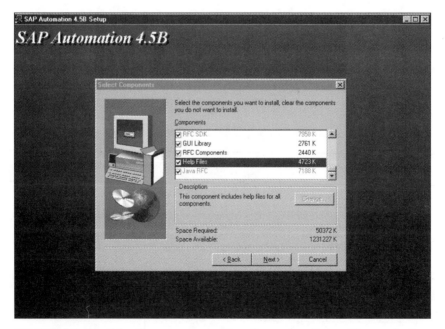

FIGURE 4.5 *The Select Components screen for a Custom installation. Choose only the components that you really need.*

The components are as follows:

◆ **SAP Assistant**. The SAP Assistant allows you to view and execute BAPIs and RFCs. The SAP Assistant requires the SAP DCOM (*Distributed Component Object Model*) connector that is included in the RFC SDK (*Software Development Kit*). If you select this option, the RFC SDK (described below) is automatically selected. Selecting this module also requires you to have Microsoft Transaction Server installed on your machine. Microsoft Transaction Server is available for Windows NT and Windows 95.

◆ **C++ BAPI**. This component includes the C++ BAPI source files; it requires the SAP Assistant and RFC SDK (which are automatically selected if you choose this option).

◆ **Java BAPI**. This component includes the Java BAPI source files; it requires the SAP Assistant, RFC SDK, and the Java RFC module (which again are automatically selected if you choose this option).

◆ **IDoc Class Library**. This component is intended for C++ application programmers who write programs that use IDocs (*Intermediate Documents*) via direct RFC calls.

◆ **RFC Class Library**. This module simplifies the programming of external applications that communicate with SAP R/3. The module comprises the C++ classes that have all the functionality of the RFC API (*Application Programming Interface*).

◆ **RFC SDK**. This component includes the RFC libraries for software developers. It also contains the SAP DCOM Connector installation files.

◆ **GUI Library**. This component provides the technology that allows you to communicate to the SAP R/3 system directly via the SAP GUI.

◆ **RFC Components**. Includes SAP Logon, RFC, Table Factory, Table Tree, Table View, and Transaction Controls.

◆ **Help Files**. This component contains Help files for all components in the setup. You cannot select specific Help modules; it is all or none.

◆ **Java RFC**. Installs the Java RFC, which is required for the Java BAPI calls.

What Is Microsoft Transaction Server?

Microsoft Transaction Server (MTS) enables a programmer to easily develop and deploy high-performance, scalable, and reliable distributed applications (such as Internet applications). Therefore, you can develop your solution with a single user in mind and not have to worry about scalability when it is running in a client/server relationship. Threads (the link between the client and the server), caching of data, and security are some of the features that MTS manages for you.

After you select your installation method, the setup program displays a list of the information you have entered along with the components that you have selected, as shown in Figure 4.6. At this point you have the opportunity to change the entered values if necessary.

When you select Next on the screen shown in Figure 4.6, the installation program takes over and begins installing the desired components (see Figure 4.7). The

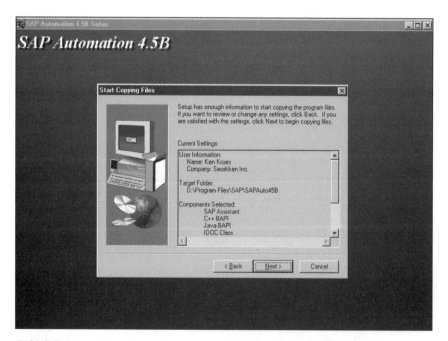

FIGURE 4.6 *Listing of selected options during SAP Automation installation*

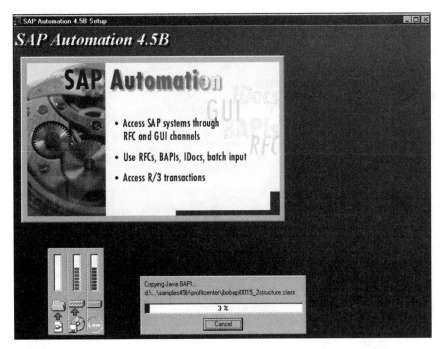

FIGURE 4.7 *SAP Automation installation screen as files are copied to your system*

time required for installation depends on the machine, but is typically less than five minutes.

When this step is complete, you are asked to reboot your computer. If you selected the Java RFC components, they are installed after the computer reboots. After your computer restarts, a screen similar to that shown in Figure 4.8 should appear.

After you work through the initial screens of the installation (in which you specify your name, company, and installation directory), you can select the parts of the Java RFC package you want to install, as shown in Figure 4.9.

If you want to have the same computer do both the client and server sides (on your first development machine, for instance), you need to select both the client and the server applications. Otherwise, select only the server or select the client if the server is already set up on a different machine. The installation of both components takes about 18MB of disk space.

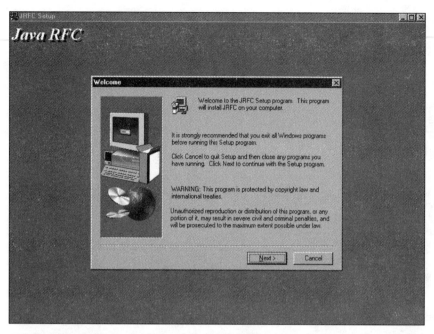

FIGURE 4.8 *Beginning of the Java RFC installation*

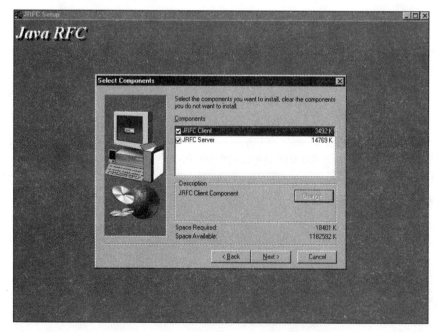

FIGURE 4.9 *Component selection screen for Java RFC installation*

TIP

To restart the Java RFC installation or install it on a different machine, go to the directory that you specified in the first part of the Automation installation (default to /Program Files/SAPAuto45B/Auto2/JRFC), and start the program JRFC45B.EXE, which is the install program for the Java RFC package.

This process is similar to the Automation load. After you select the components, you are shown what you have selected, and you are given the opportunity to change your entries or proceed with the installation. When the installation is complete, you must reboot your computer one more time to finish the process. The next step is to register your software with the middleware and to make the initial configuration settings.

As you can see, the installation of both the client and server software is fairly simple. But what have you really installed? If you examine the directories, you will see references to the Orbix Daemon, Server Manager, and CORBA (*Common Object Request Broker Architecture*). The next sections explain what these components are and how they are used in your environment.

Special Considerations for Server Installation

When you are installing the server software for the first time, you are asked whether you want to install the Orbix Daemon as a Windows NT service. Basically, if you choose to install the Orbix Daemon as a Windows NT service, it automatically starts at system startup and runs in the background. This configuration is desired for a production system, but for a stand-alone development system where the client and server software are installed on the same system, you probably won't want to install the Orbix Daemon as a Windows NT service. For more details on the Orbix Daemon, see the section titled "Component Explanation" later in this chapter.

Finishing the Installation

The final step in the installation process is to register and configure the server software with the Orbix Daemon. To register the server, click on the Register Server program in the Windows Start menu. Doing so enables the Orbix Daemon to handle requests to the Java RFC server and allows you to configure how your server works by using the Orbix Server Manager utility. If you execute the Register Server program, you should get screens that look like those shown in Figure 4.10.

 TIP

You need to run the Register Server operation once. If you re-execute it, it simply overwrites any values that you may have changed through the Server Manager utility.

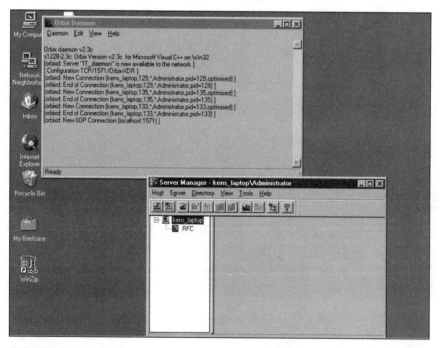

FIGURE 4.10 *Results of executing the Register Server operation*

You can perform the following activities through the Orbix Server Manager utility:

- Specify the number of Java RFC servers that can be launched.
- View and control the authorization for invoking and calling a Java RFC server.
- Control server timeout and thread pool size.
- Manually stop or start a Java RFC server.

The Server Manager Utility starts automatically when you register, or you can start it manually through the Windows Start menu. After the program starts, you can click on the RFC server to access the configuration options, as shown in Figure 4.11.

The important aspects of the configuration settings are covered next.

Name Tab

The Server Name must be RFC for Java RFC clients to connect properly, as shown in Figure 4.12. The No. of Servers parameter controls how many instances of the Java server can be launched at the same time. Each new client results in a new server process until the maximum number of processes is available. Subsequent client connections are routed to existing server processes using a round-robin algorithm.

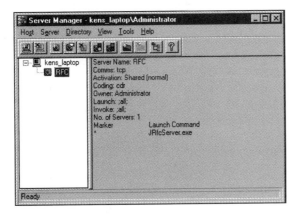

FIGURE 4.11 *Accessing the RFC server configuration through the Server Manager*

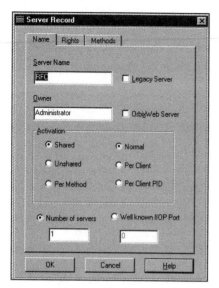

FIGURE 4.12 *Configuration parameters for RFC server—Name tab*

Rights Tab

Under the Rights tab (see Figure 4.13), you control who can create a new server process and who can use existing servers. The default installation allows all users to launch (create new) and invoke (use existing) server processes.

Methods Tab

The Methods tab (see Figure 4.14) allows you to modify the launch commands associated with a server. The Marker/Method text box controls which methods are accepted from the Java client. You can use this input field only if the server activation mode is unshared or per method.

Regardless of the server activation mode, you can enter the launch commands for the server in the Launch Command text box. You can change the timeout value between the server and the client and the number of concurrent threads that can be active in one server session; the values are initially set to no timeout and five concurrent threads. The switches used for these parameters are –t and –p, where t is used for the timeout and p is used for the number of threads.

```
Jrfcserver.exe -t 30 -p 10
```

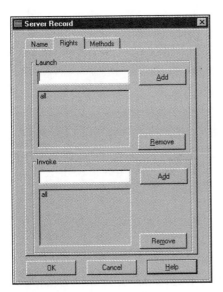

FIGURE 4.13 *Configuration parameters for RFC server—Rights tab*

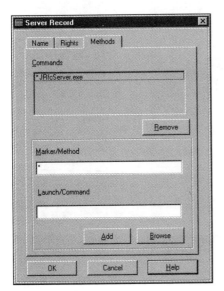

FIGURE 4.14 *Configuration parameters for RFC server—Methods tab*

The preceding example sets the timeout value to 30 seconds and the number of threads to 10. You must remember when adding a new launch command to remove the old value that is set.

Component Explanation

Some readers may already be familiar with the terms *client, server, daemon,* and *CORBA.* For everyone else, here are brief descriptions of these terms. A general overview of the flow of an RFC from your workstation to the SAP R/3 system is shown in Figure 4.15.

Client

The *client* is the system that initiates a call or transaction. Typically, the client is the workstation that executes the initial RFC call to R/3.

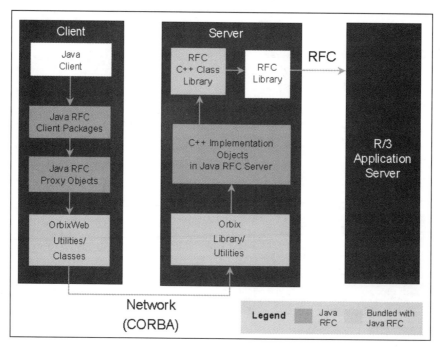

FIGURE 4.15 *Transaction flow from workstation to SAP R/3 system*

Server

The *server* is the system that receives the call from the client. In our case, as Figure 4.15 shows, the server resides between the client and the R/3 system.

CORBA

CORBA (*Common Object Request Broker Architecture*) is a technology for creating, distributing, and managing distributed program objects (such as our client/server Java RFG software). The essential concept in CORBA is the ORB (*Object Request Broker*). ORB support in a network of clients and servers on different computers means that a client program can request services from a server program or object without having to understand where the server is in a distributed network, or what the interface to the server program looks like. To make requests or return replies between the ORBs, programs use the GIOP (*General Inter-ORB Protocol*); for the Internet, they use the IIOP (*Internet Inter-ORB Protocol*).

Orbix Daemon

The *Orbix Daemon* is the software that runs on the client and server sides and is the middleware between the Java RFC client and server software. Daemon software programs communicate to each other via the CORBA networking technology.

The Difference between CORBA and DCOM?

CORBA was developed by a consortium of vendors through the Object Management Group, whereas DCOM (*Distributed Component Object Model*) was developed by Microsoft; it's basically the same concept as CORBA. DCOM is based on COM (*Component Object Model*). The problem with the DCOM solution is that you are somewhat tied to Microsoft technology. Translators allow CORBA and DCOM systems to communicate with each other.

Summary

This chapter walked you through the installation of the Java RFC software. If you are just starting out on your own, you will typically put both the client and server software on the system you use to develop programs. Larger development teams or consolidation/production systems have to consider using separate systems and perhaps even multiple server stations. Though other tools are available for developing Java-based SAP applications, the Automation Suite works and is supported by SAP. This support helps considerably because you know that the tools will work on future releases of the SAP software.

The next chapter focuses on getting a few simple Java programs working so that you can see the entire process. The step-by-step approach of this chapter and the next is intentional; if you cannot set up your environment or compile and run your programs, you won't be able to develop your application or learn much about using Java with SAP!

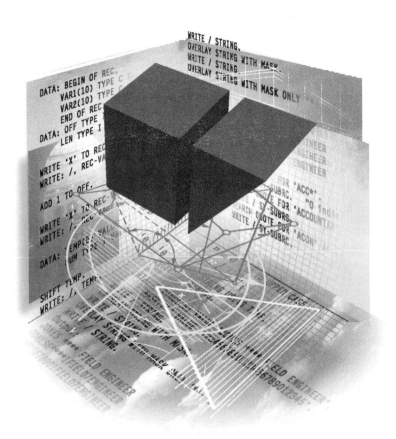

Chapter 5

A Few Simple Java/SAP Examples

In This Chapter

- ◆ Simple Ping of an R/3 System
- ◆ Simple Material Data Retrieval
- ◆ Applet Example

This chapter contains three examples of fairly simple Java programs that access SAP. Each example takes you step by step through the creation of the Java code, compilation, and finally execution of the program. The basics of the Java language, along with how to integrate it with SAP, are presented in much more detail elsewhere in this book. The purpose of this chapter is to show you the entire picture through simple examples. This approach prepares you to understand the details provided in subsequent chapters.

Even these simple examples may look intimidating if you have not done much Java programming, because quite a bit of code is necessary for even the most rudimentary command. However, a great deal of this code is required only once, and much of it is reusable. For instance, in the example on retrieving data from the material master, just a few more lines of Java would be required to create a material master or to read in or create a customer record. You will also notice that the connection code is the same in both the ping and reading the material master records examples.

Simple Ping of an R/3 System

The purpose of this example is to make sure that your systems and software are correctly configured. The code checks the compiler, client software, middleware, server software, and the connection between the server and the R/3 system itself. The program simply sends a ping down to the R/3 system and responds with a message indicating whether the program was successful in connecting to the system. The example contains no graphics, and it skips several error messages and cleanup routines, in order to keep it as simple as possible. A fully functioning version of this program is provided in the "Connecting to the SAP System" section in Chapter 11, "Integrating Java with SAP through RFCs and BAPIs."

Step 1: Getting an SAP Login

The first step in this example is to get an SAP login and to log in to the SAP system via the SAP GUI (*Graphical User Interface*). After you get your login from your system administrator and have successfully logged in to the SAP system, you will need to get the properties for the GUI, as shown in Figure 5.1 and Figure 5.2. You will need the following:

◆ Login ID

◆ Password

◆ SAP system URL

◆ System number

◆ Client number

◆ Login language

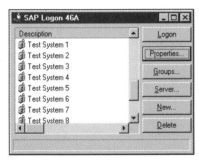

FIGURE 5.1 *Getting the properties of the SAP GUI login*

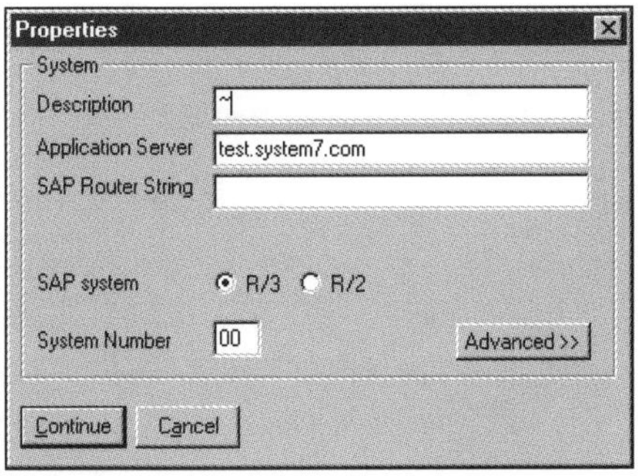

FIGURE 5.2 *The Properties page of the SAP GUI*

Step 2: Compiling the Code

This step involves the creation of a Java class named JavaPing, as well as a runtime version of this class. When you create the new project in the Microsoft Java Compiler, you should choose Console Application, as shown in Figure 5.3.

After the project has been created, you must rename the default name (Class1) JavaPing. To do so, right click on the Class1 object (on the right side of the screen) and then select Rename. This step is shown in Figure 5.4.

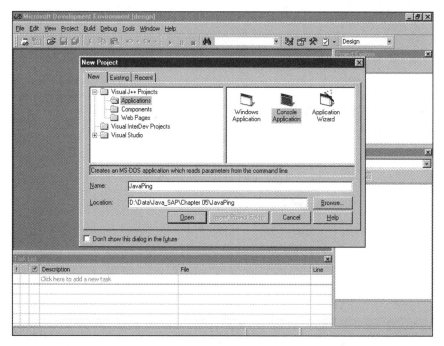

FIGURE 5.3 *Creation of the project JavaPing*

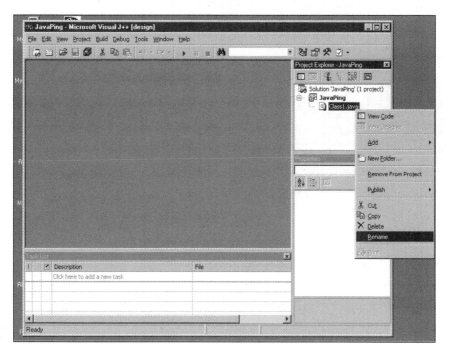

FIGURE 5.4 *Renaming the default class to JavaPing*

The Java code for this class follows.

```
// JavaPing, test the connection to a SAP instance and report
// back the status.  This is similar to the SAP samples example
// RFCPING but is simpler.

import com.sap.rfc.*;
import com.sap.rfc.exception.*;
import java.io.*;

public class JavaPing
{
    public static void main (String[] args)
    {
```

```
// Simple declaration of variables
String  rfcHost = "testsystem",          // Java RFC Host
        r3Host  = "test.system.com",     // SAP System Name
        r3SysNo = "00",                  // System Number
        client  = "001",                 // SAP Client Number
        user    = "kenkroes",            // Your User Name
        password = "scoobydoo",          // Your Password
        language = "EN";                 // Your Login Language

FactoryManager facMan = null;
IRfcConnection connection = null;

// Establish the connection to the Orbix Middleware
MiddlewareInfo mdInfo = new MiddlewareInfo();
mdInfo.setMiddlewareType(MiddlewareInfo.middlewareTypeOrbix);
mdInfo.setOrbServerName(rfcHost);

// let the global factory manager use the middlewareInfo
// to create all object factories by binding to the server
facMan = FactoryManager.getSingleInstance();
facMan.setMiddlewareInfo(mdInfo);

// Define The User information
UserInfo        userInfo      = new UserInfo();
ConnectInfo     connectInfo   = new ConnectInfo();

userInfo.setClient(client);
userInfo.setUserName(user);
userInfo.setPassword(password);
userInfo.setLanguage(language);

// Set up the Connection
connectInfo.setRfcMode(ConnectInfo.RFC_MODE_VERSION_3);
connectInfo.setDestination("xxx");
connectInfo.setHostName(r3Host);
connectInfo.setSystemNo((short)Integer.parseInt(r3SysNo));
connectInfo.setLoadBalancing(false);
```

```
connectInfo.setCheckAuthorization(true);

// Try to establish the connection

try
{
    connection = facMan.getRfcConnectionFactory()
                    .createRfcConnection(connectInfo, userInfo);
    connection.open();
}
catch (JRfcRfcConnectionException re)
{
    System.out.println("Unexpected RfcError while opening connection.\n"
                        + re.toString());
    return;
}
catch (JRfcBaseRuntimeException je)
{
    System.out.println("Unexpected JRFC runtime exception:\n"
                        + " while opening connection.\n"
                        + je.toString());
    return;
}
System.out.println("Congratulations, Connection Established !");
    }
}
```

Figure 5.5 shows the Microsoft Java Compiler with the JavaPing class. After you enter the code, select Build from the pull-down example. Any errors will be shown in the bottom window. To get more details about the errors, place the cursor on the error message and then press the F1 key. Any errors you get probably will be due to a typographical error resulting in a Java syntax error. In addition to an explanation of the error, the error message will also indicate the line number that is close to the error (sometimes an error on one line may be due to an error on the lines above or below). Once the program is compiled successfully, you will be able to see the JavaPing executable program in Windows Explorer, as shown in Figure 5.6.

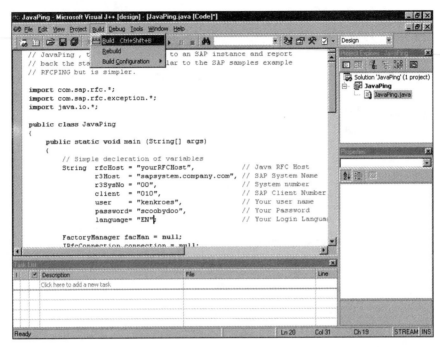

FIGURE 5.5 *The JavaPing example*

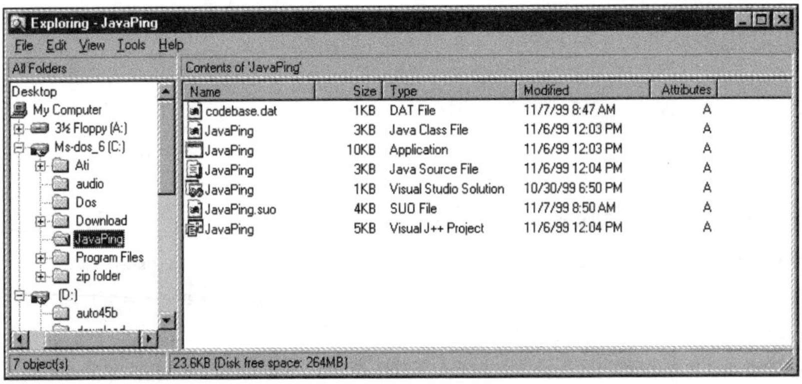

FIGURE 5.6 *Windows Explorer view of the Project directory showing the JavaPing executable program*

Step 3: Starting the Orbix Middleware

This step assumes that you are installing the server software without having the Orbix Daemon set up to start automatically as a Windows NT service. If the daemon starts up automatically on your system, or if the Java RFC (*Remote Function Call*) is already configured at your installation, you can skip this step.

To start the Orbix Daemon, simply go to the Windows Start menu and select Start Orbix Daemon, as shown in Figure 5.7. You can also select Server Manager at this time. If the Server Manager does not appear as shown in Figure 5.7, turn back to Chapter 4, "Setting up the Development and Operating Environments," and review the setup procedure for the Java RFC server.

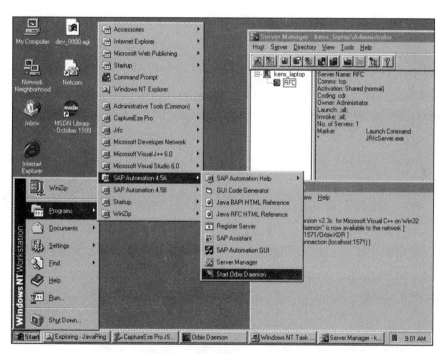

FIGURE 5.7 *Starting the Orbix Daemon and Server Manager*

Step 4: Testing the Java Class

During this final step, you'll execute your newly created code by double-clicking on the JavaPing executable program. If all goes well, your screen should look like that in Figure 5.8.

You will also notice that the daemon has started another DOS window that displays the trace of the connection to the JAVA RFC server. You can control the level of trace through the Orbix Daemon window from the Daemon menu of the Daemon window, as shown in Figure 5.9

That does it for our first example. Although it required quite a few steps, if you have this example working, the rest of the examples should work well and should be easy to do. We've attempted to make this example simple enough for you to correct any problems you might have with it.

 NOTE

Three samples come with the Java RFC you installed on your system. One of these examples is called RFCPING and is located by default in the following path:

c:\Sap\SAPAuto45B\Auto2\Jrfc\Client\Samples\JrfcSamples\

You can try this example as well, but you will have to create a project and place all of the required classes in the project before you can build it; then you can execute the program. You will be prompted for your login ID, system, and so on. Finally, you will get a confirmation message telling you that the call was successful.

```
A:\>javaping
[OrbixWeb warning: failed to load the configuration file "OrbixWeb.properties"
using defaults]
Congratulations. Connection Established !

A:\>_
```

FIGURE 5.8 *Execution of the JavaPing executable*

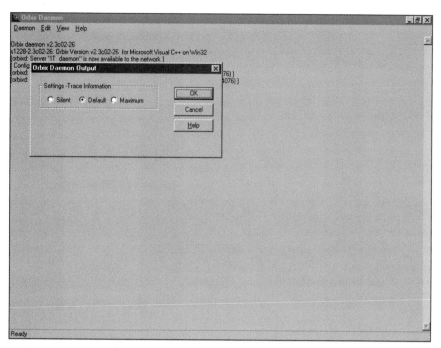

FIGURE 5.9 *Setting the level of trace for the Orbix Daemon*

Simple Material Data Retrieval

In this example we are actually going to query for a material number within SAP and report whether or not the number exists. If it does exist, we will print out the description. We've kept this example as simple as possible; it has no graphics and skips some of the detail in the steps that were performed in the first example, such as getting your SAP login and setting up the Orbix Daemon. Please refer to the first example if you require more details on these steps.

Step 1: Building up the JavaGetMat Class

Start this example by creating a new console application in the Java Compiler and adding one class to it, JavaGetMat, as shown in Figure 5.10.

The code for this example is similar to the first example but has some additional calls to get the material information through a few BAPI calls.

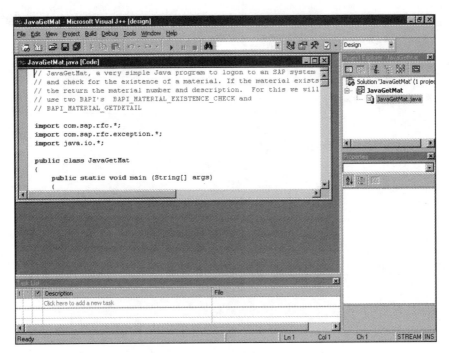

FIGURE 5.10 *Project JavaGetMat in the Java Compiler*

Step 2: Entering and Compiling the Code

The complete listing for the JavaGetMat program follows. Enter the code and compile it through the build operation (see the JavaPing example earlier in this chapter).

```java
// JavaGetMat, a very simple Java program to log in to a SAP system
// and check for the existence of a material. If the material exists,
// then return the material number and description.  For this we will
// use two BAPIs:  BAPI_MATERIAL_EXISTENCE_CHECK and
// BAPI_MATERIAL_GETDETAIL

import com.sap.rfc.*;
import com.sap.rfc.exception.*;
import java.io.*;

public class JavaGetMat
{
```

```
public static void main (String[] args)
{
    // Simple declaration of variables
    String   rfcHost = "testsystem",         // Java RFC Host
             r3Host  = "test.system.com",    // SAP System Name
             r3SysNo = "00",                 // System Number
             client  = "001",                // SAP Client Number
             user    = "kenkroes",           // Your User Name
             password = "scoobydoo"          // Your Password
             language = "EN";                // Your Login Language

    FactoryManager facMan = null;
    IRfcConnection connection = null;

    // Establish the connection to the Orbix Middleware
    MiddlewareInfo mdInfo = new MiddlewareInfo();
    mdInfo.setMiddlewareType(MiddlewareInfo.middlewareTypeOrbix);
    mdInfo.setOrbServerName(rfcHost);

    // let the global factory manager use the middlewareInfo
    // to create all object factories by binding to the server
    facMan = FactoryManager.getSingleInstance();
    facMan.setMiddlewareInfo(mdInfo);

    // Define The User information
    UserInfo       userInfo    = new UserInfo();
    ConnectInfo    connectInfo = new ConnectInfo();

    userInfo.setClient(client);
    userInfo.setUserName(user);
    userInfo.setPassword(password);
    userInfo.setLanguage(language);

    // Set up the Connection
    connectInfo.setRfcMode(ConnectInfo.RFC_MODE_VERSION_3);
    connectInfo.setDestination("xxx");
    connectInfo.setHostName(r3Host);
    connectInfo.setSystemNo((short)Integer.parseInt(r3SysNo));
```

```
connectInfo.setLoadBalancing(false);
connectInfo.setCheckAuthorization(true);

// Try to establish the connection

try
{
    connection = facMan.getRfcConnectionFactory()
                    .createRfcConnection(connectInfo, userInfo);
    connection.open();
}
catch (JRfcRfcConnectionException re)
{
    System.out.println("Unexpected RfcError while opening connection.\n"
                    + re.toString());
    return;
}
catch (JRfcBaseRuntimeException je)
{
    System.out.println("Unexpected JRFC runtime exception:\n"
                    + " while opening connection.\n"
                    + je.toString());
    return;
}
//      Simple routine to get data from user for the material number
//      if the user types in 'bye' the routine stops.
System.out.println("Congratulations, Connection Established !");
StringBuffer buf = new StringBuffer(50);
int c;
Character inChar = null;
while(true)
{
    buf.setLength(0);
    try
    {
        while((c = System.in.read()) != '\n')
        {
            if (inChar.isLetterOrDigit((char)c) ||
```

```
                                c == ' ')
                            buf.append((char)c);
                  }
                  if (buf.toString().equals("bye")) break;
            }
            catch(IOException io)
            {
                  System.out.println("Problem reading keyboard");
                  return;
            }
//      Now setup the parameters for the BAPI call.  This is a very simple
//          (yet inefficient) way to do this. More information on setting up
//          RFC parameters through "Factories" is discussed in Chapter 11
//          Build up object for the RFC Module
            IRfcModuleFactory moduleFac = facMan.getRfcModuleFactory();
            IRfcModule theModule = null;
            try
            {
                  theModule = moduleFac.
                        autoCreateRfcModule(connection,
                        "BAPI_MATERIAL_EXISTENCECHECK");

theModule.getSimpleImportParam("MATERIAL").setString(buf.toString());
//            Make the Call !!
                  theModule.callReceive();
            }
            catch(JRfcRemoteServerException je)
            {
                  System.out.println("Unexpected JRFC runtime exception:\n"
                                    + " while Calling RFC.\n"
                                    + je.toString());
                  return;
            }
            catch(JRfcRfcConnectionException je)
            {
                  System.out.println("Unexpected JRFC runtime exception:\n"
                                    + " while Calling RFC.\n"
                                    + je.toString());
```

```
                return;
            }
        catch(JRfcRfcAbapException je)
        {
            System.out.println("Unexpected JRFC runtime exception:\n"
                            + " while Calling RFC.\n"
                            + je.toString());
            return;
        }
        catch(JRfcRemoteAutoCreateException je)
        {
            System.out.println("Unexpected JRFC runtime exception:\n"
                            + " while Calling RFC.\n"
                            + je.toString());
            return;
        }

    //      Display the results
        char    bapiReturn;
        bapiReturn = theModule.getStructExportParam("RETURN").
                        getSimpleField("TYPE").getChar();

        if ( String.valueOf(bapiReturn) != "S" )
            System.out.println("Return =" + bapiReturn);
        //      Material Exists get description
        try
        {
            theModule = moduleFac.
                autoCreateRfcModule(connection,
                "BAPI_MATERIAL_GET_DETAIL");

    theModule.getSimpleImportParam("MATERIAL").setString(buf.toString());
            theModule.callReceive();
        }
        catch(JRfcRemoteServerException je)
        {
```

```
            System.out.println("Unexpected JRFC runtime exception:\n"
                              + " while Calling RFC.\n"
                              + je.toString());
        return;
    }
    catch(JRfcRfcConnectionException je)
    {
        System.out.println("Unexpected JRFC runtime exception:\n"
                              + " while Calling RFC.\n"
                              + je.toString());
        return;
    }
    catch(JRfcRfcAbapException je)
    {
        System.out.println("Unexpected JRFC runtime exception:\n"
                              + " while Calling RFC.\n"
                              + je.toString());
        return;
    }
    catch(JRfcRemoteAutoCreateException je)
    {
        System.out.println("Unexpected JRFC runtime exception:\n"
                              + " while Calling RFC.\n"
                              + je.toString());
        return;
    }
    // Print the material number and description
    String matDesc;
    matDesc = theModule.getStructExportParam("MATERIAL_GENERAL_DATA").
            getSimpleField("MATL_DESC").getString();
    System.out.println(buf.toString() + " " + matDesc );
        }
    }
}
```

Step 3: Running the Program

Start the Orbix Daemon as described in the JavaPing example. Open a DOS window on your system and change directories to the one that contains your JavaGetMat application. Type **JavaGetMat** at the prompt; your screen should look like that in Figure 5.11.

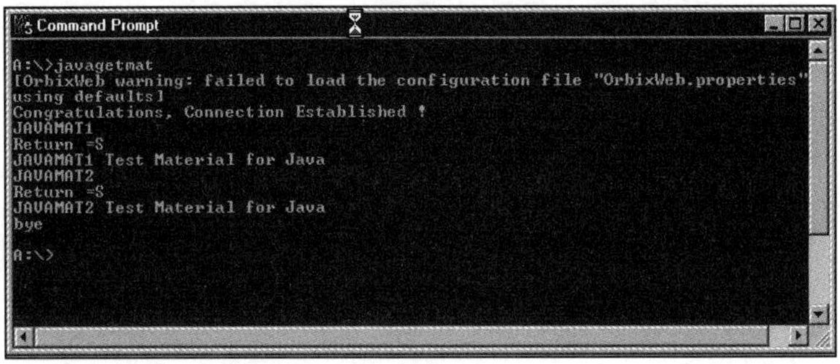

FIGURE 5.11 *Output from the JavaGetMat example*

Applet Example

This example walks you through setting up an applet using one of the sample pieces of code that comes with the Java RFC toolkit. The specific example is the RfcGetCustomer sample, which logs in to a SAP system and then retrieves data on customers that you specify. The easiest way to set up this applet is to build an HTML page that points to the class files that come with the Automation toolkit. Using the default path, they are located at

```
\Sap\SAPAuto45A\Auto2\Jrfc\client\classes\JrfcSamples\
```

When building the HTML page, you also need to set the CODEBASE parameter for the APPLET tag to point to the classes directory, as shown in the sample HTML that follows. For this example I created the HTML file in the directory that contains the applet code.

```
<!-Test HTML page for Java Sap Applet functions —>

<html>
<head>
```

```
<title>Test Page for Java Sap Applets</title>
</head>
<body>

<applet code=JRfcSamples/RfcCustomerGet/Applet/GetCustomerApplet.class
        codebase=/Sap/SAPAuto45A/Auto2/Jrfc/Client/classes
    height=500
    width=750 >
Java not supported with this browser
</applet>
</body>
</html>
```

Executing this HTML file will produce a screen similar to that in Figure 5.12.

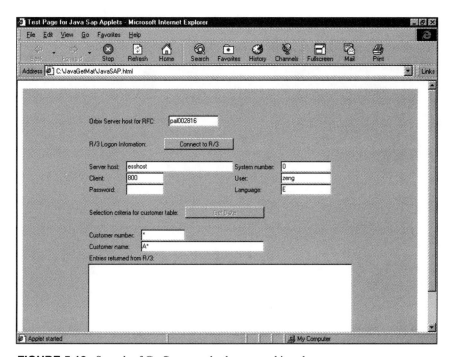

FIGURE 5.12 *Sample of GetCustomerApplet executed in a browser*

This example can also be modified so that certain variables, such as login and password, are set up in the HTML script instead of through the input prompts. More details on setting up applets in HTML and the HTML language in general are given in Appendix B, "Basic HTML Reference."

Summary

This chapter presented a few simple examples of how Java programs integrate with SAP. These examples will be especially useful after you learn about the various RFC and BAPI calls within SAP, because you can plug in new calls with little other modification. The next few chapters cover the basics of object-oriented programming and the Java language. Later chapters get into more detail on the various calls that are available within SAP, the use of BAPIs, and the classes that are available through the Java RFC toolkit.

Chapter 6

**Object-Oriented
Programming
Concepts**

In This Chapter

◆ Definition of an Object

◆ Classes

◆ Inheritance

The concept of OOP (*object-oriented programming*) has been around for a while, but was not really an important development methodology until the last decade. Its relative obscurity was at least partly due to the lack of a common programming language that truly used the OOP principles. With the introduction of C++ and now Java, true OOP is becoming more widely used and understood.

In this chapter we cover the basic building blocks of OOP—objects, classes, and inheritance—and consider how they fit specifically into the Java language.

Definition of an Object

As its name implies, OOP is centered around objects. For the purposes of OOP, an object is simply a combination of code and data that can be used together. Examples of code objects are subroutines, buttons, and screens. SAP has the BOR (*Business Object Repository*), which contains objects like material and sales orders.

Two mechanisms handle the communication to and from most objects. The first way to communicate between objects is through *variables* that can be passed back and forth from the calling object. The second approach consists of a predefined set of procedures that can be called to cause the object to do something. These procedures are more commonly known in the Java world as *methods*. Methods use the variables to determine the exact operation that the object is to perform. A graphical representation of an object can be seen in Figure 6.1.

With OOP you only have to know two things about each object:

◆ The communication process for the object, which basically means the format and content of both the incoming and outgoing variables

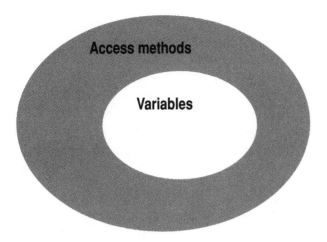

FIGURE 6.1   *A simple representation of an object-oriented environment*

◆ What the object does, or how the object behaves based on a specific set of input data

You, as programmer, do not have to know how the object is built. Consequently, you save a considerable amount of time when developing an application because you do not have to write and support every single line of code in an application. Because complete object-oriented applications are simply collections of objects that work together, you only have to code the new objects that you create and the glue that binds all of the objects together.

Objects in OOP have another advantage in addition to reusability of code; this advantage concerns how variables are treated within objects. In OOP, the object always controls which of its variables and methods other objects can see and use. This is called *encapsulation*, and it is the fundamental part of OOP.

The benefits of encapsulation are that objects can be written and maintained independent of the source code for other objects, and can easily be shared by different objects. Another benefit is simplicity, because a complicated piece of code can be written just once and then called many times. One more benefit is that data can be protected from other objects so that both integrity and security of the object are maintained.

Classes

In terms of OOP, a *class* is a grouping of like objects, and each object within a class is called an *instance* of that class. A simple programming example of the class concept is a class called Button; you may have several buttons, such as Save, Close, Open, and Cancel, in an application. Each button belongs to the Button class, yet each one can contain different variable values, such as the label or shape. Note that although the variable of each button object can contain different values, all buttons have the same variable declaration and also have the same methods as the Button class. Object variables are often called *instance variables*.

To reinforce the idea of objects and classes, we will build a simple Java program that defines a class with a few variables and a method and then declares two objects from this class.

 NOTE

The purpose of the code example is to demonstrate the class-to-object relationship, not to go through the details of Java syntax. The basics of Java syntax are covered in Chapters 7 through 10 in this book.

```
public class jsap0601
{
/* Declare some instance variables.            */
    String name;
    int age;
/* Declare a method for the class           */
    void out()
    {
        System.out.println("\n " + name + " is " + age + " years old.");
    }
/* Main declaration, required for application (instead of applet) */
    public static void main (String[] args)
    {
        System.out.println("Demonstration of Classes and Objects");
/* Declare 1st instance of class JSAP0601 */
        jsap0601 person1 = new jsap0601();
```

```
/* Declare 2nd instance of class JSAP0601 */
        jsap0601 person2 = new jsap0601();
/* Assign values to both instances */
        person1.name = "Ken";
        person1.age  = 36;
        person2.name = "Donna";
        person2.age  = 35;
/* Call method from class jsap0601 for each instance */
        person1.out();
        person2.out();
    }
}
```

The output of this program follows.

```
Ken is 36 years old.
Donna is 35 years old.
```

To make everything a bit more complicated, you can declare variables and methods that belong to the class itself. These variables and methods can be accessed directly or from an instance of the class; however, class methods cannot access instance variables or methods. This relationship is shown in Figure 6.2. Class methods must access class variables.

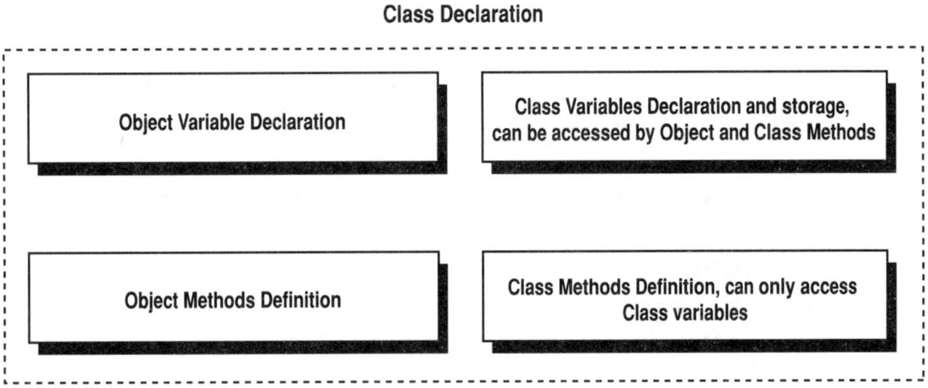

Class Declaration

FIGURE 6.2 *Variable and method relationships between class and object*

An example of a class variable is the total number of instance objects created. Then, as objects are added or deleted from the class, the accumulator can be adjusted accordingly. The following code example demonstrates the use of both class variables and methods.

```java
public class jsap0602
{
/* Declare a Class Variable                      */
    static int total;
/* Declare some instance variables.       */
    String name;
    int age;
/* Declare a Class method for the class       */
    static void add()
    {
        total = total + 1;
    }
    static void total_out()
    {
        System.out.println("\nTotal number of people = " + total);
    }
/* Declare an instance method for the class          */
    void out()
    {
        System.out.println("\n" + name + " is " + age + " years old.");
    }
/* Main declaration, required for application (instead of applet) */
    public static void main (String[] args)
    {
        System.out.println("Demonstration of Classes and Objects");
/* Declare 1st instance of class JSAP0602 */
        jsap0602 person1 = new jsap0602();
/* Declare 2nd instance of class JSAP0602 */
        jsap0602 person2 = new jsap0602();
```

```
/* Assign values to both instances and add to class variable */
        person1.name = "Ken";
        person1.age  = 36;
        jsap0602.add();
        person2.name = "Donna";
        person2.age  = 35;
        jsap0602.add();
/* Call method from class jsap0602 for each instance */
        person1.out();
        person2.out();
/* Write out the total class variable which is totaling people */
        jsap0602.total_out();
    }
}
```

The preceding code has the following output:

```
Ken is 36 years old.
Donna is 35 years old.
Total number of people = 2
```

When designing classes, keep the following elements in mind.

◆ The class should have a well-defined interface, or way that other programs can access it.

◆ If possible, a class should not have to rely on another class to perform the intended function.

◆ The class should be bulletproof, so that any input, bad or good, will have a predictable response.

◆ The purpose of the class must be well defined. Hence the class should have an easy-to-understand function or solve a specific problem in the application.

Objects help programmers by providing modularity and the ability to encapsulate data. Classes provide the benefit of reusability because the code is written once and then objects can be declared multiple times and reuse the same code.

Inheritance

The concept of inheritance is what really makes OOP a powerful tool in application development. In OOP, *inheritance* simply means that classes can inherit the variables and methods of other classes. The classes that inherit these characteristics are called *subclasses,* and the class that is being inherited from is called the *superclass.*

A simple example of this hierarchy is in the computer industry, where you can have a Computer superclass with Desktop and Server subclasses, as shown in Figure 6.3. Both the Desktop and Server classes have many of the same variables and methods, and these common variables and methods can be assigned to the Computer superclass. Then the Desktop class will contain only variables and methods that are specific to the desktop, and the Server class will contain only variables and methods that are specific to the server.

Inheritance does not have to stop at one layer. Classes can be nested as deeply as required for the problem at hand. When the system is trying to resolve a variable or method name for a low-level subclass, it starts with the instance values. If it finds a value that matches the same name and type, the search stops; if a match is not found, the system looks in that class's superclass, and so on until the variable or method is found. From this information, we know that subclasses can override

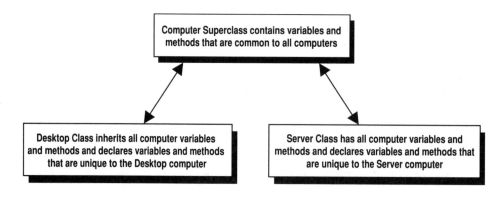

FIGURE 6.3 *Class Hierarchy example*

variables and methods from superclasses as long as the name and type declaration are the same.

Inheritance allows the programmer to build abstract objects at a high level, and then to develop more detail about the object as the classes are developed down the class hierarchy. In the automobile industry, for example, you can have a class called Vehicle that defines many of the variables and methods common to all vehicles. Under Vehicle, you can have a class called Car that contains only the variables and methods that make cars distinct from other vehicles. Under the Car class, you can then define classes for sport, luxury, and economy cars; again, each class contains only the variables that make it unique under the Car class. If you need to define a new type of car, for example electric, you can simply add a new class under the Car class. Most of the work is already completed. Because an electric car is not too different from a regular car, your only job is to define the Electric class with the variables and methods that make it unique in the Car superclass.

Does This Terminology Sound Familiar?

Even if you have never used OOP, you might recognize a lot of the concepts and terminology in this chapter. SAP's variant configurator is based on object-oriented design. Dependency rules are the methods, characteristics are the variables, and SAP's classes and class hierarchy fit the OOP mold exactly. Of course, the flip side is also true; if you do not have any experience with SAP's variant configuration module, you can now say that you understand the basics of how it works!

Summary

This chapter presents an overview of OOP. We started with the concept of objects and examined how like objects can be grouped together into classes. Within a class, we define the variables and methods that are common to all the objects in the class. When we declare a new object, it is referred to as an *instance* of the class from which we created it. We also discussed how classes can be nested within each other to form a class hierarchy. A class that is subordinate to another class is called a *subclass*, and a class that has subordinates is called a *superclass*.

Each major aspect of OOP—object, class, or inheritance—has its own features. Objects enable programmers to use encapsulation and modularity in programs. Classes allow programmers to reuse code and group logically similar objects together. Inheritance supports abstract code construction and the reuse of code because it can be shared across classes that contain common aspects.

Chapter 7

The Basics of the
Java Language

In This Chapter

- ◆ Variables, Data Types, and Declarations
- ◆ Operators
- ◆ Strings and Arrays
- ◆ Literals
- ◆ Comments
- ◆ Control Flow Statements

The basic building blocks of Java, like those in most other advanced programming languages, make up intrinsic data types, operators, and flow control statements. Readers familiar with languages such as C or C++ will find many similarities in the Java programming language.

Variables, Data Types, and Declarations

Java supports three kinds of variables: instance variables, class variables, and local variables. *Instance variables* are defined when you create the class and apply it to all instances (objects) made from that class. *Class variables* are also defined when you create the class, but they are global to the class. *Local variables* are defined within a method or other code block and can be used only within that code block. This type of variable definition really defines the scope of the variable and where it can be used.

Variable Types

Variables can basically be declared two ways: via a primitive declaration or by typing the variable after a class. Table 7.1 outlines the basic data types of the Java language. To see how Java data types compare to ABAP (Advanced Business

Application Programming) data types, please refer to Appendix C, "ABAP/4 Data Types to Java Cross-Reference."

Table 7.1 Basic Data Types for Variables in Java

Type	Size	Description
byte	8 bits	+/- 2^7 integer values
short	16 bits	+/- 2^15 integer values
int	32 bits	+/- 2^31 integer values
long	64 bits	+/- 2^63 integer values
float	32 bits	Single-precision floating-point
double	64 bits	Double-precision floating-point
boolean	1 bit	True or false
char	16 bits	Single Unicode character

If you are going to type a variable as a class, the class must obviously be defined either as part of standard Java (such as string in the java.lang package) or in your own program.

Variable Naming

The standard convention in Java is to start all variable names with a lowercase letter and all class names with an uppercase character. Variable names should be descriptive enough to indicate what the variables contain. Naming a variable "i" forces people to read through your code to determine the variable's contents, whereas naming the variable "rowsSelected" gives the reader at least some idea of the contents. When variable names contain multiple words, by convention each word begins with an uppercase character (except for the first one). Here are some examples:

```
isEnabled
totalAmountSpent
abortDueToError
```

Variable names must also follow these rules:

◆ Names must start with a letter, an underscore (_), or a dollar sign ($). Variable names cannot start with a number.

◆ Names can contain a valid Unicode character. Unicode characters comprise all standard character sets plus many others that can represent languages such as Greek, Russian, and Hebrew.

◆ Names cannot be the same as a Java keyword.

◆ Names cannot be the same as another variable in the same scope. Hence you cannot have two class variables named isEnabled (provided that both variable data types are the same); you can, however, have a class variable named "isEnabled" and a local variable named "isEnabled".

Variable Declaration and Assignment

Variables are defined by putting either the primitive data type or class first, giving the variable name, and then (optionally) adding the initialization value. Following are some examples:

```
int numberOfAccounts;
String interfaceName = "Finance_Inbound";
boolean applyDiscount = false;
```

You can also declare multiple variables of the same type in a single statement by separating the variable names with commas, as shown here:

```
String person1 = "Joe", person2 = "John";
```

It is always a good practice to assign an initial value to a variable. In Java it is mandatory to do so with local variables. If you have a class or instance variable, the following default values are used if the variable is not initialized before being used.

◆ **Booleans**—False

◆ **Characters**—\0

◆ **Integer and floating-point**—0

Operators

The operators that are used in Java are very similar to those used in C or C++. We can classify operators into five basic types: arithmetic, increment/decrement, logical, comparison, and assignment.

The order of precedence on these operators is as follows:

1. Increment or decrement
2. Arithmetic
3. Comparisons
4. Logical
5. Assignment

As with most other languages, parts of an expression can be given higher precedence by using parentheses.

Increment and Decrement

Similar to the C programming language, Java allows you to increment and decrement variables using the increment (++) and decrement (--) operators either before or after the variable name.

```
int x = 5;          // initialize 'x' to the value '5'
x++;                // after this line, 'x' is equal to '6'
```

Whether the operators are placed before or after the variable can make quite a difference in how the code functions. If the operator is placed before the variable, the increment or decrement happens before any other operation in the statement. If the operator is placed after the variable, the increment or decrement happens after all other operations in the statement.

```
int x1 = 5, y1 = 3, z1;
int x2 = 5, y2 = 3, z2;
/* Case # 1 */
z1 = ++x1 * y1;     //  After this statement z1=18 & x1=6
/* Case # 2 */
z2 = x2++ * y2;     //  After this statement z2=15 & x2=6
```

Arithmetic Operators

Table 7.2 shows the basic arithmetic operators that can be applied to all numeric data types.

Table 7.2 Java Arithmetic Operators

Operator	Use	Description
+	x + y	Addition
-	x - y	Subtraction
*	x * y	Multiplication
/	x / y	Division
%	x % y	Modulus

 NOTE

The addition operator (+) can also be used for string concatenation. Strings and arrays are discussed in more detail in the "Strings and Arrays" section later in this chapter.

Comparison Operators

Comparison operators are used to perform some type of test on two variables and then return a simple true or false Boolean result. The comparison operators for Java are listed in Table 7.3.

Table 7.3 Java Comparison Operators

Operator	Use	Returns true If
>	x > y	x is greater than y
<	x < y	x is less than y
>=	x >= y	x is greater than or equal to y
<=	x <= y	x is less than or equal to y
==	x == y	x is equal to y
!=	x != y	x is not equal to y

Logical Operators

The comparison operators in Table 7.3 can be combined to form a more complex expression through the use of logical operators. Table 7.4 summarizes the logical operators.

Table 7.4 Java Logical Operators

Operator	Use	Returns true If
&&	exp1 && exp2	Both expressions are true
||	exp1 || exp2	At least one of the expressions is true
!	! exp1	The expression is false
^	exp1 ^ exp2	One expression is true and the other is false
~	~ exp1	Bitwise complement

There is one catch with the && and || operators. You can use & instead of && and | instead of ||; these elements are bitwise operators. In these cases, Java evaluates the second expression only if necessary. This approach can save on execution time if you have very complicated expressions, but can also lead to unexpected results if you combine other operators in your expressions, as shown here:

```
int x = 5, y = 4, z = 3;
boolean testResult1 = ( x < 4 ) & ( y > ++z);
boolean testResult2 = ( X < 4 ) && (y > ++z);
```

In the preceding code sample, both testResult1 and testResult2 return false. z is not incremented (because x < 4 is not true) in the first case, but it is in the second case.

Assignment Operators

Assignment operators are the tools that allow us to change the value of variables. Table 7.5 summarizes the Java assignment operators.

Table 7.5 Java Assignment Operators

Operator	Use	Results
+=	x += y	x = x + y
-=	x -= y	x = x - y
*=	x *= y	x = x * y
/=	x /= y	x = x / y
%=	x %= y	x = x % y
&=	x &= y	x = x & y
|=	x |= y	x = x | y
^=	x ^= y	x = x ^ y
>>	x >> y	Shift bits of x right by y places
<<	x << y	Shift bits of x left by y places
>>>	x >>> y	Shift bits of x right by y places (unsigned)

Strings and Arrays

Java supports the storage and manipulation of multiple values through arrays. *Strings* are simply arrays of characters (strings are actually classes of the java.lang package). *Arrays* are similar to internal tables in ABAP.

Arrays

Arrays in Java can be declared with the following general statement:

```
datatype[] arrayname = new datatype[arraysize];
```

This statement both declares the array and allocates memory for it. After the array has been declared, each element can be accessed through the use of the square brackets, as shown here:

```
int[] arrayInts = new int[10];   // 10 array elements
int        x;
arrayInts[0] = '0';              // 1st element = '0'
arrayInts[1] = '1';              // 2nd element = '1'
x = arrayInts.length;            // x is set to 10.
```

NOTE

You can see in the preceding example that Java arrays are indexed starting at '0'. Also note that whenever you declare an array, regardless of type, the instance variable "length" can be used to determine the overall length of the array.

Multidimensional arrays in Java are declared as follows:

```
int[][] multiArray = new int[10][10];
multiArray[0][0] = '456';
multiArray[9][9] = '123';
```

Strings

Java has two different classes for character arrays: String and StringBuffer. The String class holds strings that do not change after they have been initialized or set, whereas the StringBuffer class holds arrays of characters that do change. Usually, you will use the String class for constants and for passing character arrays to and from methods where the array will not be changed.

```
String newString = "Hi there";              // Allocates a simple constant
StringBuffer newBuffer = new StringBuffer(10);  // Allocates  a 10 character
                                            // array
```

Methods for the String Class

Here are the most commonly used methods associated with the String class:

- **.length()**. Returns the length (in characters) of the string.
- **.charAt(x)**. Returns the character of the string at position x.
- **.indexof(x)**. Returns the first index of the string that contains the character equal to the value passed in.
- **.indexof(x,from)**. Returns the first index of the string that contains the character equal to the value passed in, starting at the index passed to the function in the from variable.
- **.lastindexof**. Same as .indexof but looks backward (toward the left of the string instead of the right).
- **.subtring(from,to)**. Returns a string that starts at the from index and ends at the to index.

◆ **.valueOf(var)**. Returns the string equivalent of the value contained in var regardless of data type.

 NOTE

The valueOf method is associated with most data types, so, for example, if you need to represent the value 5 as a float, you can simply say float.valueof('5').

Methods for the StringBuffer Class

Here are the most commonly used methods associated with the StringBuffer class:

◆ **.length()**. Returns the length (in characters) of the string.

◆ **.charAt(x)**. Returns the character of the string at position x.

◆ **.capacity()**. Returns the amount of space allocated to the array.

◆ **.append(x)**. Appends the character x onto the end of the StringBuffer variable; if the capacity is exceeded, more memory is allocated (although this method is not very efficient).

◆ **.insert(pos,x)**. Inserts the character specified in x at the position pos; again, if the capacity of the variable is exceeded, more memory is allocated.

◆ **.toString()**. Converts the StringBuffer to a String. This method is useful when it is necessary to pass a String to a method (instead of a String-Buffer).

The following program uses many of the methods just described.

```
public class Jsap0701
{
    public static void main (String[] args)
    {
/* Declare a Constant String and a StringBuffer */
        String str1 = "c:\testdir\file01.exe";
        StringBuffer str2 = new StringBuffer(60);
        StringBuffer str3 = new StringBuffer(20);
```

```
/* Get the length of the String      */
        System.out.println(str1.length());
/* Get the length and Capacity of the Stringbuffer */
        System.out.println(str2.length());
        System.out.println(str2.capacity());
/* Get the Drive letter from the path in str */
        str2.append(str1.substring(0,str1.indexOf(':')));
        System.out.println(str2);
/* Convert a floating point number to a string */
        str3.append(String.valueOf(1.325));
        System.out.println(str3);
    }
}
```

This program has the following output:

```
21

0
60

c
1.325
```

Literals

A *literal* is any term that directly represents a value in the code. Examples of literals are

```
X = 5;
Str = "Test";
```

Table 7.6 shows a series of special cases that demonstrate the rules to follow when you want to use numeric literal values in your Java program, along with the values to use with Boolean variables.

Table 7.6 Examples of Numeric/Boolean Literals

Example	Description
123	Integer value literal
123L	Long value literal
0123	Octal literal, prefix literal with a 0
0x123	Hexadecimal literal, prefix literal with 0x
12.3F	Floating-point literal
12.3	Double literal
12.3e12	Double literal with exponents
true	Boolean "True" literal value
false	Boolean "False" literal value

Compared to numeric literals, character and string literals are a little more complicated. A *character literal* is a single character that is enclosed in single quotes. A *string literal* is enclosed in double quotes. A string literal can contain any of the character literals that are described in Table 7.7.

Table 7.7 Special Character Literal Symbols

Code	Description
\n	New line
\\	Backslash character
\t	Tab
\b	Backspace
\r	Carriage return
\f	Form feed
\'	Single quotation
\"	Double quotation
\val	If val is a number, it is interpreted as octal
	If val starts with an x, it is interpreted as a hex value
	If val starts with a u, it is interpreted as a Unicode character

An example of a string literal with embedded characters follows.

```
String str = "This\nis\na test\nof the \\n\nliteral";
```

If the preceding variable is printed, the output will look something like this:

```
This
Is
A test
Of the \n
literal
```

Comments

You can add comments to a Java language program in three ways.

◆ `// Comment Tex`

The compiler ignores everything from the // to the end of the physical line.

◆ `/* Lots of documentation */`

The compiler ignores everything between the /* and the */. This type of comment can span multiple physical lines.

◆ `/** Official Documentation */`

The compiler ignores everything between the /** and the */. Like the preceding comment type, this one can span multiple physical lines. The difference between this type of comment and the last one is that programs like javadoc (from JDK) can read in the latter. This type of comment usually describes the purpose of a class or method.

Control Flow Statements

So far we have spent most of this chapter talking about variables, data types, arrays, and literals. To make Java programs useful, though, we need ways to control the logic flow of the software. Flow control can basically be broken up into four areas:

- ◆ Decision making
- ◆ Looping
- ◆ Exception handling
- ◆ Miscellaneous

Decision Making

Decision making in Java is usually controlled with the if-else or switch commands. The switch command is basically a fancy if-else statement, so we start our explanation with the if-else command.

The basic syntax of the if-else is as follows:

```
if (expression) statement;
```

In this simple case, if the expression evaluates to true, then the statement is executed. The statement can be a series of lines surrounded by curly brackets ({}).

```
If (expression)
{
    statement 1;
    statement 2;
    . . .
}
```

 NOTE

The curly brackets {} can be used anywhere in the Java language and indicate that all of the statements between the brackets are to be treated as one statement.

The else portion of the if-else statement is executed if the expression associated with the previous if is evaluated as false.

```
If (expression1)
{
    . . .
```

```
statements executed if expression1 is true;

. . .

}
else if (expression2)
{

. . .

statements executed if expression1 is false and expression2 is true

. . .

}
else
{

. . .

statements executed if expression1 and expression2 are both false.

. . .

}
```

As mentioned previously, the switch statement is just a derivation of the if-else statement. Using the switch statement makes your code easier to read because you do not have to code a series of else statements. A simple example of the same logic coded with both an if and a switch follows.

```
// If Statement to print first three months of the year
if month == 1
    System.out.println("January");
else if month == 2
    System.out.println("February");
else if month == 3
    System.out.println("March");
Endif
// Same logic, but using the switch statement instead
switch (month)
{
    case 1: System.out.println("January");
    case 2: System.out.println("February");
    case 3: System.out.println("March");
}
```

In a switch statement, the value right after the switch statement is evaluated against each value in each case statement. If the values are equal, then all of the following statements are executed until the end of the case statement or until the Java break command is encountered.

 NOTE

C programmers should take note that the switch command in Java is not quite the same as it is in C. In Java, the switch command evaluates only simple integer conditions, not more complicated data types like floats or strings.

The break command terminates the switch and moves execution to the line following the switch statement. Curly brackets are not required when using multiple statements in each case statement. You can also use the term *default* in the last case statement to handle any expression that does not match one of the previous case statements. The following example demonstrates a slightly more complex switch statement.

```
Switch (month)
{
    case 2:
        if ((year % 4 == 0) && ((year % 100 != 0) ||
        ((year % 400) == 0))
        System.out.println("Number of days = 29");
        else
            System.out.println("Number of days = 28");
        break;
    case 4:
    case 6:
    case 9:
    case 11:
        System.out.println("Number of days = 30");
        break;
    default: System.out.println("Number of days = 31");
}
```

Notice that if the month is June, the program still prints that the number of days is equal to 30 because all statements are executed until the next break statement is encountered.

Looping

Java has three different types of looping commands: do-while, while-do, and for.

The do-while and the while-do commands work in a similar fashion—the only difference is when the condition of the loop is evaluated. With the while-do, the expression is evaluated first, and then the statement block is executed if the expression is true. The do-while evaluates the expression block after the statement block has executed, and therefore the statement block is always executed at least once. The following is an example of a while-do loop:

```
int I = 4;
while(i < 4)
{
System.out.println(i);
i = i + 1;
}
```

The preceding loop prints out nothing because the value of i fails the test i < 4. Consider the following do-while loop:

```
int i = 4;
do
{
System.out.println(i);
i = i + 1;
}while (i < 4)
```

In the preceding example, the program prints out the value 4 because the statements in the loop are executed before the loop condition is processed.

The other type of loop condition in Java is the for loop, which has the following general syntax:

```
For(initialization code, termination evaluation, increment code)
{
statements
}
```

In the initialization code, you can both initialize and declare variables before the loop is executed. Variables that are declared here can be used inside the loop only and cease to exist when the loop has finished. Multiple variables must be separated by commas. The evaluation section of the for loop is tested once per pass and works like the while-do loop. The increment code is a statement (or a series of statements separated by commas) that is executed after each execution of the loop and before the evaluation for the loop is performed. Some examples of for loops follow:

```
// A simple FOR loop
for(int i = 1; i < 4; ++i) system.out.println(i);
// a bit more complex example
int i;
for(i= 1, int j = 3; i < j; ++ i)
{
    System.out.println(i);
}
```

 CAUTION

One of the most common programming mistakes is the misplaced semicolon (;), especially in if and loop statements. Look at the following code segment and take a guess at the output.

```
for(int i = 1; i < 4; ++i);
        System.out.println(i);
```

If you guessed that the code would print "1 2 3," you are wrong! The semicolon after the for statement terminates the for loop, and the System.out.println statement is executed as a simple Java statement; the output is "4." This mistake is easy to make because in Java (and in C) you get in the habit of putting the semicolon behind every line. Use caution whenever you build an if or a loop statement—make sure that the semicolons are placed correctly!

Other Ways to Control Program Flow

The break statement, which can be used in any loop, causes the loop to stop processing immediately and continue the program with the statement right after the loop block. For a more elaborate form of the break command, you can break out of a loop to a specific piece in the code. This technique puts a label on a piece of Java code before the loop. When you use a label with the break command, the label must be outside the loop that contains the break, as shown in the following example:

```
. . .
testLabel:
    If (userInput < 0)
    {
            System.out.println("invalid userInput");
            UserInput = 1;
    }
    for(int i = 1; i< 10; ++i)
    {
            if (userInput < 0) break testLabel;
            result = userInput / i;
            System.out.println(result);
    }
. . .
```

Another way to control program flow in loop processing is to use the Java keyword *continue*. The continue statement stops processing the current loop iteration and starts processing the next loop pass from the top of the loop logic, as shown in the following code example:

```
. . .
for( I = -5 ; I < 5; ++I )
{
    if ( I == 0) continue;
    result = 1 / I;
    System.out.println(result);
}
. . .
```

One other way to control program flow is with the Java return statement. The return statement terminates processing of the current method and returns the program call to the calling method. An addition to the return statement can be the return value of the method. In Chapter 8, "Objects, Classes, and Interfaces," we discuss how methods can return values in detail, but for now you can think of a method as being declared as a type of variable. If a method is declared as a type void, there is no return value. A method could also be declared as a type int and, in this case, would be expected to return an integer value. When you use the return keyword in a method, it must return a variable with the same type declaration as the method from which it is called.

Exception Handling

An *exception* can be defined as an event that causes a change in the normal flow of a program. Examples of exceptions are a file not being found, or unexpected input from a user. When an exception occurs in a program, the system tries to find a way to handle this event by going through the methods until it finds one that is set up to handle the exception that has occurred. The methods that handle exceptions are called *exception handlers*. When an exception is raised, it is said to be "thrown," and when an appropriate method is found, it is said to have "caught" the exception.

The general format for Java code that is set up to handle exceptions is as follows:

```
. . .
try{
statements
}catch (exception1 variable) statement to handle exception;
 catch (exception2 variable) statement to handle exception;
. . .
```

As you can see, exception handling is achieved by grouping some statements in a try block and then handling any exceptions that may occur in this block with one or more catch blocks. Inheritance also takes part in the process of exception handling in that the first catch block that matches a generated exception is executed, and any other catch blocks that may exist are ignored.

 NOTE

The exception process in Java is similar to the ABAP exception process of calling function modules. In a function module, you raise an exception, and then the calling program handles the exception through the sy-subrc return code. The difference is that in Java the exception is an event and does not automatically stop processing the current method, as the raise command in ABAP does.

Exceptions in Java are really objects of the Java class throwable. This class has two subclasses: error and exception. The error subclass is used for internal errors to the Java run-time environment, whereas the exception subclass is used for all other error types, such as I/O exceptions or class not found. To raise a generic exception in your program, you can simply create a new instance of the exception class and use the Java command throws.

```
. . .
// Example #1
Exception() myException = new Exception("Descriptive Text");
Throw myException;
return;   // Usually added
// Example # 2
throws new Exception("Descriptive Text here");
return;   // Usually added
. . .
```

To catch a generic exception like the one generated in the preceding example, you would use a piece of code like this:

```
. . .
Try{
// Statements that could generate the Exception
}catch(Exception e){
System.out.println(e.string);
}
. . .
```

The one other Java keyword associated with the try block is the finally block. The finally block is used like a catch block, as shown in the following example, and is executed regardless of how the try block is finished (exception or not).

```
. . .
try{
statements
}catch (exception1 variable) statement to handle exception;
 catch (exception2 variable) statement to handle exception;
 finally  statement to process regardless of the try block finishes
. . .
```

A full explanation of the declaration, creation, and use of exceptions is beyond the scope of this book. This section exists to make you aware of the concept and to explain how it can and should be used to handle unexpected events in your programs. The following sample program ties together all the exception-related topics discussed in this chapter. The program reads in a file and prints the value of each byte to the screen.

```
public class Jsap0702
{
    public static void main (String[] args)
    {
        FileInputStream fStr;
        Boolean endOfFile = false;
        Int  input;
        try{
            fStr = new FileInputStream("C:\test.txt");
            while (!endOfFile)
            {
                byte = fstr.read();
                System.out.print(byte + " ");
                If ( byte == -1 ) endOfFile = true;
            }
            fstr.close();
        }catch (IOException e){
         System.out.println("I/O error encounter:" + e.toString());
        }
    }
}
```

One final note about exceptions. You should write your code to catch errors that will prevent your program from executing, such as an end of file, but you should not use exception processing to handle events that you know will take place. Exception processing is very resource intensive and should not be used for things like verifying user input, which can easily be checked by other means.

Summary

This chapter covers the use of the basic Java commands. A great deal of information is presented here, and if you are not familiar with a programming language like C or C++, you should probably review this chapter again after you have gone through the next few chapters. They cover the creation of classes and methods and explain how the core elements from this chapter are used to develop real Java programs or applets.

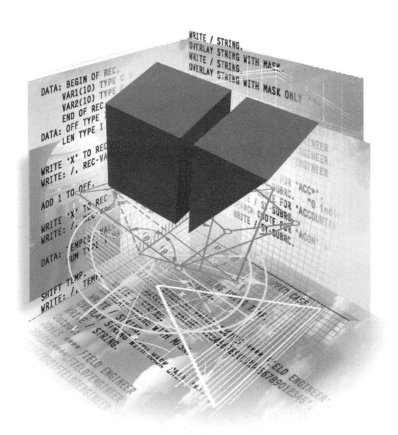

Chapter 8

Objects, Classes, and Interfaces

In This Chapter

- ◆ Creating and Using Objects
- ◆ Creating and Using Classes
- ◆ Creating and Using Interfaces and Packages

Chapter 6, "Object-Oriented Programming Concepts," covers the fundamentals of object-oriented programming; Chapter 7, "The Basics of the Java Language," discusses the basics of the Java language syntax. This chapter ties together these two areas so that you will be able to write real Java object-oriented programs.

Creating and Using Objects

Most of the work in Java programming is done with objects. This work includes creating the object, using both the variables and the methods of that object, and finally, destroying the object when it is no longer needed.

Instantiating an Object

You can create an object simply by telling the Java program the type of object and its name, as shown here:

```
// Example of creation of an object using "type name"
Rectangle myrec;
```

The preceding example does not declare an object, but simply says that the variable myrec is a reference to an object of type Rectangle. This approach is very similar to the declaration of a pointer in the C language because the variable does not point to any specific object. Java is rather strict about the use of objects, though, so before you can use the variable myrec, you need to assign it to a real object. In Java the primary way to assign a variable to a real object is through Java's "new" operator, as shown next.

```
Rectangle myrec;
myrec = new Rectangle(0,0,100,200);
```

This operator does the job of creating the object. New allocates the memory for the object and calls the constructor for the class from which the object is being created. Constructors are covered in more detail later in this chapter in the context of classes, but the point to remember here is that you can pass variables to the constructor through variables included between the parentheses.

Usually, the creation of the reference to the object and the allocation of this reference to an actual object is done in one line, as shown in the following examples:

```
Rectangle myrec = new Rectangle(0,0,100,100);
Random rand1 = new Random();
```

Declaring arrays of objects is similar to declaring primitive objects. To make an array of a certain object, first you need to make an array of references and then point each of these references to objects. The following code segment demonstrates this technique.

```
// Example of declaration of an Array of Objects
Rectangle[] manyrec = new Rectangle[5];
for (int i = 0; i < 5; i++ )
{
    manyrec[I] = new Rectangle();
}
```

 NOTE

You can determine the class of any object by using the getClass method that is available to all objects. If the object name is tempobj, its class can be determined as follows:

```
String name = tempobj.getClass().getName();
System.out.println("Class is:" + name);
```

That pretty much covers the creation of objects. As Chapter 6 points out, objects comprise two parts: variables and methods. Now that you have created an object, you are ready to learn how to access and use these parts of the object.

Using an Object's Variables

An object's variables are declared in the class definition and are accessed through the object by using the dot notation. For example, the class Rectangle has four member variables: height, width, x, and y. These variables can be accessed as follows:

```
myrec.height = 10;
myrec.width = 200;
System.out.println("the x coordinate is " + myrec.x = 10);
Myrec.y = 20;
```

From this example you can see that you can do both the assignment and display of the variables through the dot operator. Even if you have compound objects (objects within other objects), the dot notation is still used to access the inner object's variables and is evaluated from left to right, as shown here:

```
outobject.innerobject.variable = 5;
```

Remember that the new operator creates a reference to an object, and an object's variable is also an object itself (either a primitive like int or an object that is more complex). You can therefore create new instances (or objects) of the variables of an object, as shown in this example:

```
myheight = new Rectangle().height;
```

Using an Object's Methods

The second part of an object consists of the methods associated with it. *Methods* are pieces of code that the object can use; they are accessed the same way that variables are, through the dot notation.

```
object.method(arguments)
```

 NOTE

Note that parentheses are required; if no arguments are to be passed to the method, just use empty parentheses.

Examples of method calls follow:

```
int x;
int y;
y = 5;
TextArea text1 = new TextArea();
text1.setrows(y);
x = text1.getrows();
```

Java is very fussy about the arguments that are passed into methods because in Java you can have different code for the same method; the code that is executed is based on the arguments that are passed into the method. Take, for example, the String class and its method indexOf.

```
indexOf(int)
indexOf(int,int)
indexOf(String)
indexOf(String,int)
```

When the Java compiler encounters the indexOf method of an object that references the String class, the compiler evaluates the arguments to see which piece of code to execute. It is therefore important for you to use the correct types of arguments whenever you call a method. If a method requires a float, the Java compiler responds with an error if you try to send an int value to the method.

You can pass a variable of an incorrect type to a method using a process called *casting*. In casting you take an existing object and create a new value of a different type. Casting can take on three forms:

◆ Casting between primitive types such as integers and floats
◆ Casting between objects
◆ Casting between primitives and objects

When casting with primitives, you must take care as to the precision of the resulting value. A general rule of thumb is that if you cast from a smaller type to a larger type, the precision of the value is retained. However, if you cast from a larger to a smaller value, that is, from a double to a float, then you may experience a loss in the precision of your value. Thus, Java allows you to do implicit casting if you are casting to a larger type and insists that you do explicit casting if you are casting to a smaller data type. Explicit casting between primitive types is accomplished by declaring the destination type in parentheses followed by the variable or expression that you want to cast. Examples of casting between primitive data types are as follows:

```
int x;
long y;
y = x;      // no cast needed since Y is a larger data type
x = (int)y; // explicit casting is required here
```

NOTE

Boolean data types cannot be used in a cast. They must always be either true or false.

Compared with casting between primitives, casting between objects is a bit more complicated. In general, you can cast between objects only if they are related by inheritance. Take care when casting from a subclass to a superior class; the subclass will have information that is not contained in the superior class, and a loss of data or precision may result. As with primitive object type casting, you can use implicit casting if you are casting a subclass to a superior class, but you must use explicit casting if you go from a superior class to a subordinate one.

NOTE

You can find out whether an object is related to another object by using the Java operator instanceof as shown here:

```
if (obj1 instanceof Class1)
{
    Class1 obj2 = (Class1)obj1;
}
```

The last type of casting is when you want to cast a primitive to an object, or vice versa. Java does not really allow this procedure; however, you are allowed to convert the primitive to an object (or vice versa) and then perform the casting. This step is accomplished by using the classes in Java that have the same name as the primitive data type, except that the first letter is capitalized (for example, int data type and Int class).

Certain methods associated with these primitive classes allow for the conversion of values to primitive data types. In the following example, for instance, you have a String object that contains a number, and you want to put this number into a variable of type int.

```
int  tempvar;
String tempstr = "-3456";
tempvar = Integer.parsInt(tempstr);
```

Garbage Collection

One of the nice features about Java is that you do not have to worry about cleaning up objects after you are finished using them. The Java run-time environment will delete an object upon determining that it is no longer being used. This process is called *garbage collection*. Garbage collection is performed on a periodic basis and can also be called by using the System.gc() method. You normally do not need to start this process, but you may want to do so if you are going into a memory-intensive routine. You can also force an object to be collected by assigning it a value of NULL.

Creating and Using Classes

Now that you have created an object, you need to define the template for it. Templates for objects are called *classes*, and they include variables, methods, and hierarchy.

Defining a Class

A simple class can be defined with the Java keyword class as shown here:

```
class TestClass
{
    // Class components go here
}
```

The convention normally used for a class is to capitalize the first letter. The components that are in a class are typically called *members* of that class and come in the two broad categories of variables and methods. By default, all classes become public classes. Therefore, the class can be used by other classes in the class hierarchy. You can also declare two other types of classes. The first is an abstract class that cannot be instantiated to an object but is meant to contain other classes (subclasses). To declare an abstract class, use the keyword abstract before the keyword class in the declaration, as shown next.

```
abstract class HighLevel
{
    // Class Members
}
```

The other type of class is called *final*. Declaring a class as final means that no other class can be subclassed to it. Thus, by definition, a final class is the lowest class in the class hierarchy.

```
final class LowestLevel
{
    // Class Members
}
```

Declaring Member Variables

As you may recall from Chapter 6, two types of variables can be included in a class: instance variables and class variables. Instance variables are copied each time a new object for a class is created; class variables are not copied, but are global to all objects that are instantiated from the class. You define instance variables within the class definition, as shown in the following example:

```
class Test1
{
    int x;
    boolean flag;
}
```

Any object that is created from this class will have its own variables of x and flag. Class variables are defined by putting the keyword static before the declaration of the variable.

```
class Test2
{
    int x;
    boolean flag;
    static int total;
}
```

Here, each object that is created from class Test2 will have its own variables (x and flag) and will share the variable total with all other objects created from the class Test2.

If you want to declare a variable with a constant value in a class, use the keyword final before the data declaration. This keyword indicates that the value of the variable will not change.

```
class Test3
{
    int x;
    boolean flag;
    static int total;
    final  int maxobject = 10;
}
```

Later, in the section "Controlling Access to Members of a Class," you will see how to further control access to variables of a class, using access specifiers like Private and Protected.

Methods

Methods are simply pieces of code that perform a specific task. In other programming languages, methods are called *subroutines*, *forms*, or *functions*. The simple form of a method declaration is as follows:

```
class Test4
{
    static total;
    method addOne()
    {
        ++total;
    }
}
```

In this example any object created from Test4 can use the addOne method to increment the class variable total.

```
Test4 obj1 = new Test4();
obj1.addOne();
```

If you are familiar with other programming languages, the concept of methods may seem rather routine so far. However, Java does depart from many other languages in that the name of the method is not enough to uniquely define it among other members. Java also looks at the types of the arguments that are declared with the method. You can, therefore, declare two methods with the same name within one class as long as each method has a different set of arguments associated with it.

 NOTE

The concept of using the name of the method along with its arguments to uniquely define the method is called *method overloading*.

To indicate that a method will be expecting arguments, you declare the arguments in the definition of the method.

```
exampleMethod(int arg1, float arg2 . . .);
```

If you declare arguments in the definition of the method, they are valid only within that method. If the name of an argument variable is the same as that of a variable declared in the class, the class variable is hidden by the local argument variable. The following example demonstrates this concept.

```
public class Test5
{
    int x = 2;
    void method1()
    {
        System.out.println("Method1 X = " + x);
    }
    void method2(int x)
    {
```

```
        ++x;
        System.out.println("Method2 X = " + x);
    }
    public static void main (String[] args)
    {
        Test5 obj1 = new Test5();
        obj1.method1();
        obj1.method2(2);
        obj1.method1();
    }
}
```

When executed, the example produces the following output:

```
Method1 X = 2;      // The initial value of instance variable X
Method1 X = 3;      // The value of the local variable x
Method1 X = 2;      // The instance variable has not changed value
```

If you need to access a class variable in a method where both the class variable and the argument for the method have the same name, you can use Java's "this" operator. When you use "this," you are referring to the object itself and hence are accessing the instance variables of the object. You can also call other methods from that object with Java's "this" operator. The following full code example demonstrates "this":

```
public class Test6
{
    int x = 1;
    void method1(int x)
    {
        this.x = x;
        ++x;
        System.out.println("Local X = " + x);
        this.printx();
    }
    void printx()
    {
        System.out.println("Instance X = " + x);
    }
```

```
    public static void main (String[] args)
    {
        Test6 obj1 = new Test6();
        obj1.method1(5);
    }
}
```

The results from the example are as follows:

```
Local X = 6;
Instance X = 5;
```

It is important to understand how Java passes variables into methods. In Java, variables are passed by value, and you are not allowed to change these values in the method. Therefore, if you pass in primitive data arguments, they cannot be changed, and if you pass in objects (which are really references to an object), you cannot change the object. However, you are allowed to call methods of the object to change values within the object.

The default return value for a method is void or no return at all. If your method is going to return some value, you must define what type it will be when you declare the method. The next example again uses the addOne method, but this time addOne returns the total after incrementing it.

```
class Test7
{
    static int total;
    int addOne()
    {
        ++total;
        return total;
    }
}
```

You can declare instance methods and class methods, just as you can with variables. Class methods differ from instance methods in that you do not need to have an object instantiated from the class before you use the method. The declaration of a class method is just like that of variables, through the keyword static. This keyword is used to define many methods in Java's core classes like Math.abs().

Constructor Methods

A constructor method is called when a new instance of the class is created. Java performs this step automatically; constructor methods cannot be called directly. You usually use constructor methods to initialize variables for new objects. Constructor methods are not required when you create a class.

You create a constructor method just like any other method except that a constructor method will have the same name as the class and cannot have any return value (constructor methods are typed as a void). You can also overload constructor methods so that you can call up different pieces of code based on the types of the arguments passed in.

```
class Test8
{
    int x;
    Test8(int y)
    {
        x = y;
    }
    Test8()
    {
        x = 1;
    }
}
```

In the preceding example, a new instance of the class Test6 can be created with either of the following lines of code:

```
Test8 obj1 = new Test8();   // obj1.x = 1;
Test8 obj1 = new Test8(3); // obj1.x = 3;
```

There is one more type of method to discuss: the finalize method. However, to fully understand how the finalize method works, you need to understand a little more about class hierarchy and access control. The finalize method is covered in the "Finalizer Methods" section later in the chapter.

Subclasses, Superclasses, and Inheritance

Chapter 6 introduced the concept of class hierarchy. Basically, a class hierarchy allows you to define a high-level class with variables and methods that are common to many other classes; you can then nest these other classes under the high-level class, and they will all have access to the high-level class' members. A hierarchy can have any number of levels.

In Java the lower-level class is referred to as a *subclass,* and the upper-level class is referred to as the *superclass.* Members that are defined in the superclass but are used in the subclasses are referred to as *inherited members.*

A class hierarchy is created by creating the superclass first and then creating the subclass as an extension of the superclass, as shown next.

```
class test9
{
    int x;
}
class test10 extends Test9
{
    int y;
}
```

If an object is instantiated with class test10, the object will have both the x and y variables.

As with instance and method argument variables, if a variable is named the same in both the superclass and subclass, the subclass member is used as a local member. If you want to access the variable in the superclass, you can use the Java operator super, as shown in the following example:

```
class Test11
{
    int x = 2;
}
class Test12 extends Test11
{
    int  x = 3;
```

```
    void printsuperx()
    {
        System.out.println("Super X = " + super.x);
    }
}
```

If an object is instantiated from class Test12, a call to the printsuperx method will return "Super X = 2," even though the value of x in the subclass is 3.

In the case of methods, if you have methods with the same name and argument list in both the superclass and subclass, the subclass method is called instead of the superclass method. This process of using the local method instead of the one in the superclass is referred to as *method overriding*. If you want to access the superclass method instead of the subclass method, you can use the Java operator super as described in the preceding example with variables.

Controlling Access to Members of a Class

One advantage of object-oriented programming is that an object should be able to control access to members such as variables and methods. Java breaks access control into four distinct levels: private, protected, public, and package. Each level can be assigned to all declarations including classes, variables, and methods.

One key point about access levels is that they do more than just protect information from being seen. Access levels can prevent other classes from modifying variables that are critical or that should be modified only by routines within a class or group of classes.

Private Access

Private access is the most restrictive form of access that you can use. Members with Private access can be accessed only by that class or by objects initiated from it. The following code example declares Private access and states what is legal and what is not.

```
public class Test13
{
    public static void main (String[] args)
    {
```

```
        Test14 obj1 = new Test14();
        obj1.setx();        // You can set X this way
        obj1.printx();      // You can print X this way
        obj1.x = 3;                 // Syntax error since x is private
        obj1.secretx();     // Syntax error since secretx is private
        obj1.setsecret()    // Ok since setsecret is not private
    }
}
public class Test14
{
    private int x;
    void setx()
    {
        x = 2;
    }
    void printx()
    {
        System.out.println("In Test14, X=" + x);
    }
    private void secretx()
    {
        x = 3;
    }
    void setsecret()
    {
        this.secretx();
    }
}
```

Protected Access

The next level of access is Protected access. Protected access is a bit less restrictive than Private access. Protected access allows the class, subclasses, and all classes that are in the same package to access the member. Packages are discussed later in this chapter, but for now you can think of a package as a collection of classes.

Public Access

If a member is defined as public, then all classes have access to it. Therefore, any other class can set and display variables or execute methods that are declared this way.

Package Access

Package access is the default access level that is assigned to a member if no other access level is declared. Package access means that any other class of the same package has full access to a member defined with this type of access.

Finalizer Methods

Now that we have finished discussing access control and how to define hierarchy among classes, we can discuss the finalizer methods. Finalizer methods are called just before an object is destroyed during a garbage collection. Remember that Java automatically and periodically performs garbage collection on objects that no longer have a valid reference in the system. Finalizer methods are generally used to clean up references in other objects that are affected by this object. An example might be a class variable that keeps track of the number of objects instantiated with this class; in this case the finalizer method could be used to decrement the class variable just before an object is destroyed.

Creating and Using Interfaces and Packages

Interfaces and packages control how classes are declared and interact with each other. Usually, in object-oriented programming the class hierarchy controls this type of behavior. However, this approach is restrictive because to enjoy the advantages of the class hierarchy, such as inheritance, a class must become part of the hierarchy, which can cause problems with access to variables. Java has extended the functionality of the class hierarchy through interfaces and packages.

Defining an Interface

An interface can be thought of as a template that a class can use in its declaration of methods and constants. An interface is a group of method declarations (with no code) and the constants that a class may adopt. Unlike the class hierarchy, no further link exists between classes that use the same interface.

As the following example shows, the declaration of an interface is similar to that of a class.

```
interface CommonStuff
{
    int maxentries = 100;
    void printvar();
    void addvars();
}
```

The rules for interface declaration are as follows:

- ◆ All variables declared within an interface are assumed to be static and final. (Basically, they are constants.)
- ◆ Though an interface can extend another interface (in a fashion similar to the way classes can extend other classes), an interface cannot implement other interfaces.
- ◆ All methods declared within an interface default to abstract and public.
- ◆ Interfaces cannot be used to declare class methods, instance variables, or constructor methods.

Implementing an Interface

Interfaces are implemented within a class, as shown in the following code:

```
interface CommonStuff
{
    int maxentries = 100;
    void printvar();
}
```

```
class Test15 implements CommonStuff
{
    int x;
    void printvar()
    {
        System.out.println("Maxentries = " + maxentries);
    }
}
```

Interfaces can also be implemented as a data type, as shown here (with the same interface declaration as above):

```
class Test16
{
    CommonStuff obj1;
}
```

Creating and Using Packages

A *package* allows you to link several classes or interfaces without using the class hierarchy system. Packages are generally used to provide access control to the members of the class.

Packages are implemented by using the keyword package before the declaration of the class or interface.

```
package testpackage;
class Test17
{
}
class Test18
{
}
```

Summary

This important chapter covers a great deal of material. The basics of the creation and implementation of objects and classes are explained in detail, along with ways to control access to methods and variables. Other topics covered here are the class hierarchy, ways to nest classes together, the creation of interfaces and packages, and the use of interfaces and packages to interrelate classes without the class hierarchy system. The next chapter introduces user interfaces and contains a few examples that tie together these various elements.

Chapter 9

**Building Simple
User Interfaces**

```
public class AwtTest extends Applet
{
    TextField text;
    public void init()
    {
        text = new TextField();
        text.setEditable(false);
        text.setText("Ready for AWT examples");
        add(text);
    }
}
```

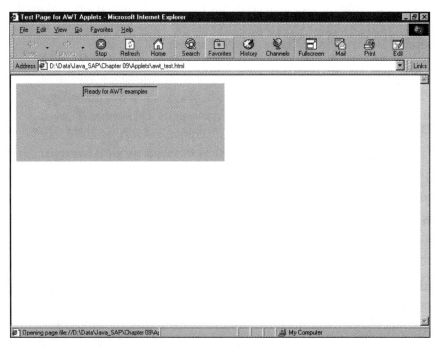

FIGURE 9.1 *Browser displaying introductory applet for AWT examples*

Basic AWT Components

AWT components consist of objects like buttons, check boxes, text fields, and menu items.

Buttons

Buttons are simple components that generate events when clicked; they are created through the Button class. A few common methods are used for the Button class.

- **setEnabled(Boolean).** Calling this method enables the button if the argument is true or disables it if the argument is set to false.
- **setlabel(String).** Sets the text on the button.
- **getlabel().** Retrieves the text that is on the button.
- **addActionListener(ActionListener).** This method registers the button so that if it is clicked, the ActionListener specified is called. The Action-Listener is usually ActionPerformed(), as shown in the next example.

The following Java applet demonstrates the use of buttons by creating a screen with two buttons. Initially, one of the buttons is active; if the user clicks on this button, it becomes disabled and activates the other button (see Figure 9.2).

 NOTE

The "Handling Events" section later in this chapter describes how the ActionListener and other interfaces work. Concentrate on the button declaration and method calls in this example.

```
import java.awt.event.*;

import java.awt.*;

import java.applet.*;

// Extend the Applet class & implement the Actionlistener

public class AwtTest extends Applet implements ActionListener

{

// Declare 2 Button Class References

    Button b1,b2;

// Declare reference to TextField Class

    TextField text;

// Setup the Applet Init method to display buttons

    public void init()

    {
```

```
// Point the references to New objects
        b1 = new Button();
        b2 = new Button();
        text = new TextField();
//  Set up the initial values
        b1.setEnabled(false);
        b1.setLabel("Left");
        b1.addActionListener(this);
        b2.setEnabled(true);
        b2.setLabel("Right");
        b2.addActionListener(this);
        text.setEditable(false);
        text.setText("Click Right Button");
//  Add the components to the Applet Container
        add(b1);
        add(b2);
        add(text);
    }
// Define the Action Event which will be called each time
// a user clicks one of the buttons
    public void actionPerformed(ActionEvent event)
    {
        Object target = event.getSource();
        if (target == b1)
        {
            b1.setEnabled(false);
            b2.setEnabled(true);
            text.setText("Left button pressed");
        }
        if (target == b2)
        {
            b1.setEnabled(true);
            b2.setEnabled(false);
            text.setText("Right button pressed");
        }
    }
}
```

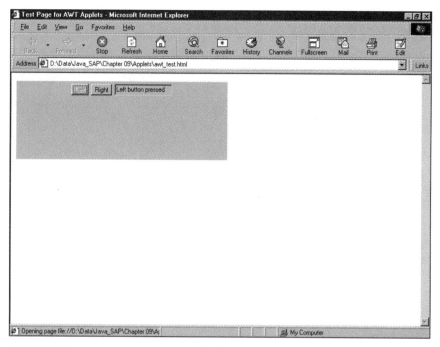

FIGURE 9.2 *An applet demonstrating the Button class*

Check Boxes

Check boxes usually allow the user to turn options on and off. Though the user can trigger code by toggling the check box, having them do so should not be the norm. The goal here is to put the check box on the screen and read the value from it when the user presses a button.

Check boxes can also be grouped together so that only one check box in the group can be marked at any one time. This approach basically gives you a group of radio buttons.

The following methods are used most often with the Checkbox class:

◆ **setLabel(string).** Sets up the text that will be positioned beside the check box.

◆ **setState(boolean).** Deselects the check box if the Boolean expression false is passed in; selects the check box if the expression true is passed in.

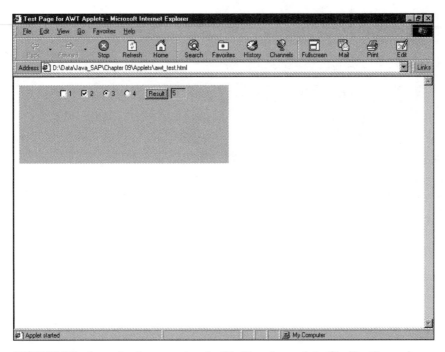

FIGURE 9.3 *An applet demonstrating the Checkbox class and the CheckboxGroup class*

Check boxes can be grouped together by passing a reference from the class CheckboxGroup to the constructor of the Checkbox class. In the following example, four check boxes are defined: two that are grouped and two that are not grouped. The check boxes are labeled 1 through 4, and the text box on the screen shows the sum of the labels for the marked check boxes. A working example is shown in Figure 9.3.

```java
import java.awt.event.*;
import java.awt.*;
import java.applet.*;

public class AwtTest extends Applet implements ActionListener
{
// Declare 4 Checkbox Class References and a CheckboxGroup Reference
    Checkbox chk1, chk2, chk3, chk4;
    CheckboxGroup chkgrp;
    Button    b1;
```

```
// Declare reference to TextField Class
    TextField text;
// Setup the Applet Init method to display checkboxes
    public void init()
    {
// Point the references to New objects
        chkgrp = new CheckboxGroup();
        chk1 = new Checkbox();
        chk1.setLabel("1");
        chk2 = new Checkbox("2");   // Label set through Constructor
        chk3 = new Checkbox("3",chkgrp,false);
        chk4 = new Checkbox("4",chkgrp,true);
        text = new TextField();
        b1   = new Button("Result");
//  Set up the initial values
        text.setEditable(false);
        text.setText("4");
        b1.addActionListener(this);
//  Add the components to the Applet Container
        add(chk1);
        add(chk2);
        add(chk3);
        add(chk4);
        add(b1);
        add(text);
    }
// Define the Action Event which will be called each time
// a user clicks one of the buttons
    public void actionPerformed(ActionEvent event)
    {
        int    result;
        Object target = event.getSource();
        if (target == b1)
        {
            result = 0;
            if (chk1.getState() == true) result += 1;
            if (chk2.getState() == true) result += 2;
            if (chk3.getState() == true) result += 3;
```

```
            if (chk4.getState() == true) result += 4;
            text.setText(String.valueOf(result));
        }
    }
}
```

Labels and Text Fields

Nearly all Java applications need to place text on the screen and allow the users to type in input. The most common classes used for this purpose are Label, TextField, and TextArea. Labels place static text on the window, TextFields create single line input fields, and TextAreas create multiple line text input boxes.

The Label class has only one commonly used method (other than the alignment method, which is covered a little later in this chapter). That method, Label.SetText(String), sets the text that you want to display.

TextField and TextArea share many methods because they are both subclasses of TextComponent.

- ◆ **setText(String)**. Inserts the value of String into the input field.
- ◆ **setEditable(Boolean)**. Makes the field noneditable if false is passed in; opens the field for user input if true is passed in.
- ◆ **getText()**. Returns the current string in the input field.

The following methods are specific to the TextArea class:

- ◆ **appendText(String)**. Appends text to the current text in the TextArea field.
- ◆ **getRows()**. Returns the number of rows currently used in the TextArea field.
- ◆ **getCols()**. Returns the number of columns currently declared in the TextArea field.
- ◆ **replaceText(String)**. Replaces the current contents of the TextArea field with the value in String.
- ◆ **insertText(String, position)**. Inserts the String at the specified position in the TextArea field.

The following example has all three text classes, along with a few buttons to control the entry of text; an example is shown in Figure 9.4.

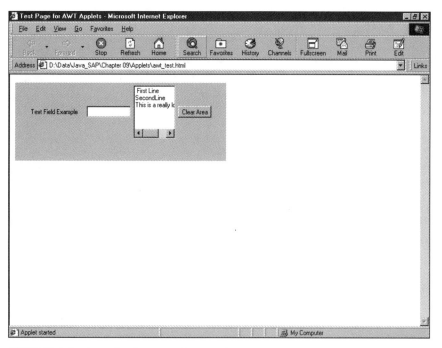

FIGURE 9.4 *An applet demonstrating text classes*

 NOTE

Take note of how the constructors are used for the TextField and TextArea classes in this example. Previous examples used empty parentheses (`b1 = new Button();`), but this example begins to use parameters. The number and type of parameters determine which constructor is called. For example, the TextField constructor can be called in the following ways:

- ◆ **().** No arguments.
- ◆ **(String).** Sets the initial string.
- ◆ **(Integer).** Sets the number of columns to display.
- ◆ **(String,Integer,Boolean).** Sets the initial string and number of columns. The Boolean flag determines whether the field is editable or not.

NOTE

The examples in this book use the most common forms of the constructors; you can refer to the online help in your Java compiler to see and get information about less common, more specific constructors.

```java
import java.awt.event.*;
import java.awt.*;
import java.applet.*;

public class AwtTest extends Applet implements ActionListener
{
//   Declare References to Class Objects
     TextField txt;
     TextArea  txta;
     Label     lab1;
     Button    b1;
// This is the initialization routine for the Applet
     public void init()
     {
// Setup the Object's initial values
          b1  = new Button("Clear Area");
          b1.addActionListener(this);
          txt = new TextField();
          txt.setColumns(10);
          txt.addActionListener(this);
          lab1 = new Label("Text Field Example");
          txta = new TextArea(6,10);
          add(lab1);
          add(txt);
          add(txta);
          add(b1);
     }
// This method will handle the events from the text box
// and the button
```

```
      public void actionPerformed(ActionEvent event)
      {
          Object target = event.getSource();
// If the button is pressed clear the text area
          if (target == b1)
          {
              txta.setText(" ");
          }
// If the user presses enter in the textfield move the
// contents to the text area plus a newline character
          if (target == txt)
          {
              txta.append(txt.getText() + "\n");
              txt.setText("");
          }
      }
}
```

Choice and List Classes

The Choice class is somewhat like a text field, except that it offers the user a limited number of choices of field entries. The Choice class is similar to the F4 functionality in SAP and Select elements in HTML. The difference between the Choice class and List class is that the Choice class is displayed on one line; to see the possible selections, a user must click on a down arrow. In the List class, all choices are shown on multiple lines. If there are more choices than the size of the object, a vertical scroll bar is used for navigation.

The most commonly used methods for the Choice class are as follows:

- ◆ **addItem(String).** Adds the string to the choice.
- ◆ **getSelectedItem().** Returns the string selected by the user.
- ◆ **getSelectedIndex().** Returns an integer that points to the row the user has selected.
- ◆ **countItems().** Returns the number of items in the choice.
- ◆ **select(String or Integer).** Selects the choice specified by String or row.

List boxes have many of the same methods as the Choice class, but also allow you to have multiple selections and to manipulate the list by deleting items and determining which items to show.

◆ **delItem(Integer)**. Deletes the indicated row.

◆ **getSelectedIndexes()**. Returns an array containing the indexes of the selected items.

◆ **setsMultipleSelections(Boolean)**. Determines whether the user can select multiple items.

◆ **makeVisible(Integer)**. Forces the indicated row to be visible.

The following example demonstrates these two classes (see Figure 9.5).

```java
// Example for Choice and List Classes
import java.awt.event.*;
import java.awt.*;
import java.applet.*;


public class AwtTest extends Applet implements ItemListener
{
// Declare Class References
    Choice      ch1;
    List        list;
    TextField   text;
// Initialization Routine for Applet
    public void init()
    {
// Instantiate the class references
        ch1   = new Choice();
        list = new List();
        text  = new TextField(15);
//  Set up the initial values for the objects
        ch1.add("Numeric");
        ch1.add("Alpha");
        ch1.addItemListener(this);
        list.addItemListener(this);
```

```
        text.setEditable(false);
        ch1.select("Numeric");
        for(int i = 1; i < 10; ++i)
            list.addItem(String.valueOf(i));
//  Add the items to the Applet Container
        add(ch1);
        add(list);
        add(text);
    }


    public void itemStateChanged(ItemEvent event)
    {
        Object target = event.getSource();
        if (target == list)
        {
            text.setText(list.getSelectedItem());
        }
        if (target == ch1)
        {

            list.removeAll();
            if (ch1.getSelectedItem() == "Numeric")
            {
                for(int i = 1; i < 10; ++i)
                    list.addItem(String.valueOf(i));
            }
            else
            {
                for(int i = 65; i< 91; ++i)
                    list.addItem(String.valueOf((char)i));
            }
        }
    }
}
```

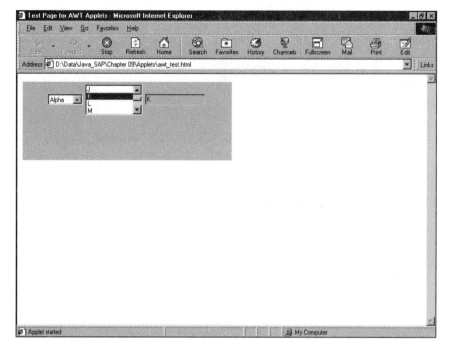

FIGURE 9.5 *An applet demonstrating the Choice and List classes*

This example completes the basic components that allow you to make simple interfaces for your users. We'll defer discussion of one more component, the Menu class, until you know a bit more about containers.

Basic AWT Containers

A *container* is simply an object that can hold components of the AWT. Containers are objects themselves, and thus containers can hold other containers. An applet is a good example of a container, as it usually contains other objects, such as text fields and radio buttons. The two basic types of containers are Panel and Window, both of which are subclasses of the Container class. Because they are subclasses of Container, they share methods that are defined to the Container class. The most often used Container methods follow.

- ♦ **add()**. Adds a component to a container.
- ♦ **remove()**. Removes a component from a container.
- ♦ **dispose()**. Removes all components from a container.

Also remember that if a container is deleted, all of the components within that container are deleted as well. This is an important point, especially when you start to group containers within one another on more complex windows.

Panel

A *panel* is a general-purpose container; the Applet class is a subclass of the Panel class. The Constructor method for a panel can be called with no arguments or with a layout manager as the argument (layout managers are covered in the "Basic AWT Layout" section later in this chapter).

A simple example of multiple panels follows (see Figure 9.6).

```
// Example for AWT
import java.awt.*;
import java.applet.*;

public class AwtTest extends Applet
{
// Declare Class References
    Panel       p1;
    Label       l1,l2;
// Initialization Routine for Applet
    public void init()
    {
// Instantiate the class references
        p1 = new Panel();
        l1 = new Label("Panel 1 (the applet panel)");
        l2 = new Label("Panel 2 (created from within the applet)");
        this.setBackground(Color.white); // background for applet
        p1.setBackground(Color.black);
        p1.setForeground(Color.white);
// Add the panels to the Applet Object
        add(p1);
        add(l1);
        p1.add(l2); // Add 2nd label to panel
    }
}
```

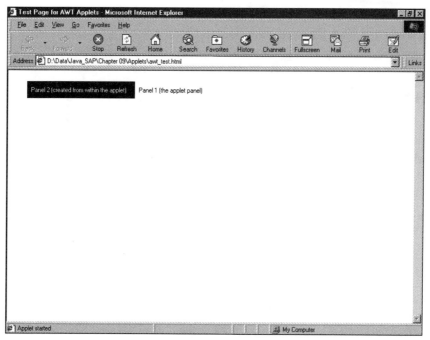

FIGURE 9.6 *A simple example of multiple panels*

Window

The Window class can be broken down into two more subclasses, Dialog and Frame. The Frame class allows you to build a window with most of the features of a standard window that are available in your operating system. These features include window titles, menu bars, and minimize and close functions. Dialogs are like frames except that they are more limited in function and are dependent on other windows.

Frame

The Frame class allows you to build windows that are independent of the calling program. Because Frame is a subclass of Window, which is a subclass of Container, which is a subclass of Component, you can use many of the functions that you have already seen, such as the add() method.

Frames can be created by using either Frame() or Frame(String), where string is the title of the frame. When you initially create a frame, it is invisible and you need to call a method to make the frame appear or to hide it again later. The most commonly used methods for the Frame class are as follows:

- ◆ **add()**. Adds components to the frame.
- ◆ **pack()**. Resizes the frame to the smallest size that allows all the components to be visible. In another method, called resize(), the arguments are in pixels, which means that the screen's appearance is different on different machines.
- ◆ **show()**. Makes the frame visible.
- ◆ **hide()**. Hides a currently visible frame.
- ◆ **dispose()**. Destroys the frame and sets it up for garbage collection.

The following is a simple example of a frame, called by an applet with a few buttons on it, as shown in Figure 9.7.

```
// Example for AWT
import java.awt.event.*;
import java.awt.*;
import java.applet.*;


public class AwtTest extends Applet implements ActionListener
{
// Declare Class References
    Frame       win1;
    Button      b1,b2;  // Buttons on Applet
// Initialization Routine for Applet
    public void init()
    {
// Instantiate the class references
        b1   = new Button("Show Frame1");
        b2   = new Button("Hide Frame1");
//  Initialize some of the stuff for the objects
        b1.addActionListener(this);
        b2.addActionListener(this);
//  Add the objects to the applet
        add(b1);
        add(b2);
        win1 = new FrameExample("Test Frame");
    }
```

```java
// Setup the code that is executed when an Action is performed
    public void actionPerformed(ActionEvent event)
    {
        Object target = event.getSource();
        if (target == b1 && !win1.isShowing())
        {
            win1.setVisible(true);
            b1.setEnabled(false);
            b2.setEnabled(true);
        }
        if (target == b2 && win1.isShowing())
        {
            win1.setVisible(false);
            b1.setEnabled(true);
            b2.setEnabled(false);
        }
    }
}
import java.awt.event.*;
import java.awt.*;


public class FrameExample extends Frame implements ActionListener


{
// Object Declaration
    Button b1;
    WindowListener wl;
// Constructor for FrameExample
    FrameExample(String title)
    {
        super(title);  // This calls the superclass's constructor
        b1 = new Button("Resize");
        b1.addActionListener(this);
        wl = new WindowAdapter()  // This Class is discussed in the Event
            {                        // Section of this chapter
                public void windowClosing(WindowEvent e)
                {
```

```
                dispose();
            }


        };
    addWindowListener(wl);
    add(b1);
    setSize(100,100);
    }
// Analysis of Actions
    public void  actionPerformed(ActionEvent event)
    {
        Object target = event.getSource();
// If the button is pressed clear the text area
        if (target == b1) pack();
    }
}
```

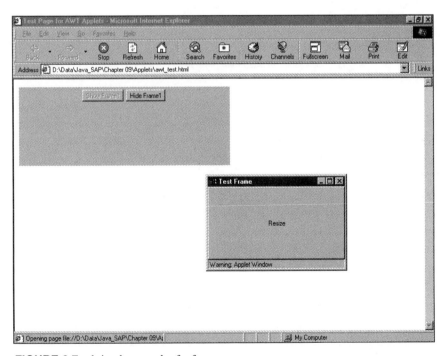

FIGURE 9.7 *A simple example of a frame*

NOTE

If you close your browser window after you start the frame, you will see that the frame remains open even after the browser is gone. The ability of frames to stand alone is the fundamental difference between frames and dialog windows.

Dialog Windows

Through the AWT you can also create dialog windows. Like pop-up dialogs in SAP, a dialog window is called up by another window, and if the source window is destroyed, the dialog window is destroyed as well. If you decide to minimize the parent window, then the child window is minimized as well. You usually use dialog windows to tell users about events or to prompt users to enter a value before the main window performs an action. With Java you don't need to worry about the code that handles this parent/child relationship between these windows because the AWT takes care of it automatically.

The capability to create dialog windows also allows you to access the FileDialog class, which contains some neat dialogs for selecting files. Many times, though, the system that is executing the Java code prohibits the use of the FileDialog class because it can be a security issue. Another problem with the Dialog class is that no mechanism exists to trigger an applet to start within a dialog window (however, an applet can use the dialogs).

Using dialog windows in your programs is very similar to using frames. The main difference is in the way the constructors are built. The examples in Figures 9.7 and 9.8 use the same Java code, except that in Figure 9.8 the dialog window replaces the frame. You will notice in the following dialog window example that the dialog is called from within an applet. This process is not as simple as it sounds because you must pass a Frame object to the constructor of the dialog to indicate the dialog's parent window. Because applets are a subclass of the Frame class, you can use the method getParent() to get the Frame object of the applet. You can then cast this object as a type Frame when you make the call to the constructor.

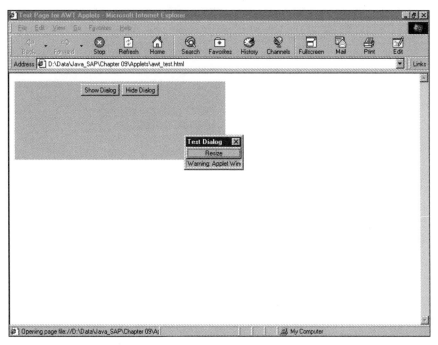

FIGURE 9.8 *A simple example of a dialog*

```
// Example for AWT
import java.awt.event.*;
import java.awt.*;
import java.applet.*;

public class AwtTest extends Applet implements ActionListener
{
// Declare Class References
    Dialog      win1;
    Button      b1,b2;  // Buttons on Applet
    Object      appletframe;
// Initialization Routine for Applet
    public void init()
    {
// Instantiate the class references
        b1   = new Button("Show Dialog");
        b2   = new Button("Hide Dialog");
```

```
//  Initialize some of the stuff for the objects
        b1.addActionListener(this);
        b2.addActionListener(this);
//  Get the Frame of the applet
        appletframe = getParent();
        while(!(appletframe instanceof Frame))
            appletframe=((Component)appletframe).getParent();
//  Add the objects to the applet
        add(b1);
        add(b2);
        win1 = new DialogExample((Frame)appletframe, "Test Dialog", true);
    }
// Setup the code that is executed when an Action is performed
    public void actionPerformed(ActionEvent event)
    {
        Object target = event.getSource();
        if (target == b1 && !win1.isShowing())
        {
            win1.setVisible(true);
            b1.setEnabled(false);
            b2.setEnabled(true);
        }
        if (target == b2 && win1.isShowing())
        {
            win1.setVisible(false);
            b1.setEnabled(true);
            b2.setEnabled(false);
        }
    }
}
import java.awt.event.*;
import java.awt.*;

public class DialogExample extends Dialog implements ActionListener
{
// Object Declaration
    Button b1;
// Constructor for FrameExample
    DialogExample(Frame parent,String title,boolean modal)
```

```
    {
        super(parent, title, modal);   // This calls the superclass's constructor
        b1 = new Button("Resize");
        b1.addActionListener(this);
        add(b1);
        setSize(100,100);
    }
// Analysis of Actions
    public void  actionPerformed(ActionEvent event)
    {
        Object target = event.getSource();
// If the button is pressed set the size of the Dialog
        if (target == b1) pack();
    }
}
```

The FileDialog class allows you to program platform-independent code to handle opening and saving files. As mentioned before, this class is often prohibited because it allows the applet to write files to the local system, which can cause a security problem. If your application allows you to use the FileDialog class, it works just like a regular dialog with a few extra methods for setting paths or file name filters. Because many browsers do not allow you to access the FileDialog class, an example is set up as a stand-alone application in Chapter 10.

Menu Items

Menu items are the last of the commonly used components covered in this chapter. Menus are a combination of objects from different classes and are used most often in frames (rather than in dialogs). A standard menu comprises the following classes:

◆ **MenuItem**. An object on a menu.

◆ **CheckboxMenuItem**. A menu object that can have a check mark beside it.

◆ **Menu**. A collection of menu items.

◆ **MenuBar**. A collection of menus.

Because menus are related to windows, you cannot have a menu in an applet. However, if the applet calls up a window, then menus can be implemented there. The following example shows how to set up a simple menu with a few options. Figure 9.9 shows this example in action.

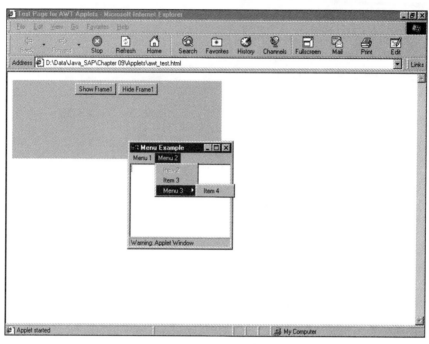

FIGURE 9.9 *A simple example of a menu in a frame called by an applet*

```
// Example for AWT
import java.awt.event.*;
import java.awt.*;
import java.applet.*;

public class Jsap0911 extends Applet implements ActionListener
{
// Declare Class References
    Frame        win1;
    Button       b1,b2;  // Buttons on Applet
// Initialization Routine for Applet
    public void init()
    {
// Instantiate the class references
        b1   = new Button("Show Frame1");
        b2   = new Button("Hide Frame1");
```

```
//  Initialize some of the stuff for the objects
        b1.addActionListener(this);
        b2.addActionListener(this);
//  Add the objects to the applet
        add(b1);
        add(b2);
        win1 = new MenuExample("Menu Example");
    }
// Setup the code that is executed when an Action is performed
    public void actionPerformed(ActionEvent event)
    {
        Object target = event.getSource();
        if (target == b1 && !win1.isShowing())
            win1.setVisible(true);
        if (target == b2 && win1.isShowing())
            win1.setVisible(false);
    }
}


import java.awt.event.*;
import java.awt.*;


public class MenuExample extends Frame implements ActionListener


{
// Object Declaration
    TextField txt1;
    WindowListener wl;
    MenuBar mb;
    Menu    menu1, menu2, menu3;
    MenuItem item1, item2, item3;
    CheckboxMenuItem item4;
// Constructor for FrameExample
    MenuExample(String title)
    {
        super(title);   // This calls the superclass's constructor
```

```
txt1 = new TextField(20);
wl = new WindowAdapter()  // This Class is discussed in the Event
        {                      // Section of this chapter
            public void windowClosing(WindowEvent e)
            {
                dispose();
            }

        };
    addWindowListener(wl);
    add(txt1);
    // Build up our simple Window Example
    mb = new MenuBar();
    setMenuBar(mb); // Ties menu to this frame
    // Menu 1
    menu1 = new Menu("Menu 1");
    mb.add(menu1);
    item1 = new MenuItem("Item 1");
    item1.addActionListener(this);
    menu1.add(item1);
    // Menu 2
    menu2 = new Menu("Menu 2");
    mb.add(menu2);
    item2 = new MenuItem("Item 2");
    item2.setEnabled(false);
    menu2.add(item2);
    item3 = new MenuItem("Item 3");
    item3.addActionListener(this);
    menu2.add(item3);
    // Menu 3 (a sub menu under menu 2)
    menu3 = new Menu("Menu 3");
    item4 = new CheckboxMenuItem("Item 4");
    item4.addActionListener(this);
    menu3.add(item4);
    menu3.addActionListener(this);
    menu2.add(menu3);
```

```
        // Set the initial size of the Apple
        setSize(200,200);
    }
//  Analysis of Actions
    public void  actionPerformed(ActionEvent event)
    {
        if(event.getSource() instanceof CheckboxMenuItem)
        {
            CheckboxMenuItem citem = (CheckboxMenuItem)event.getSource();
            txt1.setText(citem.getLabel() + ":" + citem.getState());
        }
        else if(event.getSource() instanceof MenuItem)
        {
            MenuItem item = (MenuItem)event.getSource();
            txt1.setText(item.getLabel());
        }
    }
}
```

Basic AWT Layout

So far we have explored building user interfaces by looking at containers—and the components inside them—without really considering the placement of the components on the screen. The layout manager controls the position and size of components within a container. All Java containers have a layout manager, implemented through the LayoutManager interface.

 NOTE

Another way to position items within a container is to use absolute positioning. This method is not commonly used because it can become platform dependent; most screens can be built by using one of the standard layout managers.

Java has five standard layout managers; they are described in the sections that follow.

BorderLayout

BorderLayout is the default layout manager of all Window objects. BorderLayout contains five areas to hold components: north, south, east, west, and center. An example of a BorderLayout (see Figure 9.10), along with the sample code, follows.

```java
import java.awt.*;
import java.applet.*;

public class Applet1 extends Applet
{
    public void init()
    {
        setLayout(new BorderLayout());

        add("North",new Button("NORTH"));
        add("South",new Button("SOUTH"));
        add("East",new Button("EAST"));
        add("West",new Button("WEST"));
        add("Center", new Button("CENTER"));
    }

}
```

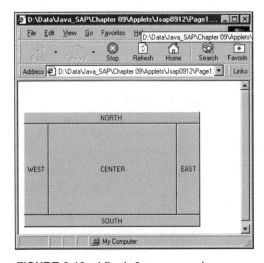

FIGURE 9.10 *A BorderLayout example*

By default there is no gap between components. The outside edge of the border is just large enough to hold its components, and the center of the window takes the rest of the space. You can set both horizontal and vertical gaps between components through the BorderLayout constructor.

CardLayout

The CardLayout layout manager allows you to stack components on top of one another. You can then select the component to display by using one of the following methods: first(), next(), previous(), last(), or show().

FlowLayout

The FlowLayout layout manager is the default manager for panels. The FlowLayout manager works just like sentences in a book. The containers are added in a single row from left to right at their preferred size (if the LEFT alignment is used), as seen in Figure 9.11. When the row is filled, the layout manager creates a new row underneath the current row and continues.

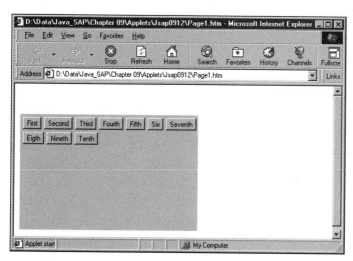

FIGURE 9.11 *A FlowLayout example*

```
import java.awt.*;
import java.applet.*;

public class Applet1 extends Applet
{
    public void init()
    {,
        setLayout(new FlowLayout(FlowLayout.LEFT));

        add(new Button("First"));
        add(new Button("Second"));
        add(new Button("Third"));
        add(new Button("Fourth"));
        add(new Button("Fifth"));
        add(new Button("Six"));
        add(new Button("Seventh"));
        add(new Button("Eigth"));
        add(new Button("Ninth"));
        add(new Button("Tenth"));
    }
}
```

The alignment of components on each row is determined through the constructor of the FlowLayout manager (LEFT, RIGHT, CENTER), as are the horizontal and vertical gaps that determine the space between the components.

GridLayout

With the GridLayout constructor, you specify the number of rows and columns you want, along with optional horizontal and vertical component gaps. The layout manager creates the grid with equal-size cells. If the window is resized, then the manager resizes the cells to get the maximum possible constant cell size. The components are filled from right to left and from top to bottom, as shown in Figure 9.12.

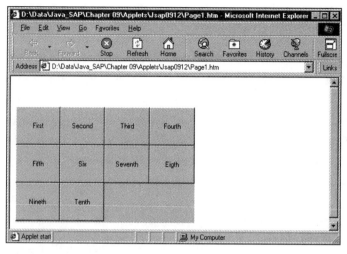

FIGURE 9.12 *A GridLayout example*

```java
import java.awt.*;
import java.applet.*;

public class Applet1 extends Applet
{
    public void init()
    {
        setLayout(new GridLayout(3,4));

        add(new Button("First"));
        add(new Button("Second"));
        add(new Button("Third"));
        add(new Button("Fourth"));
        add(new Button("Fifth"));
        add(new Button("Six"));
        add(new Button("Seventh"));
        add(new Button("Eigth"));
        add(new Button("Ninth"));
        add(new Button("Tenth"));
    }
}
```

GridBagLayout

The GridBagLayout layout manager is both the most flexible and the most complicated of the layout managers. Like the GridLayout manager, the GridBagLayout places components in rows and columns; however, the size and number of components per row or column can be controlled at the component level.

Because the GridBagLayout method is so complex, it is not discussed in this introductory-level book. If you need more flexibility than the preceding four layout managers can provide, you can try the form generator that comes with most Java compilers.

Common Layout Manager Methods

Every layout manager, whether provided by the AWT or custom written, must have the following five methods defined:

- ◆ **addLayoutComponents(String, Component).** Called by the container add() method.
- ◆ **removeLayoutComponent(Component).** Called by the remove() and removeAll() container methods.
- ◆ **preferredLayoutSize(Container).** Called by the container preferredSize() method.
- ◆ **minimumLayoutSize(Container).** Called by the container minimumSize() method.
- ◆ **layoutContainer(Container).** Called the first time a container is drawn and each time that its size changes.

Handling Events

The AWT also provides a common way to handle events. This approach enables you to write platform-dependent event code, which means that if the code is executed on different operating systems, it will work in the same fashion. Event handling is one area in Java that has changed a great deal between versions 1 and 2. Most of the old event-handling methods, such as action(), have been replaced with a concept called *event listening*. With event listening, you call a method when you want to intercept an event for an object.

Many examples in this chapter created buttons. To find out whether someone has pressed the button, call addActionListener() and pass to it the object to which you want to listen. When the button is pressed, the AWT event handler calls the processAction() method in your code. To gain access to the addActionListener() method, you need to implement the ActionListener interface.

For window events such as WINDOWS_DESTROY, you can set up an event scheme similar to the ActionListener interface mentioned earlier. The interface to use is the WindowListener; however, if you implement this interface, then you have to code all the event processing for WINDOW_CLOSE, WINDOW_ICONIZE, and so on. The menu example earlier in this chapter shows one workaround. The WindowAdapter class is an empty class that allows you to write single functions, for example, a function to handle the WINDOW_CLOSE event.

Other listeners that are available include

- **ComponentListener**. Used for processing events related to keystrokes, mouse movement, focus, and other related component events.
- **AdjustmentListener**. Used for events pertaining to adjustable objects (such as toolbars).
- **ItemListener**. Used for item-specific events, such as check boxes or radio buttons.

Summary

This chapter develops a simple user interface that uses components, containers, layout managers, and events, all of which are provided by the AWT, or Application Window Toolkit. Using this tool to develop user interfaces ensures that they are platform independent. Though this chapter focuses on the basics of user interfaces, it provides enough pieces to develop fairly complicated interfaces containing many components.

This chapter is the first to include several code examples. In preceding chapters we did not have enough pieces to show a useful example, but now we can display things on the screen via a user interface. The examples in this chapter use several techniques to accomplish similar results. Review these examples to get an idea of the flexibility available in the Java language.

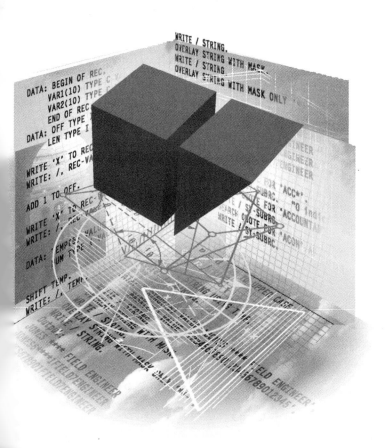

Chapter 10

JavaBeans,
ActiveX, Applets,
and the Internet

In This Chapter

- ◆ Java Streams
- ◆ Using Java and the Internet
- ◆ Sockets
- ◆ The Difference between an Application and an Applet
- ◆ Creating and Using Applets
- ◆ What Is a JavaBean?
- ◆ Comparison of ActiveX and JavaBeans

In this chapter we'll discuss certain advanced Java topics that are useful even to the novice Java programmer. Most of these topics deal with the concept of streams. *Streams* are what Java uses to read and write data to devices and other applications. With a fundamental understanding of the stream concept, you can write Java applications that read and write files and communicate with other servers and other Java programs. Using JavaBeans, the relationship of ActiveX to Java, and applets are also covered in this chapter.

Java Streams

Many Java programs are required to communicate with other systems or programs to get or send data. Java handles this communication through data streams.

Input streams send data from some external source to the Java program, and output streams send data from the Java program to an external area. The basic type of stream is referred to as a byte stream. *Byte streams* carry integers with values that range from 0 to 255. A derivation of the byte stream is the character stream. A *character stream* handles text data only and also supports Unicode.

Streams are fairly easy to use. You simply need to declare an object that is associated with the external system with which you want to communicate. You then use the methods associated with this class to read or write bytes, strings, and so on.

The following example shows a simple Java program that reads in a file from the user's computer and writes the contents back to the screen and to another file.

```java
import java.io.*;

public class Jsap1003
{
    public static void main (String[] args)
    {
// Instantiate the File Class for our File names and streams
        File                inFile, outFile;
        FileInputStream     inStream    = null;
        FileOutputStream    outStream    = null;
        int                 oneByte;
        boolean               eof = false;
        boolean               cool = false;
// Open up the data files, catch the exception if we cannot
// do this for some reason
        try
        {
            inFile      = new File("testin.txt");
            outFile     = new File("testout.txt");
            inStream    = new FileInputStream(inFile);
            outStream   = new FileOutputStream(outFile);
            cool        = true;
        }
        catch (FileNotFoundException err)
        {
            System.err.println("Cannot open input file");
        }
        catch (IOException err)
        {
            System.err.println("Cannot open output file");
        }
// If there are errors, just quit
        if (cool == false ) return;
// Now read in the input file, write out to screen and write
// out to the new file
```

```
try
{
    while(!eof)
    {
        oneByte = inStream.read();
        if (oneByte == -1 )
        {
            eof = true;
        }
        else
        {
            System.out.print((char)oneByte);
            outStream.write(oneByte);
        }
    }
    inStream.close();
    outStream.close();
}
catch (IOException err)
{
    System.err.println("Error during read/write operation");
}
}
}
```

Using Java and the Internet

Another instance in which you might use streams is when you want to use networking in a Java program. In this context, *networking* means having your Java application or applet communicate to another system over a network, such as the Internet. Communication over the Internet is accomplished mostly through the class URL (*Uniform Resource Locator*), which is included in the java.net package.

The URL class has the following constructors:

◆ **URL(String).** Tries to create a complete URL based on the string passed in.

- ◆ **URL(String, String, String).** Attempts to create a URL for the specified protocol, host, and file name.
- ◆ **URL(String, String, Int, String).** Attempts to create a URL for the specified protocol, host, port, and file name.
- ◆ **URL(URL, String).** Attempts to create a URL for the specified base URL and a relative URL passed through as a string in the second parameter.

All of these constructors throw the exception MalformedURLException if an error occurs in building the URL.

The following methods are commonly used with URL objects:

- ◆ **GetContents().** Returns the contents of the URL
- ◆ **OpenConnection().** Attempts to open the connection to the URL
- ◆ **OpenStream().** Attempts to open an InputStream connection

Below is an example of a Java application that opens a URL connection to the specified site and then displays the HTML (*Hypertext Markup Language*) source listing from that site. This example uses two streams: one for the input from the keyboard (System.in), and the other for the communication with the URL.

```
/* Example of code to read in a URL's HTML and
   print it to the screen
*/
import java.net.*;
import java.io.*;

public class Jsap1004
{
    public static void main (String[] args)
    {
        // Declare some variables
        byte                userInput[] = new byte[256];
        URL                 ourUrl;
        String              instr;
        URLConnection       conn = null;
        Object              urlContent;
```

```
BufferedInputStream      buf;
int                      urlByte;
String                   line;
// Setup prompt for user input
System.out.println("Enter URL to retrieve:");
// Get user input
try
{
    System.in.read(userInput);
}
catch (IOException e)
{
    System.out.println("I/O Error:" + e.getMessage());
    return;
}
instr = new String(userInput);
// Write out the User Input and initialization message
System.out.println("Validating URL...");
try
{
    ourUrl = new URL(instr);
}
catch (MalformedURLException e)
{
    System.out.println("Problem with entered URL");
    System.out.println(e.getMessage());
    return;
}
// Attempt to establish a connection to this URL
try
{
    ourUrl.openConnection();
}
catch (IOException e)
{
```

```
                System.out.println("Cannot establish connection to URL");
                System.out.println(e.getMessage());
                return;
            }
            // Read in the HTML and Print to the screen
            try
            {
                urlContent = ourUrl.getContent();
                if ( !( urlContent instanceof BufferedInputStream ))
                {
                    System.out.println("Unknown input from URL");
                    System.out.println(urlContent.getClass().getName());
                    return;
                }
                buf = (BufferedInputStream)urlContent;
                urlByte =  buf.read();
                while( urlByte  != -1 )
                {
                    System.out.print((char)urlByte);
                    urlByte = buf.read();
                }
            }
            catch (IOException e)
            {
                System.out.println("Problems reading HTML");
                System.out.println(e.getMessage());
                return;
            }
            System.out.println("Program Finished");
        }
    }
```

Figure 10.1 shows the program screen of the preceding example if you try to go to the URL www.primapub.com. (This URL actually redirects you to Prima's real home page, www.primapublishing.com.)

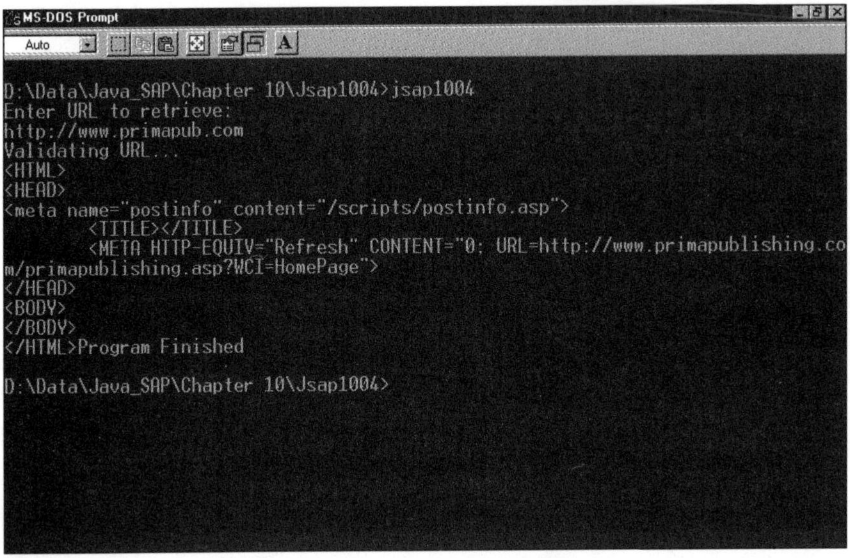

FIGURE 10.1 *Output from the sample URL reading program*

Sockets

The URL class works well if you need a high-level class for accessing data from the Internet. However, you may want to write Java applications that require lower-level network communication, such as client/server applications. For example, you may have to deal with additional security software before accessing a server, or you may need to access a legacy application that requires a more complicated communication protocol.

In typical client/server applications, a communication link exists between the client software and the server software through a mechanism called *sockets*. Client-based software uses the Java class Socket, and server-based software uses the Java class ServerSocket, both of which are in the java.net package.

To implement this type of communication, you simply need to create an instance of either the Socket or ServerSocket class and then use the stream methods introduced earlier to perform the communication. Many types of constructors are available for the Socket and ServerSocket classes, but the two that follow are the most frequently used.

◆ **Socket(String, Int).** String is the host name and Int is the port on this host to which to connect.

♦ **ServerSocket(Int).** Int is the port number used for
communication.

The next example contains two Java classes, Jsap1006 and Jsap1005; Jsap1006 is
the client code, and Jsap1005 is the server code. I have programmed this example
in the Windows 98 environment and have executed each class in a separate MS-
DOS window. If you type in a string on the client window, the client Java program sends the string to the server class, which reverses the characters and then
sends the string back to the client class for display. If you type **ServerOff** on the
client side, the server application shuts down. If you type **bye** in the client application, the client application terminates. As you can see in this example, with the
exception of the Socket and ServerSocket classes, all reading and writing is done
with streams in a fashion that is very similar to reading or writing to a file or URL.

Client Example

Listed below is the client side of the client/server example. We try to establish
communications with the server, get the user string, and finally make the call to
the server application.

```java
import java.io.*;
import java.net.*;

public class Jsap1006
{
    public static void main (String[] args)
    {
        // Try to establish a connection to the host
        Socket     mySocket = null;
        byte     userInput[] = new byte[256];
        PrintWriter os = null;
        BufferedReader is = null;
        Character inChar = null;
        try
        {
            mySocket = new Socket("localhost",9876);
            os = new PrintWriter(mySocket.getOutputStream());
            is = new BufferedReader(
                new InputStreamReader(mySocket.getInputStream()));
```

```
    }
    catch (UnknownHostException e)
    {
        System.out.println(e.getMessage());
        return;
    }
    catch (IOException e)
    {
        System.out.println(e.getMessage());
        return;
    }
    // Get input from the user and send it to the host
    try
    {
        StringBuffer buf = new StringBuffer(50);
        int c;
        String fromServer;
        while(true)
        {
            while((c = System.in.read()) != '\n')
            {
                if (inChar.isLetterOrDigit((char)c) ||
                    c == ' ')
                    buf.append((char)c);
            }
            if (buf.toString().equals("bye")) break;
            os.println(buf.toString());
            os.flush();
            buf.setLength(0);
            fromServer = is.readLine();
            System.out.println("Server:" + fromServer);
        }
        os.close();
        is.close();
        mySocket.close();
    }
    catch(UnknownHostException e)
```

```
                {
                    System.out.println(e.getMessage());
                }
                catch(IOException e)
                {
                    System.out.println(e.getMessage());
                }
            }
        }
```

Server Example

Listed below is the server side of this example. This code locks a port number for communications, waits for a message through this port, reverses the letters, and finally sends the message back.

```
import java.net.*;
import java.io.*;

public class Jsap1005
{
    public static void main (String[] args)
    {
        // Attempt to lock onto a port number
        ServerSocket serverSocket = null;
        try
        {
            serverSocket = new ServerSocket(9876);
            // Write the host name and port number
            System.out.println("Host:" +
                        serverSocket.getInetAddress().getHostName());
            System.out.println("Port:" + serverSocket.getLocalPort());
        }
        catch (IOException e)
        {
            System.out.println(e.getMessage());
            return;
```

```
    }
    // Wait for client message
    try
    {
        Socket clientSocket = null;
        clientSocket = serverSocket.accept();
        BufferedReader is = new BufferedReader(
                        new InputStreamReader(
                            clientSocket.getInputStream()));
        PrintWriter os = new PrintWriter(
                        new BufferedOutputStream(
                            clientSocket.getOutputStream(),
                            1024),false);
        String inputLine;
        while((inputLine = is.readLine()) != null)
        {
            System.out.println("Received:" + inputLine);
            StringBuffer myBuffer = new StringBuffer(inputLine);
            os.println(myBuffer.reverse().toString());
            os.flush();
            if (inputLine.equals("ServerOff"))
                break;
        }
        os.close();
        is.close();
        clientSocket.close();
        serverSocket.close();
    }
    catch (IOException e)
    {
        System.out.println(e.getMessage());
        return;
    }

    }
}
```

Figures 10.2 and 10.3 show how these two programs interact with each other.

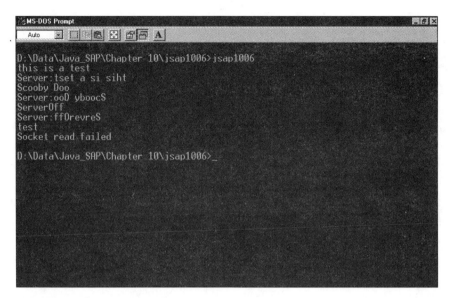

FIGURE 10.2 *Client side of sockets example*

FIGURE 10.3 *Server side of sockets example*

The Difference between an Application and an Applet

The difference between a Java application and a Java applet is how they are executed. An application is executed by a Java interpreter that loads the application's main class file, whereas an applet is executed through a Java interpreter that works with a browser and must be included on a Web page to run. Because Java applets are executed on the Web user's computer, certain restrictions limit what they can do. If these restrictions were not in place, it would be easy to write Java programs capable of planting viruses or violating the security of the Web user's computer (for example, by looking for Intuit's Quicken program and then sending all of your credit card numbers to an Internet site.)

In general, most Web browsers place the following restrictions on applets:

- ◆ They cannot read or write files to a user's file system.
- ◆ They cannot make network connections other than to the host where they originated.
- ◆ They cannot start any program on the computer on which they are running.
- ◆ They cannot load program or library files that are stored on the computer on which they are running.

A Java application must have a main( ) method, which is where the application starts to execute. An applet uses other methods, such as init( ), start( ), stop( ), and destroy( ). However, it is possible to write a class that can be used as both an application and an applet, because applets ignore the main( ) method when they are executed.

Creating and Using Applets

In previous chapters we created many applets. Applets are a subclass of the Applet class (java.applet.Applet). The five primary methods that you'll probably want to override when you write an applet are init( ), start( ), stop( ), destroy( ), and paint( ).

- ◆ **init( )**. This method is called only once in an applet's lifetime. You can use init( ) for data declaration and initialization or for loading fonts and images.

◆ **start()**. This method is called each time the applet is started, including the first time the applet is called and each time the user returns to the Web page containing the applet.

◆ **stop()**. Like the start() method, the stop() method is called each time the applet is stopped. For example, it is called when the user leaves the Web page containing the applet.

◆ **destroy()**. This method does any final cleanup before the applet is unloaded from memory.

◆ **paint()**. This method displays items in the applet window; it can be called as many times as needed. You need to pass an object of Class Graphics to the paint() method; this object is passed to the applet from the browser.

Overriding these five methods leaves you with a basic applet shell that looks like this:

```
import java.awt.*;
import java.applet.Applet;
public class AppletSample extends Applet
{
    public void init(){ . . . }
    public void start(){ . . . }
    public void stop() { . . . }
    public void destroy() { . . . }
    public void paint(Graphics g) { . . . }
}
```

Applet Communications

Applets can also communicate with other programs either by calling public methods of applets that are running in the same browser or by using certain API (*Application Programming Interface*) calls that are available in either the java.net or java.applet packages.

For two applets to communicate, the first applet needs to determine the name of the second. The name of an applet is defined during the creation of the HTML tag that defines the applet as follows:

```
<APPLET CODE=Test.class>
```

```
<PARAM NAME="NAME" VALUE="Scooby">
</APPLET>
```

The current name of an applet can be determined by using the following code segment:

```
appletName = getParameter("NAME");
```

You can check whether another applet is executing and then execute a method within that applet by using the getApplet() method. You can also query all the applets currently running by using the getApplets() method. An example of the getApplet() method is shown later in this section.

The applet can communicate with the browser and the originating server. You can also accomplish other tasks with it, such as retrieving the current host name and URL, setting the status message or displaying other documents. Some of the more popular classes and methods follow.

- ◆ **appletContext.showDocument().** This method tells the browser to either show a new window or replace the current window.
- ◆ **getCodeBase().getHost().** This method retrieves the host from which the applet came.
- ◆ **appletContext.showStatus().** This method tells the browser which string to show in the status line.

 CAUTION

Be careful about using the showDocument() method and the showStatus() method in an applet. Many browsers ignore these methods.

The following example shows many features of applet communication. It consists of one HTML page with two applets in it (see Figure 10.4). The first applet looks for the second applet, and if it is found, all messages are routed to it. The example also demonstrates some applet-to-browser communication and applet-to-server communication by retrieving various system values.

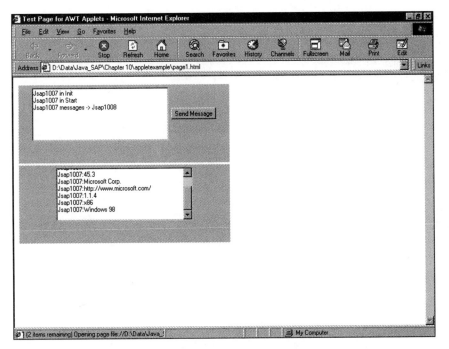

FIGURE 10.4 *Output from the communication applet example*

page1.html

```
<!-Test HTML page for Applet communications —>
<html>
<head>
<title>Test Page for AWT Applets</title>
</head>
<body>
<applet name="Jsap1007" code="Jsap1007.class" width=400 height=200>
Java not supported with this browser
</applet>
<applet name="Jsap1008" code="Jsap1008.class" width=400 height=200>
</applet>
</body>
</html>
```

Jsap1007

```java
import java.awt.*;
import java.awt.event.*;
import java.applet.*;
import java.net.*;

public class Jsap1007    extends Applet
                         implements ActionListener
{
    Applet          app2 = null;
    AppletContext   myContext;
    TextArea        txta;
    Button          but1;
    String          myName;

    public void init()
    {
        // Initialize variables and construct applet objects
        txta = new TextArea(6,40);
        but1 = new Button("Send Message");
        add(txta);
        add(but1);
        but1.addActionListener(this);
        // Get Context for this Applet
        myContext = getAppletContext();
        // Now check if the applet "Jsap1008" is running
        myName = getParameter("NAME");
        this.message(myName +  " in Init");
    }
    public void start()
    {
        this.message(myName + " in Start");
    }
    public void stop()
    {
        this.message(myName + " in Stop");
    }
```

```
    public void destroy()
    {
        this.message(myName + " in Destroy");
    }
    public void message(String str)
    {
        if (app2 != null)
        {
            ((Jsap1008)app2).message(str);
        }
        else
        {
            txta.append(str + "\n");
        }
    }
// Handle the button presses
    public void actionPerformed(ActionEvent event)
    {
        Object target = event.getSource();
        if (target == but1)
        {
            app2 = getAppletContext().getApplet("Jsap1008");
            if (app2 != null)
            {
                txta.append("Jsap1007 messages -> Jsap1008" + "\n");
            }
            this.message(myName + ":" + getCodeBase().getHost());
            this.message(myName + ":" + System.getProperty("java.class.version"));
            this.message(myName + ":" + System.getProperty("java.vendor"));
            this.message(myName + ":" + System.getProperty("java.vendor.url"));
            this.message(myName + ":" + System.getProperty("java.version"));
            this.message(myName + ":" + System.getProperty("os.arch"));
            this.message(myName + ":" + System.getProperty("os.name"));
        }
    }
}
```

Jsap1008

```java
import java.applet.*;
import java.awt.*;
import java.awt.event.*;

public class Jsap1008     extends Applet
{
    TextArea     txta;
    String       myName;

    public void init()
    {
        // Initialize variables and construct applet objects
        txta = new TextArea(6,40);
        add(txta);
        myName = getParameter("NAME");
        // Now check if the applet "Jsap1008" is running
        this.message(myName + " in Init");
    }
    public void start()
    {
        this.message(myName + " in Start");
    }
    public void stop()
    {
        this.message(myName + " in Stop");
    }
    public void destroy()
    {
        this.message(myName + " in Destroy");
    }
    public void message(String str)
    {
        txta.append(str + "\n");
    }
}
```

What Is a JavaBean?

JavaBeans are simply pieces of reusable Java code that follow a strict set of rules on how they interface with other pieces of Java code. Any Java class that adheres to the rules regarding properties of interfaces can be a Bean. The best way to learn about JavaBeans is to experiment with them. Sun offers a free Bean Development Kit (BDK) through its Web site at www.sun.com (the BDK is available in the Products and API section of this site.) This site also contains documentation and tutorials on how to create and use JavaBeans through the Java class Beans. Note that the BDK is not meant for commercial application development, but merely for learning purposes. Many other JavaBean development kits are available if you want to develop Beans for commercial use.

TIP

While you are at Sun's Web site, you may want to also download the Java Development Kit (JDK) along with many other Java utilities. The kit and documentation are free and provide an excellent way of experimenting with the Java language on a different platform, without having to pay for a compiler right away.

Comparison of ActiveX and JavaBeans

Microsoft has its own set of software components that can be reused; they are called *ActiveX* components. ActiveX is a set of technologies that enable software components to interact with one another in a networked environment, regardless of the language in which they were created. ActiveX is built on the COM (*Component Object Model*). COM is also the model upon which OLE (*Object Linking and Embedding*) is built. COM was developed by Microsoft and Digital Equipment as a standard for cross-platform development. COM is based on the object-oriented programming concepts discussed in Chapter 6, "Object-Oriented Programming Concepts." A COM object must support the IUnknown interface, which maintains the object's existence while it is being used, and provides access to the object's other interfaces.

If you are using the Microsoft Visual J++ compiler, you can import ActiveX controls into your Java programs. However, ActiveX components may not be compatible with operating systems other than Windows.

Summary

This chapter discussed the basics of using data streams in Java—for reading and writing from data files, accessing Web pages through the Internet, and for developing of a client/server communication system through the use of sockets. When you know how to use streams in one of these instances, the others are quite simple because Java handles all streams in much the same way. The Java section of this book is meant to be an introduction to the language for those who want to use it with SAP. You are strongly encouraged to experiment with the various classes and methods that are introduced in this chapter. To become familiar with related methods and classes, look through the online help that is available with your Java development system.

Applets are a very common use for Java. With Java you can develop small applications that can run on any browser, regardless of operating system. This chapter covers the basics of applets, points out the differences between applets and full-blown Java applications, and discusses how applets can communicate with other programs.

Finally, this chapter also briefly introduced JavaBeans and ActiveX. These advanced topics are not crucial for an introduction to the Java language, but the basic concepts are good to know as you start to read and learn more about the Java language.

Taken as a whole, the information in this chapter will help you to build useful, full-fledged Java applications.

PART II

Using Java with SAP

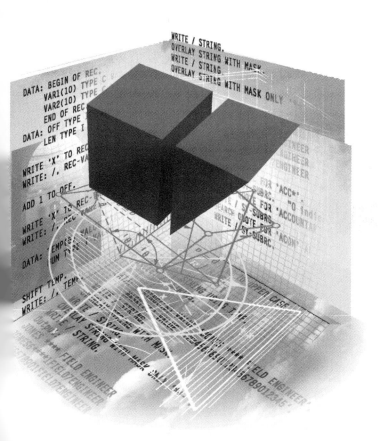

Chapter 11

**Integrating Java
with SAP through
RFCs and BAPIs**

In This Chapter

◆ Initialization to the Middleware

◆ Connecting to the SAP System

◆ The Basics of the BAPI Call

Chapter 5 includes several simple examples of accessing data within an SAP system from a Java program using the classes provided in the Java packages com.sap.rfc and com.sap.rfc.exception. These two packages contain all the classes that are used in connecting a Java program to SAP. This chapter goes through the details for this process and describes how to set up basic applications that interact with an SAP system. Comprehensive information on every class and interface in these packages is provided in Chapters 19 and 20.

Initialization to the Middleware

Communication between a Java program and an SAP system is done through a middleware software package. For the SAP Automation suite, the middleware is Orbix (see Chapter 4, "Setting up the Development and Operating Environments"). To establish a connection between the Java client and the middleware, you need to first create an instance of the MiddlewareInfo class (which is defined in the com.sap.rfc package) and tell this new object where the Orbix Daemon is running. A piece of code similar to the following does the job:

```
// Trigger the constructor for the class to instantiate the object
// mwinfo
MiddlewareInfo mwInfo = new MiddlewareInfo ();
// Set up the class variable to indicate which kind of middleware
// we are going to connect to, You can use "middlewareTypeJNI" below
// instead of "middlewareTypeOrbix" if you are using IBM's JNI middleware
mwInfo.setMiddlewareType (MiddlewareInfo.middlewareTypeOrbix);
// Now tell the new object where to find the middleware daemon.
String rfcHost = "testsystem";
mwInfo.setOrbServerName(rfcHost);
```

After you have created the MiddlewareInfo object, you are ready to use the FactoryManager class to establish the connection between the client where your Java code is executing and the middleware server.

The FactoryManager class creates objects that Java code uses to access both the middleware and the RFCs (*Remote Function Calls*) within SAP. You will use this class many times in this chapter. Here, you will use it to set up the variables in a MiddlewareInfo object. A one-to-one correspondence exists between the FactoryManager class and the MiddlewareInfo object, which means that an applet or Java application is allowed to have only one FactoryManager object. After this one-to-one relationship is established, the FactoryManager uses one of five factory interfaces in the com.sap.rfc package to actually access the SAP system. These five factories are described in Table 11.1.

Table 11.1 FactoryManager Objects

Factory	Description
IRfcConnectionFactory	Creates the initial RFC connection
IRfcModuleFactory	Creates a basic RFC function module object
ISimpleFactory	Creates single-value RFC parameters
IStructureFactory	Creates structured RFC parameters
ITableFactory	Creates RFC table parameters

To set up the connection between the FactoryManager and the Middleware, use the methods getSingleInstance and setMiddlewareInfo, as shown in this partial code example.

```
FactoryManager facman = null;
facMan = FactoryManager.getSingleInstance();
facMan.setMiddlewareInfo(mwInfo);
```

 TIP

If your Java program will be used in different types of middleware software, you need to determine the type of middleware when you set up the MiddlewareInfo object. To do so, you can use the getMiddlewareInfo method of the FactoryManager to return the middleware that is being used at run time.

What Is a Factory?

A *factory* is an interface whose methods create objects that Java programs use to access the SAP system. The important point here is that these factories are interfaces, not classes. One of the main differences between interfaces and classes is that you cannot create an instance of an object through an interface. For example, the following declaration creates a variable that is assumed to have the methods that are included in the interface; the declaration does not create the object itself.

```
IRfcConnection connection =
facMan.getRfcConnectionFactory().createRfcConnection(connectInfo,
➡ userInfo);
```

The object is actually created by the FactoryManager class through the createRfcConnection method, which then passes back a reference to the newly created object. This reference is assigned to the variable connection.

After you perform the method setMiddlewareInfo in the FactoryManager class, your program will be ready to start communicating with the SAP system.

Connecting to the SAP System

The connection to an SAP system is handled through the IRfcConnection and IRfcConnectionFactory interfaces. (See Chapter 8, "Objects, Classes, and Interfaces," for a general discussion of interfaces in the Java language.) Basically, an *interface* is a collection of methods (beyond those that the class inherits from the class hierarchy) that can be included in a class. The classes that are affected by these interfaces are described in Table 11.2. You need to instantiate and populate the classes UserInfo and ConnectInfo before you can establish the connection to the SAP system.

Table 11.2 Classes Used with the IRfcConnection Interface

Class	Description
UserInfo	Contains the SAP user information used in collection, such as login ID, language, and password
ConnectInfo	Contains information about a connection to SAP R/3, such as system name and number
SystemInfo	Contains the information about the R/3 system that is contained in the SYST SAP information structure
ConnectionEvent	Supports the ConnectionListener interface

The following portion of code shows how to set up the UserInfo and ConnectInfo objects, and then connect to a SAP system.

```
// Instantiate classes
UserInfo userInfo = new UserInfo();
ConnectInfo connectInfo = new ConnectInfo();
// Define variables within the newly created objects
userInfo.setClient("000");
userInfo.setUserName("TESTUSER");
userInfo.setPassword("abc123");
userInfo.setLanguage("E");
connectInfo.setRfcMode(ConnectInfo.RFC_MODE_VERSION_3);
connectInfo.setDestination("xxx");
connectInfo.setHostName(r3Host);
connectInfo.setSystemNo((short)Integer.parseInt (r3SysNo));
connectInfo.setLoadBalancing(false);
connectInfo.setCheckAuthorization(true);
// Call up the factory manager to create a new object and assign
// a reference to this object to the variable "connection". This object
// is assumed to have the methods that are defined in the
// IRfcConnection interface, such as open();
IRfcConnection connection = facMan.getRfcConnectionFactory()
                        .createRfcConnection(connectInfo, userInfo);
connection.open();
```

In Chapter 5 we developed a simple Java program to ping an SAP system. That example does not have a user interface, and the program is executed from a DOS shell window. To keep the program as simple as possible, it was developed as a single class. We are now going to develop a more complex program—with windowing features and multiple classes—that will log in to an SAP system and return some of the system variables contained in the system info structure SYST.

The example contains three classes: ShowSyst, SystFrame, and Sap. The ShowSyst class is the main class; it calls the other classes. The ShowSyst class handles all screen I/O, and the Sap class handles all calls to the SAP system. Java allows only one class per file; therefore, we must link these three files to form the executable program. This example is set up as previous examples have been, as a console application from the Microsoft Java Compiler. After the project is set up, we add the three classes, as shown in Figure 11.1.

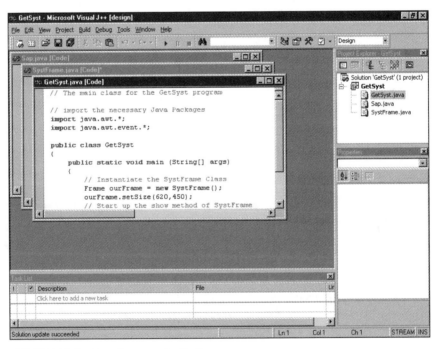

FIGURE 11.1 *Compiler screen for GetSyst*

GetSyst.Java

```
// The main class for the GetSyst program


// import the necessary Java Packages
import java.awt.*;
import java.awt.event.*;


public class GetSyst
{
    public static void main (String[] args)
    {
        // Instantiate the SystFrame Class
        Frame ourFrame = new SystFrame();
        ourFrame.setSize(340,300);
        // Start up the show method of SystFrame
        ourFrame.show();
    }
}
```

Sap.Java

```
// This class handles all communication to the
// SAP system


import com.sap.rfc.*;
import com.sap.rfc.exception.*;


public class Sap
{
    public String     rfcHost      = null,
                      r3Host       = null,
                      r3SysNo      = null,
                      r3FieldFld   = null,
                      r3InfoFld    = null,
                      client       = null,
```

```
                         user          = null,
                         password      = null,
                         language      = null,
                         errmess       = null;

public String custNo=null, custName=null;

protected    FactoryManager facMan = null;
protected    IRfcConnection connection = null;
protected    MiddlewareInfo mdInfo = null;

public boolean connect()
{
    errmess = new String("Connected to SAP System");
    //cleanup previous connection
    cleanUp();

    try
    {
        if( null == mdInfo )
        {
            // create a middlewareInfo object with rfcHost name
            mdInfo = new MiddlewareInfo();
        }

        mdInfo.setMiddlewareType(MiddlewareInfo.middlewareTypeOrbix);
        mdInfo.setOrbServerName(rfcHost);

        // let the global factory manager use the middlewareInfo
        // to create all object factories by binding to the server
        facMan = FactoryManager.getSingleInstance();
        facMan.setMiddlewareInfo(mdInfo);
    }
    catch (JRfcBaseRuntimeException je)
    {
        errmess = new String(je.toString());
        return false;
    }
```

```
        connection = logon();
        if( connection == null ) return false;

        return true;
    }


protected IRfcConnection logon()
{
    UserInfo userInfo = new UserInfo();
    ConnectInfo connectInfo = new ConnectInfo();
    IRfcConnection connection = null;

    userInfo.setClient(client);
    userInfo.setUserName(user);
    userInfo.setPassword(password);
    userInfo.setLanguage(language);

    connectInfo.setRfcMode(ConnectInfo.RFC_MODE_VERSION_3);
    connectInfo.setDestination("xxx");
    connectInfo.setHostName(r3Host);
    connectInfo.setSystemNo((short)Integer.parseInt(r3SysNo));
    connectInfo.setLoadBalancing(false);
    connectInfo.setCheckAuthorization(true);

    try
    {
        connection = facMan.getRfcConnectionFactory()
                        .createRfcConnection(connectInfo, userInfo);
        connection.open();
    }
    catch (JRfcRfcConnectionException re)
    {
        errmess = new String(re.toString());
        System.out.println("Unexpected RfcError while opening connection.\n"
                        + re.toString());
        return null;
    }
    catch (JRfcBaseRuntimeException je)
```

```java
        {
            errmess = new String(je.toString());
            System.out.println("Unexpected RfcError while opening connection.\n"
                            + je.toString());
            return null;
        }
        return connection;
    }


    public boolean getSystInfo()
    {
        SystemInfo si;
        ISimple    sparam;
        try { si = connection.getSystemInfo();}
        catch (JRfcRfcConnectionException je)
        {
            errmess = new String("GetSystemInfo Failed");
            return false;
        }
        sparam = si.getItem(r3FieldFld);
        r3InfoFld = sparam.getstring();
        errmess = new String(sparam.getFieldName() + ":Call Done");
        return true;
    }


    public void cleanUp()
    {
        try
        {
            if( null != connection )
                connection.close();
            connection = null;
        }
        catch (JRfcBaseRuntimeException je)
        {
            errmess = new String(je.toString());
            return;
        }
```

```
        }
    }
```

SystFrame.Java

```
// This class displays a window and handles all
// I/O from that window (like logging into SAP)

import java.awt.*;
import java.awt.event.*;

import com.sap.rfc.*;
import com.sap.rfc.exception.*;

// Frame is part of the AWT and is a subclass of the Window class. It provides a
// window with a title bar, close boxes, and other platform-specific window
// features. Our class "SystFrame" will be an extention of this class and thus
// will inherit all of its features, along with the methods that we will code
// (again like logging into an SAP system).

public class SystFrame extends Frame implements ActionListener
{
    private Sap ourSap = new Sap();    // New SAP object

    private TextField rfcHostFld,      // Java Server Name
                      r3HostFld,       // SAP System Name
                      r3SysNoFld,      // SAP System Number
                      clientFld,       // Client
                      userFld,         // Login Name
                      passwordFld,     // Password
                      languageFld,     // Login Language
                      r3FieldFld,      // Input Field for inquiry
                      r3InfoFld;       // Output Field for inquiry
    private Label     messageStr;      // Error Messages

    private TextArea resultArea;
```

```java
private final String connectStr = "Login to SAP System";

private Label rfcHostLbl  = new Label("Java Server Name:");
private Label r3HostLbl   = new Label("SAP Server host:");
private Label r3SysNoLbl  = new Label("System number:");
private Label clientLbl   = new Label("Client:");
private Label userLbl     = new Label("User:");
private Label passwordLbl = new Label("Password:");
private Label languageLbl = new Label("Language:");
private Label r3FieldLbl = new Label("Field Name:");
private Label r3InfoLbl   = new Label("Result:");

private Button connectBut;
private Button getInfoBut;

public SystFrame()
{
    // Set the Title for the Frame
    setTitle("GetSyst - Get SAP System variables");

    // For this example we will use the GridLayout layout manager
    // in the constructor we indicate the number of columns and rows
    // that we will have
    GridLayout gLayout = new GridLayout(12,5,2,5);
    // Define the input fields
    rfcHostFld       = new TextField("", 30);
    r3HostFld        = new TextField("", 30);
    r3SysNoFld       = new TextField("", 2);
    clientFld        = new TextField("", 3);
    userFld          = new TextField("", 12);
    languageFld      = new TextField("E", 2);
    r3FieldFld       = new TextField("",10);
    r3InfoFld        = new TextField("",30);
    messageStr       = new Label("");
    passwordFld      = new TextField("", 8);
    passwordFld.setEchoChar('*');

    // Define the Buttons
```

```java
connectBut = new Button("Connect");
getInfoBut = new Button("GetInfo");

// Define the initial status of input boxes and buttons
r3FieldFld.setEnabled(false);
r3InfoFld.setEnabled(false);
getInfoBut.setEnabled(false);

// add components to the frame, these are added in order,
// from left to right, top to bottom.
setLayout(gLayout);
add(rfcHostLbl);
add(rfcHostFld);
add(r3HostLbl);
add(r3HostFld);
add(r3SysNoLbl);
add(r3SysNoFld);
add(clientLbl);
add(clientFld);
add(userLbl);
add(userFld);
add(passwordLbl);
add(passwordFld);
add(languageLbl);
add(languageFld);
add(connectBut);
add(new Label(" "));
add(r3FieldLbl);
add(r3FieldFld);
add(getInfoBut);
add(new Label(" "));
add(r3InfoLbl);
add(r3InfoFld);
add(messageStr);

// subscribe to the buttons actionlistener events for the buttons
connectBut.addActionListener(this);
getInfoBut.addActionListener(this);
```

```
// subscribe to the window events, only handle close for
// right now.
addWindowListener
(
    new WindowAdapter()
    {
        public void windowClosing(WindowEvent e)
        {
            ourSap.cleanUp();
            System.exit(0);
        }
    }
);
}


// This piece of code handles the actions via the actionlistener

public void actionPerformed(ActionEvent evt)
{
    // Handle the Connection Button
    if(evt.getActionCommand().equals("Connect"))
    {
        ourSap.rfcHost = rfcHostFld.getText();
        ourSap.r3Host = r3HostFld.getText();
        ourSap.r3SysNo = r3SysNoFld.getText();
        ourSap.client = clientFld.getText();
        ourSap.user = userFld.getText();
        ourSap.password = passwordFld.getText();
        ourSap.language = languageFld.getText();
        if (ourSap.connect() == true)
        {
            dispMessage(ourSap.errmess);
            connectBut.setEnabled(false);
            getInfoBut.setEnabled(true);
            r3FieldFld.setEnabled(true);
        }
        else
        {
```

```
                    dispMessage(ourSap.errmess);
            }
    }
    // Handle the GetInfo Button
    if(evt.getActionCommand().equals("GetInfo"));
    {
        ourSap.r3FieldFld = r3FieldFld.getText();
        ourSap.getSystInfo();
        r3InfoFld.setText(ourSap.r3InfoFld);
        dispMessage(ourSap.errmess);
    }
    }
    // Display a message on the bottom of the screen
    void dispMessage(String instr)
    {
        messageStr.setForeground(Color.red);
        messageStr.setText(instr);
    }
}
```

This program enables you to query for fields in the RFCSI structure, along with CURRENT_RESOURCES and MAXIMAL_RESOURCES (the function module call RFC_SYSTEM_INFO handles these queries). An example of the Java screen appears in Figure 11.2.

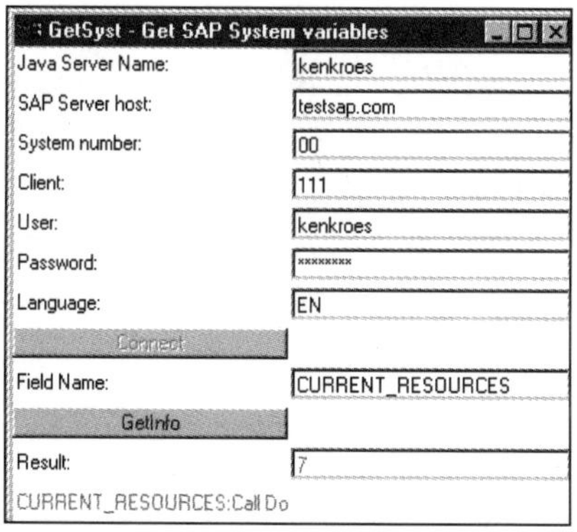

FIGURE 11.2 *A GetSyst example screen*

The Basics of the BAPI Call

Most communication between a Java program and an SAP system is done through BAPIs. As discussed in Chapter 18, the basic construct for calling a BAPI is as follows:

```
call function 'Scooby-doo'
    exporting
        Parameters
    Importing
        Parameters
    Tables
        Parameters
    Exceptions
        Parameters.
```

After the link to the SAP system is established through the IRfcConnection factory, you need the ability to set up the export and table variables, make the call to the SAP system, and then read in the import and table variables. You also need the ability to handle any exceptions that occur. All activity with the BAPI is handled through the IRfcModule Java interface.

Handling Simple Import and Export Parameters

Let's start by looking at how to populate a simple export variable (import variables are set up in an identical fashion). In other words, the export parameter for the BAPI comprises one of the basic SAP data element types, such as CHAR or NUM, and is not a structure. The export variable can be set up manually through a call to the addExportParam method of the IRfcModule object. This method expects an object containing the necessary information about the export parameter, such as data type, parameter name, and value. For a simple variable, this information is contained in an object called ISimple. The following code segment summarizes this entire process.

```
// Instantiate the Isimple Class
ISimple simpleParam;
// Instantiate the Factory Manager Class
FactoryManager facMan = FactoryManager.getSingleInstance();
// Instantiate the IsimpleFactory
ISimpleFactory simpleFac = facMan.getSimpleFactory();
```

```
// Create the Isimple object and reference it to simpleParam
simpleParam = simpleFac.createSimple(
new SimpleInfo(null, IFieldInfo.RFCTYPE_CHAR, 10, 0), "KUNNR");
// Instantiate the IrfcModuleFactory and IRfcModule
IRfcModuleFactory moduleFac = facMan.getRfcModuleFactory();
IRfcModule theModule = moduleFac.createRfcModule(connection, "RFCNAME");
// Set the value for the variable
theModule.setSimpleExportParm("KUNNR").setString("Prima");
// Assign the Export Parameter
theModule.addExportParam(simpleParam);
```

 TIP

Do not let the constructor for `Isimple`—`SimpleInfo(null, IFieldInfo.`
`RFCTYPE_CHAR, 10, z)`—intimidate you. All the parameters for constructors and
most methods are covered in Chapters 19 and 20. In this case, the first parameter is
used if this field is part of a structure, the second is the data type, the third is the
data length, and the fourth is the number of decimals.

In the preceding code segment, the constructor for SimpleInfo defines the values such
as data type and size, and the call to the simple factory ties this object to an actual
parameter in the RFC, in this case KUNNR. This method of creating the export
parameter works if you know the parameter definitions of the BAPI and you want to
hard code these into your Java program. However, you can also build this export parameter automatically, via the getSimpleInfo method of the IRfcModule interface.
Using the automatic creation mode, the same example can be coded as follows.

```
// Instantiate the Isimple Class
ISimple simpleParam;
// Instantiate the Factory Manager Class
FactoryManager facMan = FactoryManager.getSingleInstance();
// Instantiate the IsimpleFactory
ISimpleFactory simpleFac = facMan.getSimpleFactory();
// Instantiate the IrfcModuleFactory and IRfcModule
IRfcModuleFactory moduleFac = facMan.getRfcModuleFactory();
IRfcModule theModule = moduleFac.createRfcModule(connection, "RFCNAME");
// Get the values for the variable
ISimple simpleParam = theModule.getSimpleImportParam("KUNNR");
// Set the value for the variable
```

```
theModule.setSimpleExportParm("KUNNR").setString("Prima");
// Assign the Export Parameter
theModule.addExportParam(simpleParam);
```

As you can see, this approach is a little less cumbersome to use than the original, and no knowledge is required about the parameter that is to be defined. You can view or use the current value of either export or import parameters via methods of the ISimple interface, such as getFloat() or getString(). These methods return the value of the variable in the format specified (for example, getFloat() returns a float).

With the basics of simple import and export parameters out of the way, we can move on to perform the RFC itself.

Calling the Remote Function Module

The remote function module to be called by a Java program is defined through the methods autoCreateRfcModule or CreateRfcModule of the IRfcModuleFactory. The difference between the methods is in how the parameters are created. The autoCreateRfcModule automatically creates all parameters, whereas the constructor for CreateRfcModule allows you to create none, some, or all. If you are going to use all of the parameters in a BAPI call, then use the autoCreateRfcModule. Examples for both methods follow, and the full syntax for both is discussed in Chapter 19.

```
// Autocreate example
IRfcModule theModule = moduleFac.autoCreateRfcModule(connection, "RFCNAME");
// Create example
IRfcModule theModule = moduleFac.createRfcModule(connection, "RFCNAME");
theModule.addImportParam(simpleParam);
theModule.addExportParam(simpleParam);
```

After the IRfcModule object has been created and the export variables have been defined with values, the call to the RFC itself is accomplished through one of three methods:

- ◆ **Call().** A one-way call to the SAP system. Use this method when you are not receiving any values (including tables) from the function module.
- ◆ **Receive().** A one-way call from the SAP system. Use this method when you are not sending any values to the function module.
- ◆ **CallReceive().** A two-way call to and from the SAP system. Use this method when you are both sending and receiving values from the function module.

You can also remove fields from the IRfcModule object.

Handling Complex Import and Export Variables

Import and export parameters are often not simple variables, but instead are structures composed of many simple fields.

Examples of setting up structures both manually and automatically follow.

```
// Example of manual creation of structure
IStructure structParam;
IStructureFactory structFac = facMan.getStructureFactory();
structParam = structFac.createStructure();
SimpleInfo simpleInfos[] =
{ new SimpleInfo("KUNNR", IFieldInfo.RFCTYPE_CHAR, 10, 0),
new SimpleInfo("ANRED", IFieldInfo.RFCTYPE_CHAR, 15, 0),
......
};
ComplexInfo complexInfo = new ComplexInfo(simpleInfos, null);
structParam.setComplexInfo(complexInfo);
structParam.setParameterName("PARAMNAME");
// Example of Automatic Creation of Structure
IStructure structParam;
IStructureFactory structFac = facMan.getStructureFactory();
IRfcConnection connection = …;
connection.open();
structParam = structFac.
autoCreateStructure("PARAMNAME", connection, "TABNAME");
```

Handling Tables and Cursors

Defining tables is very similar to defining complex info objects and is done through the objects ITable and IRow.

Sample code for building table entries follows.

```
// Sample code for adding a row to an iTable object
ITable theTable = …;
IRow theRow = theTable.createEmptyRow();
theRow.getSimpleField("KUNNR").setString(custNo);
```

```
theRow.getSimpleField("NAME1").setString(custName);
theTable.appendRow(theRow);
// Sample code for updating a row
ITable theTable = …;
IRow rowCopy = theTable.getRow(0); //get a copy of the first row
rowCopy.getSimpleField("KUNNR").setString(custNo);
rowCopy.getSimpleField("NAME1").setString(custName);
theTable.updateRow(0, rowCopy);
```

Exceptions and Errors

You must be concerned with two types of errors when making the BAPI calls: catchable Java errors and the parameter RETURN, which is associated with all BAPIs. To write bulletproof code, you should always set up your program to catch all Java errors and to test the RETURN parameter. Information on all catchable errors for all methods is provided in Chapters 19 and 20. You can also set up your Java compiler to catch all exceptions.

Summary

The first time you set up a function module call in Java, you have to write a fair amount of code. However, you will find that all calls follow the same pattern and that you can set up methods within your Java class to perform the repetitive coding operations.

One key to a successful Java program is efficient operation. Efficiency is accomplished by setting up only the parameters that you need and by using the correct calls; these techniques avoid as much overhead as possible. You also want to catch and print out or log all errors that occur when you first start setting up RFC calls. Reviewing these errors will often tell you exactly what is wrong with your program or your setup to the function module.

Data structure is the most important thing to understand when working with RFCs. ISimple fields are the basic ones; they are used to develop the structure and table parameters. Chapters 19 and 20 provide detailed information on the methods that are available in the area of constructors for the data, along with methods that are available for the data and IRfcModule interfaces.

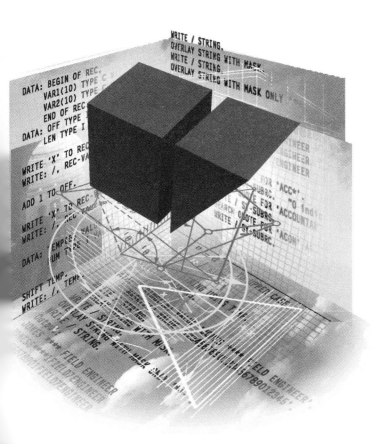

Chapter 12

*SAP's Business
Object Repository*

In This Chapter

◆ Introduction to Business Objects

◆ Navigation through the BOR

◆ Key Information in the BOR for the Use of BAPIs

◆ Finding Usable Function Modules Outside the BOR

◆ ActiveX Controls and the Business Object Broker

The BOR (*Business Object Repository*) is the heart of the SAP system. The business model is both defined and executed through the BOR, and BAPI/Java programming requires an understanding of these fundamentals. If you have not yet read Chapter 6, "Object-Oriented Programming Concepts," I urge you to do so, because the BOR is very closely modeled after this concept.

The BOR was introduced in release 3.0 of SAP and at that time was primarily used for SAP Business Workflow. This approach allowed users to build workflows that used these objects and were triggered when events such as the creation of an object occurred. Release 3.1 of SAP extends the use of the BOR to include BAPIs, which makes the BOR the central point for access from external systems, such as Java programs. Now an object can contain variables and events, and have methods assigned to it. This chapter covers the basics of the BOR and explains the various details of the objects it contains, and how they relate to your Java programs.

Introduction to Business Objects

Business objects and OOP (*Object-Oriented Programming*) are based on the same concepts. In general, a *business object* is a tangible item used in a business environment, such as a material, a customer, an employee, or a sales order. As in object-oriented programming, business objects can have variables and methods and can inherit properties from other objects. Variables and methods in the BOR can be related to the object definition or to an instance of the object. This idea is similar to the Class and Instance variables for OOP. Objects are created through a tool called the *Business Object Builder* seen in Figure 12.1.

The properties of an object can be seen through the Object Builder. Figure 12.2 shows the detail for the EMPLOYEEI object.

A business object has four parts, or levels. The first part, the kernel, represents the data or variables that actually make up the object itself. The second part, the integrity level, is where we define how the object works in the overall business model, that is, how objects are related to each other. The third part, the interface level, basically contains the methods that are implemented to access the object. The fourth and final part is the access level, which defines how external applications access the data. The levels are shown in Figure 12.3.

The Business Object Repository is used not just to define objects within SAP, but also to define outside interfaces to SAP. For instance, if an outside vendor supplies an ATP (*Available to Promise*) engine for your instance of SAP or a software

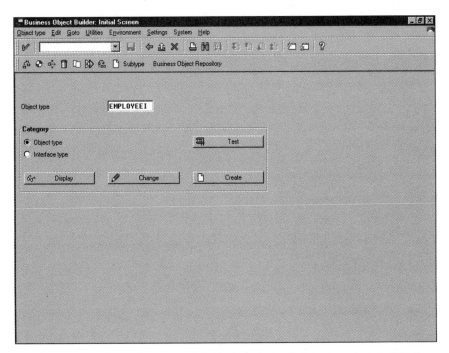

FIGURE 12.1 *The opening screen of the Business Object Builder (transaction SWO1)*

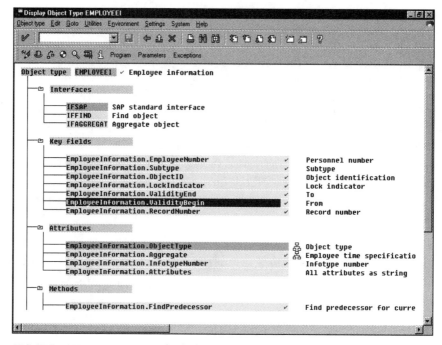

FIGURE 12.2 *The details of the EMPLOYEEI object*

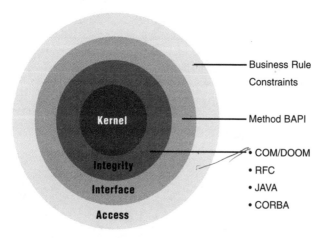

FIGURE 12.3 *The layers of an SAP business object*

package to calculate taxes based on geographic location, the applications can be configured in the BOR so that all SAP (or your Java program) has to do is call a BAPI to access the software.

You need to be able to use the correct terminology when discussing business objects. Following is a list explaining how SAP defines the various components of a business object. Note the slight difference in wording, such as *object type* instead of *class* (the object-oriented term).

- ◆ The *object type* describes the features common to all instances of that object type. This description includes information such as the object type's unique name, its classification, and the data model. In OOP, this field is called *class*.

- ◆ The *key fields* determine the structure of an identifying key, which allows an application to access a specific instance of the object type. The object type Employee and the key field Employee.Number are examples of an object type and a corresponding key field. In addition to being used to identify objects, key fields are also instance attributes (variables) for the object.

- ◆ A *method* is an operation that can be performed on a business object and provides access to the object data. A method is defined by a name and a set of parameters and exceptions which the calling program must provide. BAPIs are examples of such methods. Methods are typically implemented through function modules.

- ◆ An *attribute* contains data about a business object, thus describing a particular object property. For example, Employee.Name is an attribute of the Employee object type.

- ◆ An *event* indicates the occurrence of a status change to a business object. Generally, you use events to trigger actions, such as using a Business Workflow event if a certain operation is performed on an instance of the object type. A good example is the creation of a workflow when a material is created.

Navigation through the BOR

The BOR can be accessed either through the Business Object Builder (transaction SWO1) or, if you are interested only in BAPIs, through the transaction BAPI. The menu path for accessing the BOR is Tools, ABAP Workbench, Overview, Business Object Browser. An example of the first screen of the BOR is shown in Figure 12.4.

The Business Object Builder allows you to maintain the business objects, and the BOR helps you find more information about a specific object. The BOR lets you find the properties of an object, determine which properties are inherited, and where the object is used within the SAP system. From the BOR, you can drill down into the various SAP business areas. Figure 12.5 shows this expansion for the object Material through the Logistics General business area.

The icons in the BOR do have special meaning; they can tell you the status of a BAPI, such as whether it is released or obsolete. A sample of the legend that comes with the BOR transaction is shown in Figure 12.6.

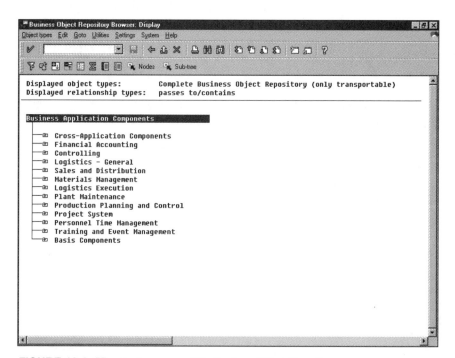

FIGURE 12.4 *The opening screen of the Business Object Repository*

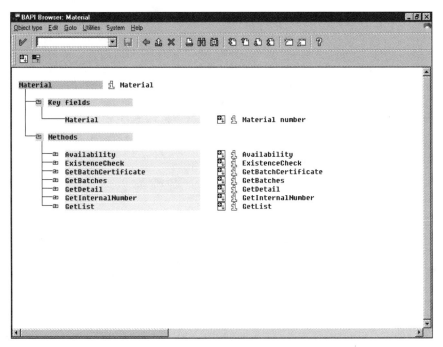

FIGURE 12.5 *A detailed view of the Material object*

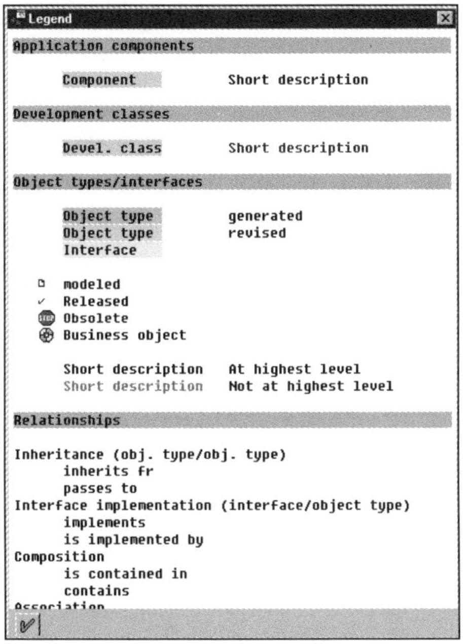

FIGURE 12.6 *The BOR legend*

TIP

When a released BAPI becomes obsolete, it remains in the BOR for at least two major revision levels of the SAP package. This practice gives customers time to port any code accessing the old BAPI to its replacement, and allows for a stable upgrade path between major versions of SAP. Consequently, you will see several SAP BAPIs with a 2 behind the name, for example, get_material and get_material2.

Key Information in the BOR for the Use of BAPIs

Before using a BAPI that you find in the BOR, you must examine the BAPI to see whether it performs the tasks that you require and whether you have sufficient information to provide to it.

The first step is to determine whether or not the BAPI is *instance-dependent*. You can differentiate between instance-dependent (instance methods) and instance-independent (class methods) BAPIs. Unlike instance-independent methods, instance-dependent methods relate to one instance (one specific occurrence) of an SAP business object type (for example, to one specific sales order). The type of BAPI is usually very apparent after examining the parameters that are transferred to and from it.

You must also examine the key fields of the object to which the BAPI is related. All key fields are required if you want to access one specific instance of the object. Depending on the BAPI, you can get away with partial keys; for instance, if you want a list of material numbers that start with TST, you can enter TST* in the material number key field.

Finally, you should check the name of the BAPI (usually a function module) and whether any documentation is available on it. The documentation can be found by clicking on the Information icon to the right of the BAPI name.

Finding Usable Function Modules Outside the BOR

Ideally, when you access SAP through a Java program, you are doing so through BAPI interfaces. However, at times you may need access to functions within SAP that are not available as BAPIs. As you have already learned, a BAPI is basically just a remote function module. To look for other function modules that are available through SAP, you can use the Find function in transaction SE37 to list the modules. Basically, you can perform the search by excluding function modules that start with BAPI and by looking for functions that have the RFC flag set in the attributes section. The screen sequence for looking up these RFCs is shown in Figures 12.7, 12.8, and 12.9.

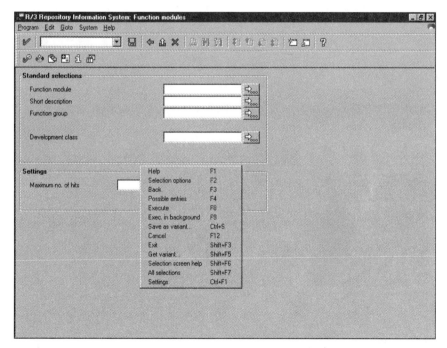

FIGURE 12.7 *The initial Find function in SE37. To set the correct filter, you need to expand all selection conditions.*

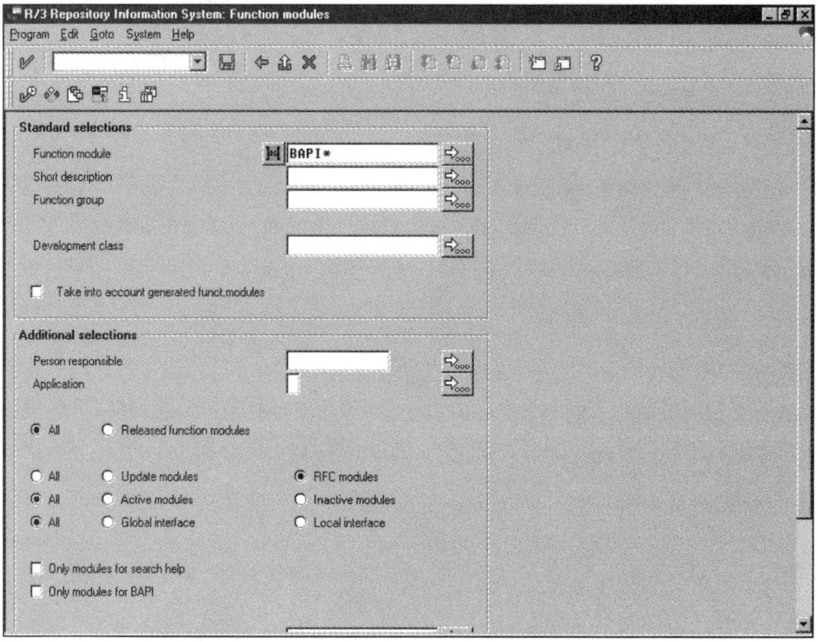

FIGURE 12.8 *The expanded selection screen, filled in with the required values*

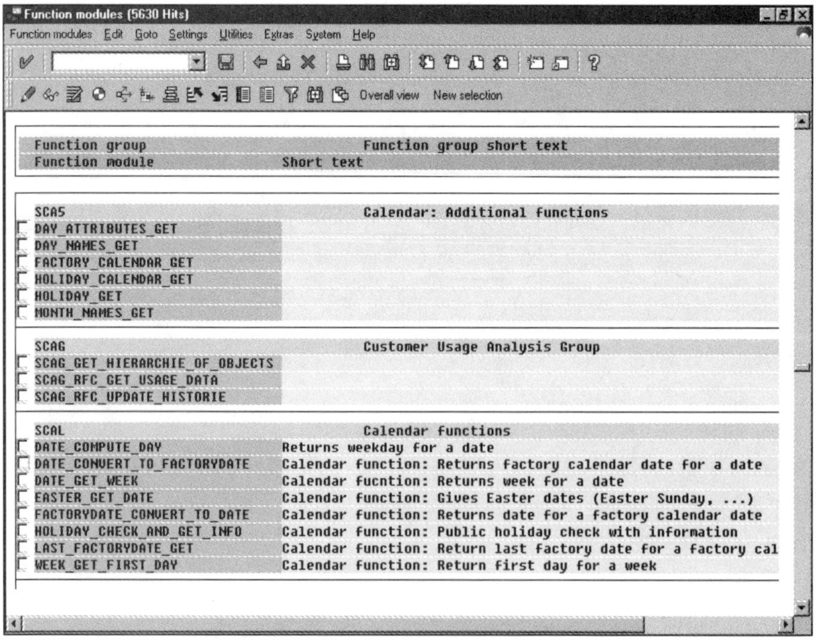

FIGURE 12.9 *Sample results from the selection*

Figure 12.9 shows RFC functions that let you work with the factory calendar within SAP. Currently, no BAPI functions are available for this purpose; if your Java program needs to look at the factory calendar, you can use these function modules.

ActiveX Controls and the Business Object Broker

The BAPI ActiveX control can be used by external applications to access business functions in the R/3 system by calling BAPIs through OLE Automation. Client programs access *proxy objects*, which are local instances of SAP business objects managed by the BAPI ActiveX control. These proxy objects correspond to the real SAP business objects stored in R/3's BOR.

The core of the BOR run-time system is the BOB (*Business Object Broker*), which executes on the client system. Client programs send requests to the BOB, which takes the following actions:

- ◆ Creates the addressed run-time object
- ◆ Chooses the correct method implementation
- ◆ Calls the method found
- ◆ Transports the results back to the caller
- ◆ Destroys the runtime objects

If the client calls a BAPI directly, then the BOB calls the BAPI through an RFC. If the BAPI is not defined, the BOB goes through the BOR, finds the corresponding object, and then finds the correct BAPI (for example, GetList()). The BAPI ActiveX control is currently implemented to run under Windows 95 and Windows NT.

Summary

The BOR is your guide to how the SAP system is set up, and it is modeled after the object-oriented programming concept. As a Java programmer, you are probably most interested in the BAPI area of the BOR. This area lists the BAPIs that are available, their import/export parameters, and their status, such as released or obsolete.

Sometimes, a BAPI is not available for the function you need (such as looking at the factory calendar). You can find remote function modules that are not set up as BAPIs through transaction SE37.

The BOR is closely linked to the Business Object Builder. The Business Object Builder maintains objects within SAP, whereas the BOR's sole function is to retrieve information about the objects. The final topic covered in this chapter is related to the Business Object Broker ActiveX control. This control allows OLE applications to reference objects within SAP without having a specific link to the BAPI.

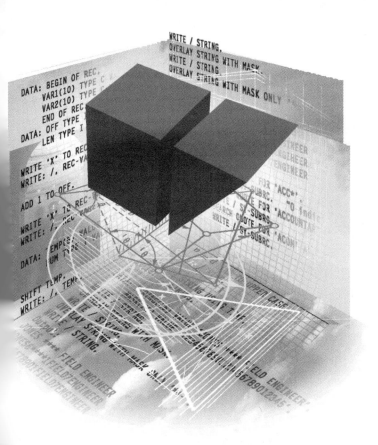

Chapter 13

Building a
More Advanced
User Interface

In This Chapter

- ◆ Abstract Windowing Toolkit
- ◆ The Swing Classes
- ◆ Swing Components

Some forms of information can be more efficiently processed in a graphical fashion than by other means. In addition, many GUI (*Graphical User Interface*) elements can be manipulated via a mouse, eliminating the need for advanced typing skills. This chapter discusses the AWT (*Abstract Windowing Toolkit*), and explains how to create GUIs in Java by using JFC (*Java Foundation Classes*).

Abstract Windowing Toolkit

AWT is a platform-independent interface that allows developers to create GUIs that run on all major platforms. AWT uses the "common functionality/specific implementation" approach. This approach is very object-oriented in that the functionality is the superclass (high-level abstraction) and each platform's look and feel is a subclass. The common functionality/specific implementation approach allows the application to take advantage of a platform's unique GUI and makes Java applications look and feel just like other native applications. AWT also encourages innovation by allowing third parties to develop variations of GUI components.

The Java AWT uses three concepts to implement the common functionality/ platform-unique look and feel: abstract objects, toolkits, and peers. Every AWT-supported GUI element has a class, and objects of that class can be instantiated. For example, a Button object can be instantiated from the Button class—even though there is no physical display of a button—because the Button call in AWT does not represent a specific look and feel. A specific look and feel would be a Solaris button, a Macintosh button, or a Windows button. AWT GUI objects are platform-independent abstractions of a GUI in the same way that Java byte codes are platform-independent assembly language instructions for a virtual operating system display. The toolkit is the platform-specific implementation of all the GUI elements supported by AWT. Each toolkit implements the platform-specific GUI elements by creating a GUI peer.

A *peer* is an individual platform-specific GUI element. Because every AWT GUI object is derived from the generic AWT object called a *component*, every component will have a peer. The peer implements the platform-specific behavior of the AWT component; it is added to the generic AWT object when the object is added to a container that has a peer.

Accessing the Default Toolkit Properties

Let's examine some code that demonstrates toolkits and peers. The following code demonstrates how to access the default toolkit properties:

```
import java.awt.Toolkit;
import java.awt.Dimension;

class ToolkitTest
{
    public static void main(String args[])
    {
        Toolkit toolkit = Toolkit.getDefaultToolkit();

        String name = System.getProperty("awt.toolkit");
        System.out.println("Toolkit name: " + name);

        Dimension screen = toolkit.getScreenSize();
        System.out.println("Screen Dimension : " +
                    screen.toString());
        System.out.println("Screen Resolution (dpi): " +
                    toolkit.getScreenResolution());
        System.out.println("Beep.");
        toolkit.beep();

        System.exit(0);
    }
}
```

By compiling the code and running it in MS-DOS, you produce the following:

```
C:\> java ToolkitTest
Toolkit name: sun.awt.windows.WToolkit
Screen Dimension: java.awt.Dimension[width=800,height=600]
Screen Resolution (dpi): 96
Beep.
```

Major Elements of AWT

AWT can be divided into six major areas.

- ◆ **Components**. Components are the building blocks of GUI-based applications. GUI elements are implemented via an abstract Component class; the class's associated subclasses implement specific GUI components. For X Windows programmers, an AWT component is analogous to an X Windows widget. For Windows developers, an AWT component is analogous to a CWnd object and inherits the appropriate derived object (CButton, for example).

- ◆ **Events**. A user action is translated into an Event data structure that stores the type of action and where it occurred, as well as other information. The event is then sent to the JVM (*Java Virtual Machine*) via the OS (*Operating System*). If an EventListener has been registered for this type of event, then that listener is called and may perform some action.

- ◆ **EventListeners**. The Java 2 platform uses the Delegation Event Model. Under this model, classes both register for events they would like to receive and define EventListeners to receive these events. EventListeners and the new Delegation Event Model simplify and separate the handling of events from the GUI elements that generate them.

- ◆ **Containers**. These are components that store other components. The most common container is the window. A panel is another very common Java AWT container whose purpose is to group other components inside a window.

- ◆ **Layout and Layout Managers**. A layout determines where the components will be drawn within a container. Layout managers implement specific policies for laying out components. For example, the GridLayout class lays out added components in a tiled grid.

✦ **Painting and Updating**. Although the prefabricated AWT components are useful, you will need to do some custom drawing in your applications. The Java AWT provides the paint(), repaint(), and update() methods to allow you to do just that.

The Swing Classes

JFCs, which are also called *Swings*, are sets of prebuilt classes that provide Java applications and applets with the building blocks for a sophisticated GUI. The architecture of most Swing components is based on the MVC (*Model-View-Controller*) design pattern.

Swing and AWT

Java took off faster than anyone could have imagined; the most visible of the Java APIs (*Application Programming Interfaces*), AWT, was thrust into the limelight. Unfortunately, the original AWT was not prepared for its sudden rise in popularity.

The original AWT was not designed to be anything akin to a high-powered user interface toolkit used by many developers. Instead, it was aimed at supporting the development of simple user interfaces for simple applets. The original AWT lacked many features that one would expect in an object-oriented GUI toolkit; clipboards, printing support, and keyboard navigation, for example, were all conspicuously absent. The original AWT did not even include such basic amenities as pop-up menus or scroll panes, two staples of modern user interface development.

In addition, the AWT infrastructure was flawed. AWT was fitted with an inheritance-based event model that scaled badly and a peer-based architecture that was destined to become the toolkit's Achilles heel.

One drawback of peer design is that on most platforms, each peer is rendered in a native window. A ratio of one native window per component is not exactly a formula for high performance, and applets that contained numerous AWT components paid a steep performance penalty as a result.

Because the original AWT had a high incidence of bugs, third-party companies began to offer toolkits providing more solid infrastructures and more functionality than did AWT. One such toolkit was Netscape's IFC (*Internet Foundation Classes*), a set of lightweight classes based on concepts from NEXTSTEP's user interface toolkits. IFC components did not use peer elements, and they surpassed AWT components in many respects. IFC also began to attract more than its share of developers.

Realizing that the Java community was likely to split over a standard user interface toolkit, JavaSoft struck a deal with Netscape to implement JFC (Apple and IBM have also participated in the development of JFC), or Swing. Netscape developers have worked with Swing engineers to embed considerable IFC functionality in Swing components.

Originally, Swing was meant to closely resemble Netscape's IFC. Over time, however, Swing diverged considerably from its original intent as features, such as pluggable look and feel (which provides a common look and feel across platforms and allows developers to guarantee a consistent interface for their Java applications or applets), were added and designs were modified. With release 1.0 most of Swing's outward similarities to IFC had vanished, although a great deal of IFC technology remains embedded within Swing. Today, Swing provides the best of both AWT and IFC in a comprehensive user interface toolkit.

Benefits of Swing

A common misconception about Swing is that it is designed to replace AWT; actually, Swing is built on top of AWT. Swing takes advantage of the AWT infrastructure, including graphics, colors, fonts, toolkits, and layout managers, but does not use AWT components. The only AWT components that have relevance for Swing are the frames, windows, and dialogs. In essence, Swing uses the best of AWT to build a new set of mostly lightweight components while leaving behind the heavyweight components.

To get the most out of Swing, you need a basic knowledge of AWT infrastructure. In addition to using AWT functions, all Swing lightweight components are ultimately derived from the AWT Container class, which in turn extends the AWT Component class. In other words, not only does Swing take advantage of the infrastructure provided by AWT, but all Swing components are actually AWT containers. The AWT Container class itself is *lightweight*, meaning that it has no peer element and is painted in its container's window.

The Model-View-Controller Design Pattern

The MVC design pattern, like many other design patterns, goes back to the principle of object-oriented design, which advises against making one object responsible for too much functionality. In other words, don't have a single button class do everything; instead, have the look and feel of the component associated with one object and store the contents in another object. The MVC design pattern accomplishes its goal by implementing three separate classes: the *model*, which stores the contents; the *view*, which displays the contents; and the *controller*, which handles user input.

The MVC design pattern specifies precisely how these objects interact. The model stores the contents and has no user interface. A small set of flags that indicate whether a button is currently active or inactive should suffice. The content for a text field is a bit more interesting; it is a string object that holds the current text. If the content is larger than the text field, the user sees only a portion of the text displayed.

The model must implement methods to discover what the contents are and then change them. For example, a text model has methods to add or remove characters in the current text and to return the current text as string. Again, keep in mind that the model is completely abstract. It has no particular visual representation.

The view's job is to draw the data that is stored in the model. One advantage of the MVC design pattern is that a model can have multiple views, each showing a different aspect of the full contents.

The controller handles user-input events, such as mouse clicks and keystrokes; it decides whether to translate these events into changes in the model or the view. For example, if the user presses a character key in a text box, the controller calls the Insert Character command of the model. The model then tells the view to update itself, and the view never knows why the text changed. But if the user presses a cursor key, then the controller may tell the view to scroll. Scrolling the view has no effect on the underlying text, so the model never knows that this event occurred.

Creating a Swing Applet

The following example inherits the JApplet class to create the SwingApplet class, which displays the earth.gif image. The SwingApplet overrides the JApplet init()

method. You should put all the code in the init() method you want your applet to execute before it starts. In the SwingApplet init() method, we create a container (to hold the earth.gif image and label) and display the earth.gif image in the center.

```
import javax.swing.*;
import java.awt.*;
import java.awt.event.*;

Public class SwingApplet extends JApplet
{
    public void init()
    {
        Container contentPane = getContentPane();
        Icon icon = new ImageIcon("earth.gif",
            "An earth GIF on a Swing");

        JLabel label = new JLabel("Swing!", icon,
                        JLabel.CENTER);

        contentPane.add(label, BorderLayout.CENTER);
    }
}
```

Compile this example in MS-DOS using command line *javac SwingApplet.java*. Assume that the example is in the SwingApplet.java file. The Java compiler produces SwingApplet.class. To execute SwingApplet.class at MS-DOS, use command line *java SwingApplet*, which should produce the results shown in Figure 13.1.

The JApplet class uses an instance of BorderLayout as the layout manager for its content pane. To stress this fact, the applet listed in the preceding example specifies a layout constraint of BorderLayout.CENTER, which enters the label in the content pane. The default constraint for a component laid out by BorderLayout is BorderLayout.CENTER; specifying the constraint in the applet is not strictly necessary.

FIGURE 13.1 *Results of running SwingApplet in MS-DOS*

Swing Components

Following are the current key components of Swing:

- ◆ **JApplet**. This component is an extended version of the applet that supports multiple panes (just as JFrame does) and also supports a Swing menu bar.

- ◆ **JButton**. This is a lightweight, pluggable version of the familiar AWT button. Note that all JFC components are subclasses of JComponent. JButton supports many variations of a button (for example, an image button or variable placement of text). All JFC components, even those similar to AWT components, are generally flexible. The model for this component is the ButtonModel, which is also the model for JButton, JCheckbox, and JRadioButton.

◆ **JCheckbox, JCheckboxMenuItem.** This component is a lightweight, pluggable version of Checkbox and Checkbox Menu Item.

◆ **JColorChooser.** This is a pane or dialog of controls that allow a user to graphically select a color.

◆ **JComboBox.** A combo box is a drop-down list of choices. This class has a custom combo box, an editable combo box, and a classic combo box. The model for this component is the ComboBoxDataModel.

◆ **JComponent.** All JFC components subclass (or inherit) the JComponent that extends java.awt.Container.

◆ **JDesktopPane.** This is a container that allows you to create a virtual desktop by adding JInternalFrames. The result is the familiar MDI (*Multiple Document Interface*) common in Windows applications.

◆ **JDialog.** This component is a class to create a dialog that allows multiple panes, just as JFrame does.

◆ **JEditorPane.** This is a content pane that allows you to edit different types of content, such as HTML (*Hypertext Markup Language*), RTF (*Rich Text Format*), or even the Java language, by use of an installable EditorKit class. This set of classes allows you to create powerful editors, and is well worth exploring.

◆ **JFileChooser.** This component is a pure Java version of a dialog to select and choose a file.

◆ **JFrame.** This is a lightweight, pluggable version of the AWT frame. The frame has a single child, JRootPane.

◆ **JInternalFrame.** This component allows frames within frames. This convention enables Java applications to create Windows MDI-type applications. You create and add these frames to the JDesktopPane.

◆ **JLabel.** This is a lightweight, pluggable version of the AWT label. Like other JFC components, JLabel is flexible, allowing various placements of the text and even images. JLabel has no model.

◆ **JList.** This component is a lightweight, pluggable version of the AWT list. JList has two models: ListDataModel and ListSelectionModel. JListBox is designed to make it easy to view the common collection types (for example, arrays, vectors, and hash tables).

◆ **JMenu, JMenuBar, JMenuItem**. These are lightweight, pluggable versions of the menu and menu items. The JFC Menu Items allow images on a menu and menu item.

◆ **JPanel**. This component is a lightweight, pluggable version of the AWT panel.

◆ **JPasswordField**. This is a subclass of JTextField that allows you to enter a word without revealing what is typed. Instead of showing the characters typed, the field displays an echo character, such as an asterisk.

◆ **JPopupMenu**. This menu can pop up anywhere on the screen. The best example is the right-click contextual pop-up menu in Windows, which was also recently added to Mac OS 8 via a Ctrl-click.

◆ **JProgressBar**. This is a new component that presents a graphical view of an action's progress. This element uses the BoundedRangeModel, the same model used by JSlider and JScrollBar.

◆ **JRadioButton**. This subclass of JToggleButton can be selected or de-selected and maintains (and displays) its state. It is normally used with a ButtonGroup so that only one button of a set of buttons is selected at any time.

◆ **JRootPane**. This is the fundamental component of the Swing frame, window, and pane classes. The parent containers delegate their operations to an instance of JRootPane, which has a glass pane and a layered pane. (A glass pane is a component that is laid out to fill the entire pane. By default, it is an instance of JPanel, but it can be replaced with any Component.) The glass pane sits on top of everything so that it can intercept mouse events. The layered pane manages the content pane and an optional JMenuBar. The three primary components of JRootPane are glass panes, content panes, and an optional menu bar. JRootPane is used by JFrame, JWindow, JApplet, JDialog, and JInternalFrame. Except for JInternalFrame, these elements are heavyweight components that extend their AWT counterparts.

◆ **JScrollBar, JScrollPane, JViewPort**. JScrollBar is a lightweight, pluggable version of the AWT scroll bar. It is intended to be a replacement for the AWT scroll bars. The model for this component is the BoundedRange-Model. JViewPort displays a view that is potentially larger than the viewport. JScrollPane combines JScrollBars with a JViewPort and maps them accordingly.

◆ **JSeparator**. This component is a lightweight, pluggable menu separator.

◆ **JSlider**. This element is a control that allows the user to select a value from a bounded range by dragging a selector knob. The operation is similar to that of a scroll bar. This component uses the same model as the ScrollBar: the BoundedRangeModel.

◆ **JSplitPane**. This component is used to visually divide two other components. Many applications use this element to separate a hierarchical view (using a JTree) from a second view that represents a view of one of the JTree nodes.

◆ **JTabbedPane**. A tabbed pane displays a set of labels that resemble file folders, and enables the user to store any component under that tab. When the user selects the tab, the component comes to the front. The model for this component is the SingleSelectionModel.

◆ **JTable**. This component resides in its own package, called *table*, and has numerous support classes and interfaces. A table is a graphical element to display relational data in a two-dimensional format. This format is perfect for the display of a database table.

◆ **JTextComponent, JTextArea, JTextField, JTextPane**. These components have an associated package called text, and numerous support classes and interfaces. The JTextComponent goes far beyond the AWT TextComponent by providing the building blocks for a fully internationalized text editor. JTextComponent works with the help of several other classes, such as Document interface, DocumentListener, and DocumentEvent, as well as various view classes and interfaces.

◆ **JToggleButton**. This is an implementation of the two-state button and uses a ToggleButtonModel. JRadioButton and JCheckBox extend this class.

◆ **JToolBar**. This graphics component displays icons for commonly used actions. The Action class enables the toolbar and menu bar to share common action classes.

◆ **JTree**. This class displays hierarchical data in an outline format. The most common example of a tree is the tree used in Windows Explorer to navigate Microsoft Windows file systems. JTree supports a more generic model that includes this type of view. The support classes are the TreeModel, the ListSelectionModel, and the TreeNode classes. The

TreeNode class is a simple data structure for storing hierarchical data. A JTree component will provide a default view for a TreeNode structure.

◆ **JWindow**. This is a lightweight version of a window that has a JRoot-Pane as a single child.

Using JButton, JTextArea, and JScrollPane

The following example demonstrates the use of JButton, JTextArea, and JScroll-Pane:

```java
import java.awt.*;
import java.awt.event.*;
import javax.swing.*;

class TextAreaFrame extends JFrame
    implements ActionListener
{
    public TextAreaFrame()
    {
        JPanel p = new JPanel();

        insertButton = new JButton("Insert");
        p.add(insertButton);
        insertButton.addActionListener(this);

        wrapButton = new JButton("Wrap");
        p.add(wrapButton);
        wrapButton.addActionListener(this);

        noWrapButton = new JButton("No wrap");
        p.add(noWrapButton);
        noWrapButton.addActionListener(this);

        getContentPane().add(p, "South");

        textArea = new JTextArea(8, 40);
        scrollPane = new JScrollPane(textArea);
```

```
getContentPane().add(scrollPane, "Center");

setTitle("TextAreaTest");
setSize(300, 300);
addWindowListener(new WindowAdapter()
{
    public void windowClosing(WindowEvent e)
    {
        System.exit(0);
    }
} );
}

public void actionPerformed(ActionEvent evt)
{
    Object source = evt.getSource();
    if (source == insertButton)
        textArea.append
            ("The quick brown fox jumps over the lazy dog. ");
    else if (source == wrapButton)
    {
        textArea.setLineWrap(true);
        scrollPane.validate();
    }
    else if (source == noWrapButton)
    {
        textArea.setLineWrap(false);
        scrollPane.validate();
    }
}

private JButton insertButton;
private JButton wrapButton;
private JButton noWrapButton;
private JTextArea textArea;
private JScrollPane scrollPane;
}
```

```
public class TextAreaTest {
   public static void main(String[] args)
   {
       JFrame f = new TextAreaFrame();
       f.show();
   }
}
```

Compile TextAreaTest and TextAreaFrame and run the class in MS-DOS by typing **Javac TextAreaTest**. The output is shown in Figure 13.2.

FIGURE 13.2   *The results of running TextAreaTest in MS-DOS*

Using JTextArea, JScrollPane, and JTextField

This example demonstrates the use of JTextArea, JScrollPane, and JTextField:

```
import java.awt.*;
import java.awt.event.*;
import javax.swing.*;

class TextEditFrame extends JFrame
{
    public TextEditFrame()
    {
```

```
setTitle("TextEditTest");
setSize(300, 300);
addWindowListener(new WindowAdapter()
    {
        public void windowClosing(WindowEvent e)
        {
            System.exit(0);
        }
    }
);


Container contentPane = getContentPane();


JPanel panel = new JPanel();


JButton replaceButton = new JButton("Replace");
panel.add(replaceButton);
replaceButton.addActionListener(new ActionListener()
    { public void actionPerformed(ActionEvent evt)
        {
            String f = from.getText();
            int n = textArea.getText().indexOf(f);
            if (n >= 0 && f.length() > 0)
              textArea.replaceRange(to.getText(), n,
                  n + f.length());
        }
    });


from = new JTextField(8);
panel.add(from);


panel.add(new JLabel("with"));


to = new JTextField(8);
panel.add(to);
```

```
        textArea = new JTextArea(8, 40);
        scrollPane = new JScrollPane(textArea);

        contentPane.add(panel, "South");
        contentPane.add(scrollPane, "Center");
    }

    private JScrollPane scrollPane;
    private JTextArea textArea;
    private JTextField from, to;
}
public class TextEditTest
{
    public static void main(String[] args)
    {
        JFrame f = new TextEditFrame();
        f.show();
    }
}
```

Compile TextEditFrame and TextEditTest and run the class in MS-DOS by typing **Javac TextEditTest**. The output is shown in Figure 13.3.

FIGURE 13.3 *The results of running TextEditTest in MS-DOS*

Summary

This chapter covered the advanced user interfaces, presented the benefits of using Swing and AWT, and explained the benefits of Swing versus AWT. The chapter also explained how to create graphical user interfaces in Java, using both foundation classes and Swings.

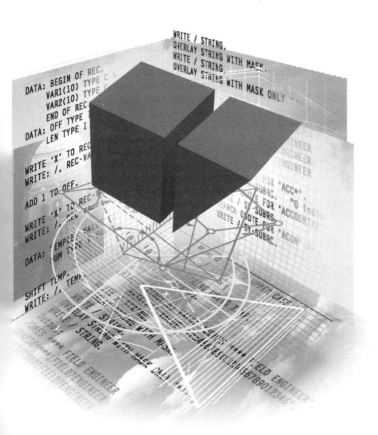

Chapter 14

SAP
Assistant

In This Chapter

SAP Assistant

SAP Assistant is a stand-alone executable program that provides an online tool for users to access R/3 objects and RFC (*Remote Function Call*) information from outside R/3. This tool allows you to perform various tasks related to SAP business objects and RFCs. You can view and search for information on SAP RFC function modules, and on business objects and their BAPIs (*Business APIs*, the methods of the business objects). You can call RFCs and use them directly online.

BAPI Wizard, another feature of SAP Assistant, enables you to generate either Java or C++ classes, which you can use to create and manipulate SAP business objects using their BAPIs.

System Requirements

To run SAP Assistant on your PC, you must have the following:

◆ SAP R/3 release 3.1F or higher

◆ SAP DCOM Connector

◆ Windows NT 4.0, Windows 95, or Windows 98

You cannot use SAP Assistant to call an RFC that invokes a SAPGUI screen, be it a dialog box or a window. You can determine whether SAP Assistant fails as a result of calling such an RFC by using transaction SE37 in R/3 and checking for a SAPGUI screen.

Internal Components of SAP Assistant

The following components of the SAP Assistant package are also available as stand-alone tools.

◆ **DCOM Connector logon component**. This component provides a logon screen and parameters for obtaining a connection from the end user. It allows the user to define the destination system.

◆ **Repository services**. This tool allows you to access business objects and RFC function modules in the R/3 system to COM-complaint programs and applications. It also lets you save a copy of the metadata in a local database. Using a local database provides a local caching mechanism to speed up access to the metadata.

◆ **BAPI Gateway**. The BAPI gateway allows you to dynamically call BAPIs and RFCs through the DCOM Connector.

◆ **Repository Browser**. The repository browser is also called the SAP Browser Control. An ActiveX control can be hosted by any ActiveX container, and consists of a window with two panes for browsing SAP BAPI and RFC metadata information. The browser supports online calling of RFC functions from within the control.

Configuring SAP Assistant

When working with SAP Assistant, you log on to an R/3 system to get its BAPIs or RFC metadata. Before you can log on to the R/3 system through SAP Assistant, you must set up a destination definition for that system. You can set up the destination definition by using the SAP DCOM Connector. Figure 14.1 shows the screen of the SAP DCOM Connector definition.

Follow these steps to get to the logon screen through SAP Assistant:

1. Select Login Online (File, Login R/3 System).

2. Click on the Administration tab.

3. Perform one of the following tasks: Add New Destination, which allows you to enter a name for the destination definition, or Edit Existing Destination, which allows you to select the destination name from the Destinations list. Figure 14.2 shows an example of the Edit Existing Destination option.

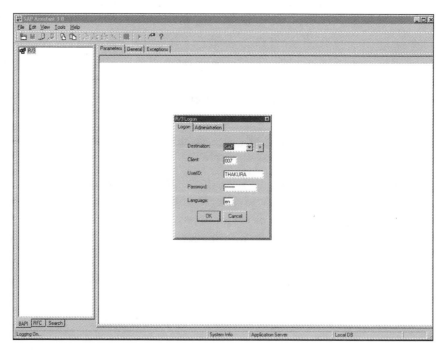

FIGURE 14.1 *SAP DCOM Connector definition*

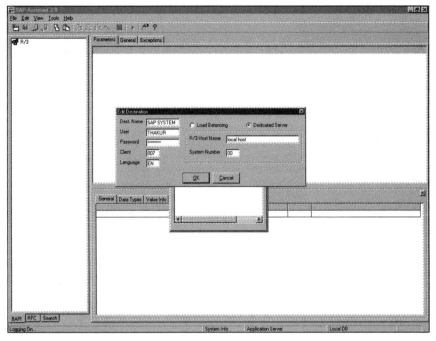

FIGURE 14.2   *Editing Destination dialog box*

4. Regardless of which task you performed in Step 3, choose either Load Balancing or Dedicated Server. If you choose Dedicated Server, when logging on, you must specify the actual R/3 application server to use; if you choose Load Balancing, you must specify a message server, which then selects the least busy application server for you to log on.

5. Enter the user name, password, client, and language to use when logging on to the system you have defined.

When all definitions are complete, you can log on to the R/3 system and view all of the RFCs and BAPIs in the SAP system.

The SAP Assistant Screen

The SAP Assistant screen area consists of the Browser window, which uses the SAP Browser control to display the RFC and BAPI information.

As Figure 14.3 shows, the SAP Assistant has three frames. The left frame of the Browser window is similar to a tree structure; it displays a list of all BAPIs or RFCs that exist in the R/3 system. From the tab (at the bottom of the frame), you can choose BAPI, RFC, or Search view. The Search tab enables you to search for a specific function group, function, or any program within SAP.

The frame on the right side of the screen changes according to your selection in the BAPI/RFC tree pane; it is called the *BAPI/RFC detail frame*. It shows the details of the BAPI or RFC you selected in the left frame. After you display a BAPI or an RFC and you see its parameters in the BAPI/RFC detail pane, you can double-click on any of the parameters or other detail items to view the item's properties. This information is displayed in a third frame, called the *properties pane*, at the bottom of the BAPI/RFC detail pane.

The properties pane consists of the following four tabs.

◆ **General Info**. The General Info tab shows basic information, such as the name, internal name, decimal position, and description of the parameter field displayed in the heading row.

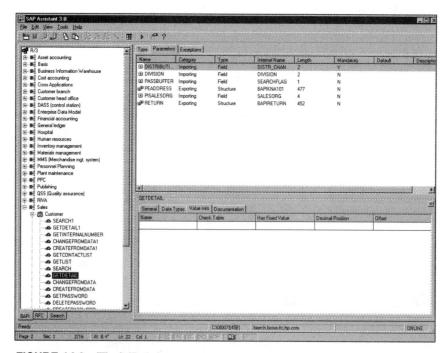

FIGURE 14.3 *The SAP Assistant screen*

- **Data Types**. Data Types gives the ABAP type and dictionary type of the parameter displayed in the heading row.

- **Value Info**. Value Info displays the check table of the parameter displayed in the heading row.

- **Documentation**. The Documentation tab provides a long text description of the selected item. A search function is also available in this tab.

Browsing on BAPIs and RFCs

From the RFC function on the SAP Assistant browser, select the desired function name on the BAPI/RFC tree pane. To do so, switch to one of the RFC views and look for the functions in the hierarchy, or use the Search tab. The Type tab of the BAPI/RFC tree pane displays general details of the function. Choose the Parameters table to list all parameters for the selected function and double-click on the name of a parameter to invoke the properties pane. You can then view all the details of a single parameter. You can also invoke the properties pane by choosing View, Properties, and then clicking on a parameter name to view its details. Use the same procedure to display the parameters of BAPIs.

SAP Assistant allows you to work with R/3 function modules (RFC functions) or business objects (BAPIs). When working with an RFC function, SAP Assistant enables you to display information on a function or to call the function online and see the output. SAP Assistant also allows you to display a list of remote functions or function groups in the R/3 system. With R/3 BAPIs, SAP Assistant lets you display a list of business objects in the R/3 system. It displays the key field of a business object and can generate the code for programming BAPIs in Java or C++.

Working on Multiple Windows through SAP Assistant

To work with multiple windows, you must open additional SAP Assistant windows; doing so allows you to work with other systems. Choose File, New Browser Window. Now you can log on to a different system or local Repository.

SAP Assistant Searching Tool

The Search tab in the BAPI/RFC tree pane supports searching for a specific business object, RFC function, or function group. The Search tab also accepts wildcards (*).

SAP Assistant Table Browser

This tool allows you to browse the R/3 table or an R/3 structure. Choose View, Table/Structure Browser, then enter the name of the table or structure in the Table/Structure field and choose display. SAP Assistant Table Browser displays all the fields for a specified table or structure. Viewing the table is not related to browsing BAPIs and RFCs and therefore is not related to any activity in the BAPI/RFC browsing area.

Downloading BAPIs or RFCs to Excel

You can export BAPIs, RFCs, or any business objects to Excel by downloading the associated data to an Excel spreadsheet. Log on to the R/3 system and select the data you want to download. Then choose Tools, View in Microsoft Excel. After you download and save the data this way, you can perform any Excel operation upon it.

Local Repository

The local repository is another way of working offline. Log on to the R/3 System through SAP Assistant, get any RFCs, functions, or BAPIs you want, and save them into the local repository file. The SAP Assistant local repository file uses the file type SDB. You can create multiple local repositories, each containing a different set of metadata.

Log on to the R/3 system from which you want to copy the business objects and highlight the items you want to save. You may save either the entire BAPI or RFC, or just a subset of it. When the business objects are in a local repository file, you can view them without logging on to the R/3 system.

Reading from a Local Repository

To read BAPI or RFC metadata from a local repository file, log on to a system in offline mode instead of from a live R/3 system. Choose File, Open File. Browse the Open Local Repository dialog box for the local repository file with which you wish to work. Select the desired file, and choose Open. If the local repository file contains data from more than one system, then you must specify a system. The Available SAP Systems dialog box displays the list of systems whose data is included in the current local repository. Select one of these systems and choose Open. Remember that the system includes only the business objects that have been saved into the local repository file, not all of the business objects that exist in the R/3 system. The practice of using the local repository is sound because BAPIs and RFCs normally do not change often. This approach allows you to work offline and to view the data more quickly.

You can create multiple local repositories that each contain a different set of RFCs, BAPIs, or functions. You can save RFCs or BAPIs into your local repository file from any R/3 system. However, if you are saving RFCs or BAPIs from various R/3 systems in one local repository file, you have to log on to the appropriate system.

You have the option to delete the business objects from a local repository file, but be sure to log off from the R/3 system first. To delete all the RFCs, BAPIs, or any business objects from a local repository file, choose File, Open File. When the Open Local Depository dialog box appears, select the desired file and choose Open. SAP Assistant selects the system whose data you want to delete. Choose Delete and confirm the deletion at the SAP Assistant dialog box.

Making a Remote Function Call

Before making an RFC from SAP, you should be connected to an R/3 system or to your local repository file. After you are connected, click on the Search tab and specify an RFC. Right-click and choose Run from the context menu, or choose Tools and run RFC/BAPI.

If you are reading from a local repository, SAP Assistant asks whether you want to log on using the last logon parameters. If you choose Yes, SAP Assistant logs on to the system you logged on to last, and you can continue to specify the parameters for running the RFC. Make sure that you are logged on to the desired system.

At the Run RFC/BAPI dialog box, enter values for any required importing parameters. You may enter data into any importing or importing/exporting parameters. If the parameter is a single field, click on the Value column next to the importing parameter name to enter a value for it. If the importing parameter is a table or a structure, click on the Table icon to get an expanded view of the table with its fields so that you can enter data into those fields. Choose Run to execute the call. When the call returns, you can check the RETURN parameter, which contains any error messages. The value of the various exporting parameters contains the data returned from the call. If an exporting parameter is a single field, its data appears in the Value column. If the returned value is a structure or a table, click on the Table icon to see its fields and their values.

Tracing Errors in SAP Assistant

If errors occur while you are running SAP Assistant, you can activate the Trace option to produce a log file. To active Trace, choose View, Options and click on the Trace tab. The tab has two options, Log Errors or Log Errors and Messages. The best way to handle errors is to report them through the SAP system.

Summary

This chapter covered the basics of using SAP Assistant. In addition, it described the screens and the internal components of SAP Assistant and the use of RFCs and BAPIs through the local repository. SAP Assistant can generate either Java or C++ classes, which you can then use to create and manipulate SAP business objects using their BAPIs.

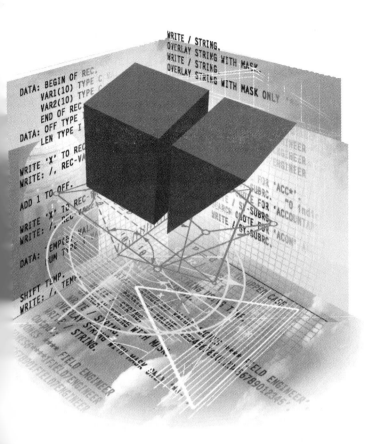

Chapter 15

Internet
Transaction
Server

In This Chapter

◆ Why Use ITS?

◆ Basics of ITS

◆ Internet Applications Components

◆ Development Environment

ITS (*Internet Transaction Server*) is a link between the World Wide Web and the SAP R/3 IAC (*Internet Application Components*). ITS can perform several functions; it can access specially designed SAP transactions, run reports, and access RFCs (*Remote Function Calls*) called BAPIs. ITS does not have to be used just for the Internet; it can also be a very useful tool for a company's intranet, providing easy and secure access to the SAP system. With the release of SAP 4.5 and ITS 2.2, the ITS development environment now also provides a controlled release environment where SAP code and HTML can be transported from the development system to the consolidation system and through to the production environment via the SAP standard transport system. The best part about ITS is that it comes with and is supported by SAP.

Why Use ITS?

So, why use ITS at all? After all, plenty of third-party systems for the development of Internet sites have many features and are easy to use. The advantages that ITS brings to Internet site development include the following:

◆ ITS is integrated with SAP and will be supported by SAP through the new versions of SAP.

◆ ITS supports a large number of concurrent users through an efficient interface to R/3.

◆ ITS is scalable.

- ◆ ITS is a single development environment with a single development language.
- ◆ ITS provides access to the R/3 data dictionary for easy future support for both SAP and Internet applications.
- ◆ ITS provides source code control for the entire solution.
- ◆ ITS security and login handling are done through R/3.
- ◆ ITS provides national language support.

In addition, ITS provides access to SAP-developed IACs, which can reduce over-all development time and cost.

Basics of ITS

ITS comes with the R/3 installation and currently runs on an Intel-based server running under Windows 4.0 NT. As shown in Figure 15.1, ITS expands SAP's

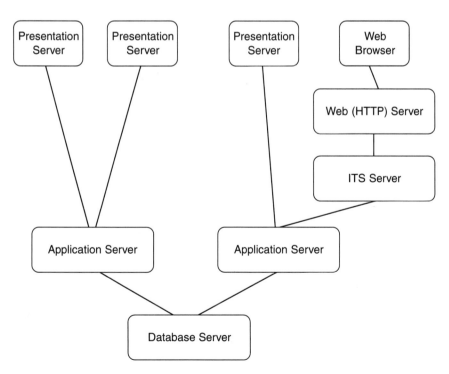

FIGURE 15.1 *A typical SAP system using ITS*

standard three-tier architecture of database server, application server, and presentation server into a five-tier system.

The extra two tiers in the overall system include the Web server, which is sometimes referred to as the *HTTP server*, and the ITS. The HTTP server is the link to the Internet/intranet, and the ITS component communicates between the HTTP server and the SAP system. ITS is composed of two components. The first is the WGate, which must reside on the same hardware as the HTTP server. The WGate communicates with the second portion of ITS, called the *AGate*, which can reside either on the same piece of hardware or on an isolated system. The AGate portion of the ITS handles the communication to SAP.

Because ITS is scalable, you can have a simple intranet scenario in which a single PC acts as your Web server and also holds both the WGate and the AGate of ITS. Alternatively, you can have a much more complicated scenario, as shown in Figure 15.2.

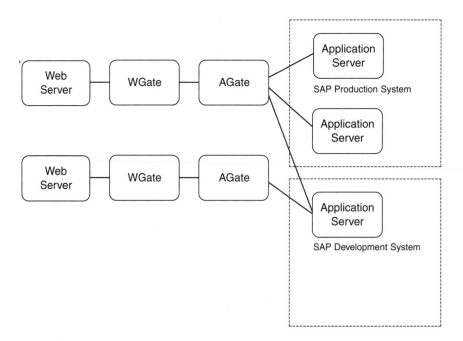

FIGURE 15.2 *An example of how ITS can be scaled up for a larger system*

Because most SAP installations contain sensitive data, security must be taken into account in any ITS installation. If the ITS system will be set up with access from the Internet, a high level of security can be maintained by placing a firewall before the Web server in order to allow a secure connection to it (that is, HTTPS). Additional security can be achieved by placing other firewalls between the WGate and the AGate and between the AGate and SAP itself. Access to the SAP system itself has also been enhanced for the IACs and can be achieved either through implicit or explicit logins. When the user is connected to the R/3 system, another Internet password system can be used to further restrict access to data. Access to this system is through transaction SU05. These different features can be implemented in any combination; a diagram depicting all of them appears in Figure 15.3.

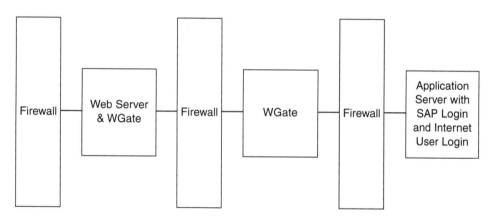

FIGURE 15.3 *All the security features of an ITS system*

Internet Applications Components

Through ITS, the Web user can access IACs from SAP. There are three types of IACs:

- ◆ **WebTransactions**. These IACs are specially designed transactions in SAP. As of release 4.5, more than 50 SAP-provided transactions are available. You can also develop your own SAP transactions for use with ITS.

◆ **WebRFCs.** These IACs are specially designed RFCs that return an HTML page to be displayed with the Web browser.

◆ **WebReporting.** This type of IAC allows users to run any ABAP report that generates a list. WebReporting also gives the user access to the reporting tree.

WebTransactions

Transactions to be used through ITS are simply enhanced SAP transactions. One of the drawbacks of ITS is that it cannot handle subscreens or pop-up dialog boxes very well. If you are expecting to see exactly the same kind of screens that you see in SAP, you will be disappointed. This situation, however, is not as problematic as it may seem. ITS was designed for use with the Internet, which means that people with little or no training should be able to use the transactions. Therefore, you should keep the transaction simple and intuitive (which, most would agree, SAP transactions are not).

For example, if you want a system that allows vendors to use the Internet to view information about your products, you would not want the vendors to have to enter the SAP material number and information such as plant or sales organization. It would be much simpler to first display the product text description and then provide more information when the user clicks on the text.

For an example of an SAP transaction designed for the Web, check out transaction MEWP (see Figure 15.4). As you can see, this transaction is much simpler to use than the standard SAP purchase order series of transactions.

When you are designing transactions to be used on the Web, the following actions and elements require additional coding or HTML:

◆ **Error handling.** You must make sure that no warning or error messages are generated in the transaction when an Internet user accesses it. Informational messages that behave like a warning or error message in SAP can be generated.

◆ **Screen control.** Because your user can navigate with the Back function of the Internet browser, special code needs to be in place to ensure that the SAP session and the Web page stay in synchronization.

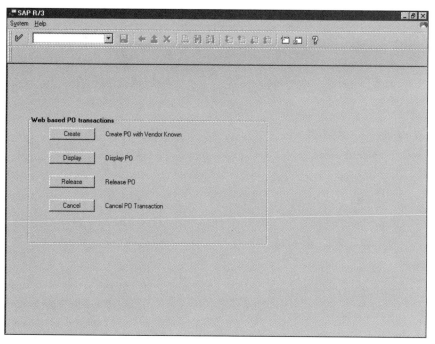

FIGURE 15.4 *A Web-based purchase order transaction*

◆ **F1 help**. This area must be handled through special HTML code on your Web page.

◆ **F4 pull-down help**. This function can be performed through ITS but requires special coding to send all possible values of a field at the same time as the main HTML is generated.

◆ **Check boxes and radio buttons**. These items require special code to be handled through the Internet properly.

◆ **Loops**. Currently, ITS does not support table controls. You must design your transaction using step loops, and you can have only one loop per SAP screen.

SAP is developing a set of transactions that meet these guidelines and are easy to use. Table 15.1 lists the current SAP IACs.

Table 15.1 SAP Developed Transactions for Web Use (SAP 4.5)

Application Scenarios	Starting in SAP Release
Consumer to business	
Product catalog	3.1G
Online store	3.1G
Sales order creation	3.1G
Sales order status	3.1G
Available to promise	3.1G
Customer account information	3.1G
Calendar of events	3.1G
Employment opportunities	3.1G
Application status	3.1G
Booked events—Web users	3.1G
Booking attendance—Web users	4.0A
Canceling Attendance—Web users	4.0A
Business to business	
Quality certificates	3.1G
Quality notification	3.1G
Service notification	3.1G
Measurement and counter readings	3.1G
Consignment stock status	3.1G
Kanban	3.1G
Requirement request	3.1G
Requirement request status	3.1G
Collective release of PO	3.1G
Collective release of requisition	3.1G
Collective release of service entry	4.0A
Procurement via catalogs	4.0A
Status display in procurement via catalogs	4.0A
Enter service performed	4.5A
Goods receipt	4.5A

Table 15.1 SAP Developed Transactions for Web Use (SAP 4.5) *(continued)*

Application Scenarios	Starting in SAP Release
Invoice verification	4.5A
Import processing	4.5A
Internal business	
Integrated inbox	3.1G
Asset information	3.1G
Internal activity allocation	3.1G
Internal price list	3.1G
Project data confirmation	3.1G
Web reporting browser	3.1G
Business object browser	3.1G
Workflow status	3.1G
Employee directory	3.1G
Project documentation	4.0A
Document search	4.5A
Customer master record creation	4.5A
Employee self-services	
Personal data	3.1G
Who is who	3.1G
Time statement form	3.1G
Booked events—R/3 users	3.1G
Booking attendance—R/3 users	3.1H
Canceling attendance—R/3 users	4.0A
Personal data	4.5A
Travel expenses	4.5A
Benefits	4.5A
Time management	4.5A
Payroll	4.5A
Training and event management	4.5A

To try out an online transaction from SAP, you can go to SAP's Internet Store, which can be accessed at http://www.sap.com/store_index.htm. From here, go to the link for the Merchandise Shop and notice that the URL contains wgate, which is the Internet link to an ITS system (see Figure 15.5).

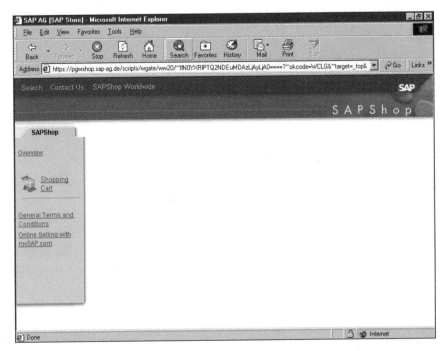

FIGURE 15.5 *An example of an ITS online transaction*

WebRFC Access

WebRFC allows users to access special function modules directly in SAP, and these function modules will return HTML pages that are displayed on the user's Web browser. This process is done through the ITS and its AGate and the call to the function module WWW_DISPATCH_REQUEST, which in turn calls the WebRFC function module. To "WebRFC enable" a function module, it must have the following items in the interface definition and be enabled through the SAP Web Repository (transaction SMW0):

```
Function . . .
* Local interface:
* TABLES
*   QUERY_STRING          STRUCTURE  W3QUERY
*   HTML                  STRUCTURE  W3HTML
*   MIME                  STRUCTURE  W3MIME


* CHANGING
*   VALUE(CONTENT_TYPE)    LIKE  W3PARAM-CONT_TYPE
*   VALUE(CONTENT_LENGTH)  LIKE  W3PARAM-CONT_LEN
*   VALUE(RETURN_CODE)     LIKE  W3PAAM-RET_CODE
```

WebRFC can handle MIME data, such as pictures and sound, and integrate these objects into HTML templates. MIME objects are contained in the SAP Web Repository, which can be accessed through transaction SMW0, as shown in Figure 15.6.

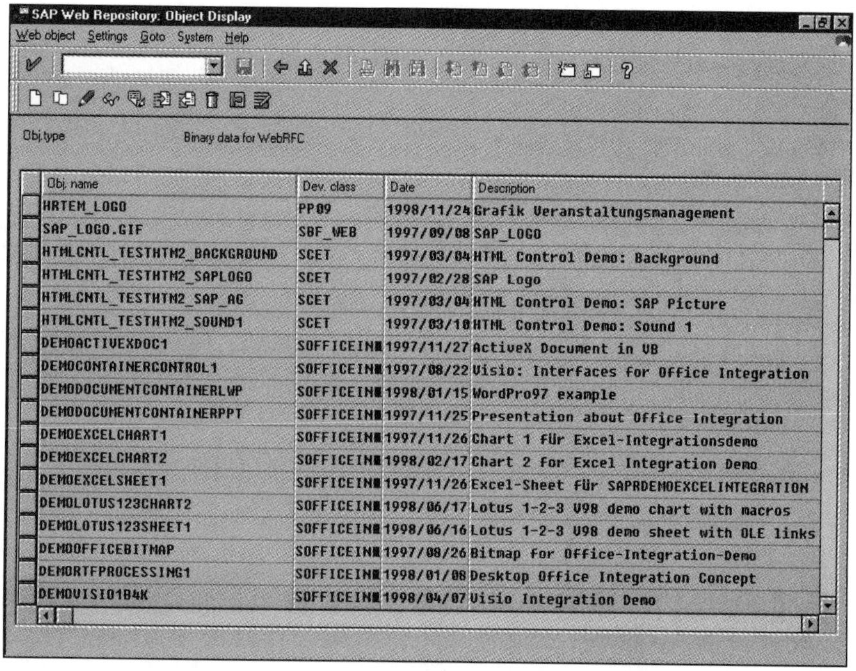

FIGURE 15.6 *A sample of a bitmap object list in transaction SMW0*

The function group SURL contains all of SAP's WebRFC-enabled function modules, which are listed in Table 15.2.

Table 15.2 A Listing of the WebRFC-Enabled Function Modules in SAP (4.5)

Function Module	Description
WWW_HTML_ECHO	Sample WebRFC function module
WWW_GET_MIME_OBJECT	Sample WebRFC that handles MIME data
WWW_MODEL_MODULE	Blank template
WWW_ITAB_TO_MODULE	Converts internal table to HTML
WWW_ERROR_MESSAGE	Creates HTML for ABAP message
WWW_URL_PREFIX	Creates URLs dynamically
WWW_PACK_TABLE	Removes blanks from filled HTML tables
WWW_HTML_MERGER	Generates an HTML page from a template and other objects
WWW_GET_TREELIST	Generates an HTML page of a report tree

WebReporting

WebReporting is simply an extension of the WebRFC function discussed in the last section. In addition to allowing users to run standard ABAP reports, it also allows them access to the reporting tree through their intranet browser.

WebReporting is implemented through the WWW_DISPATCH_REQUEST function module, which calls the two function modules WWW_GET_SELSCREEN and WWW_GET_REPORT to generate the HTML output of the report for the user. It is also possible to combine the output of a report with a template (for example, with company colors and logo).

Reports for use through WebReporting should *not* contain the following elements:

- ◆ Call Transaction
- ◆ Call Screen
- ◆ Call Selection-Screen
- ◆ Submit Report

You can also run interactive reports through WebReporting if your users use Internet Explorer running JScript. This approach works well for intranets where you have control over the browser that is used, but is not recommended for Internet solutions because a wide variety of browsers will be used to access your site.

Development Environment

Various tools, including the SAP workbench and SAP@Web Studio, are used for IAC development. Everything you need (with the exception of the SAP system, of course) is available at the SAP Labs Inc. Web site, at www.saplabs.com. The current path to the ITS area is under the Projects hyperlink on the left side of the page, but this hyperlink may change in the future. The ITS software is also included on the SAPGUI installation disc.

SAP@Web Studio

The SAP@Web Studio enables you to integrate ITS into your environment. With SAP@Web Studio, you can develop and configure *Services*, which are links to the Web-enabled IACs that you access through ITS. The typical functions for the SAP@Web Studio are template generation, Service file configuration, and source code control. Figure 15.7 shows an SAP@Web Studio screen.

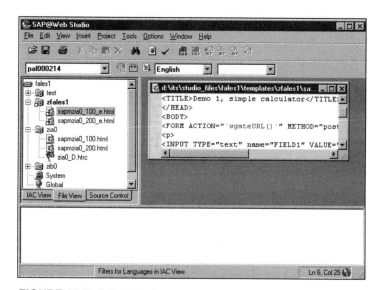

FIGURE 15.7 *SAP@Web Studio screen*

Template Development

After you develop your Web-based transaction in SAP, you need to generate the HTML templates that will be accessed by the Web. A first pass of this process can be performed through SAP@Web Studio. During this stage, SAP@Web Studio pulls the screen layout from the SAP system you specify and generates a simple HTML equivalent page. You must then go through this page and edit it to make it more visually appealing. ITS uses an enhanced HTML language called *HTML Business HTML*. With this extension, you can put SAP variables into your HTML pages and display multiple lines associated with loops, among other things.

Service Configuration

The Service file contains all of the information about a specific HTML page that references an SAP screen. This information includes the name of the called transaction, R/3 connection information, login data, language, and other session data.

Source Code Control

After you develop your Web page in the development environment, you can use SAP@Web Studio to manage your HTML files (including graphics) for movement through the consolidation and production SAP environments. This process requires you to upload all non-SAP objects to SAP and assign a change request to them. The procedure is like a check in and check out process. After items are uploaded to SAP, they can then be "checked out" and changed again in the development environment. After you move your change request to the consolidation or production environment, you can check out the objects by using SAP@Web Studio, which places them correctly on the various servers. However, SAP@Web Studio does not allow you to change these objects in a nondevelopment environment.

SAP Web Repository (SMWO)

The SAP Web Repository releases objects such as reports, function modules, reporting trees, and bitmap objects for access to the Web. You can also display and edit bitmap objects through this transaction. The first screen of the transaction is shown in Figure 15.8.

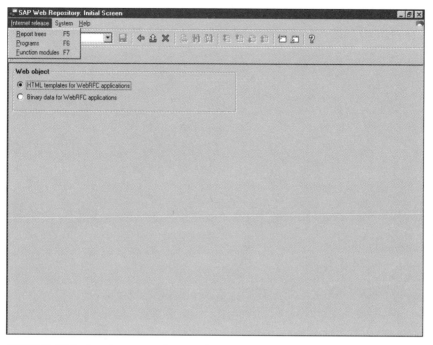

FIGURE 15.8 *Opening screen of transaction SMW0*

Summary

Overall, ITS is a comprehensive and easy way to give Internet and intranet users access to an SAP system. ITS is secure and scalable to meet any project size. It also allows users to access IACs; these components include the capability to run transactions, RFCs, and reports. Some restrictions apply to each area, but as of SAP release 4.5 and ITS 2.2, it is relatively easy to develop or find ready-made applications to use through an Internet browser. The ITS software, along with all the development tools, comes with the SAP system or is available through SAP Labs, Inc. If you are interested in using ITS, the online help in both the ITS and SAP@Web Studio provides step-by-step instructions on how to perform typical tasks, such as setting up a transaction or a report. However, if you want to use ITS for a real production environment, you should consider taking the BC440 SAP course on developing Internet transactions before starting your project. This course will help you configure your architecture and develop your transactions correctly from the beginning.

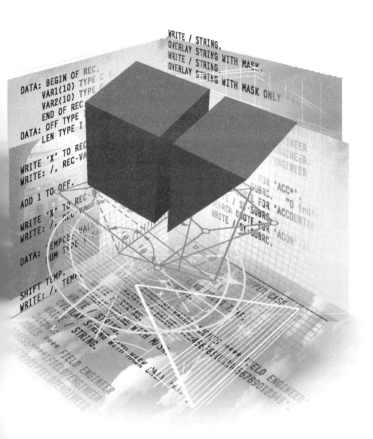

Chapter 16

Deciding Which Technology to Use for a New Application

In This Chapter

- Evaluation of Application Requirements
- GUI-Based Object-Oriented Solutions
- RFC/BAPI-Based Java
- Internet Transaction Server
- Other Object-Oriented Languages
- ABAP
- Integrating SAP with Other Software

The information in this chapter will help you decide which technology to use when you are developing a new application to be integrated with SAP. Although the basic requirements of the application usually dictate the best technology and general approach, you must also consider the people who will be using and supporting the application, the resources that are available, the time required to complete the application, and the security levels required. Each technology presented in this chapter has its own advantages and disadvantages, which must be evaluated for each situation.

Evaluation of Application Requirements

When evaluating an application, you need to consider several questions. Even though you may not have every answer at the preliminary design stage, you should be able to at least narrow the field a bit for the possible technologies. The questions generally revolve around the interface that the application will have with SAP. The application may be as simple as getting an SAP report to work through a Web browser, or as complicated as having bidirectional communications between SAP and the new application.

What Is the Server/Client Relationship between the Application and SAP?

Will the application always initiate the request to SAP, or will SAP initiate the requests from the application? Sometimes it is both ways. If the new application will at any time act like a server, then you probably should develop the interface with RFCs (*Remote Function Calls*), IDocs (*Intermediate Documents*), or something similar (for example, SAP's new Business Connector technology). If the application will act only as the client, then you can use almost any interface method.

 NOTE

In a two-system environment that includes bidirectional communication, either system can be the client or the server, depending on the initiation of the call.

Does the Application Need to Be Executed Outside the Firewall?

Though most of these technologies can be set up to work outside the corporate firewall, some are easier than others to set up. ITS (*Internet Transaction Server*), for example, is very easy to set up and provides many layers of security; in contrast, the Orbix Java server does not have a robust security set. You must also consider how the user will be allowed to connect through the firewall. One possibility is to use a secure connection, established by the user manually, and connect to a corporate system through modems and servers that are not connected to the Internet. Another way to connect through the firewall is to use the Internet (that is, through ITS).

Does the Application Need to Be Synchronous with SAP?

If the application will be waiting for responses from SAP, you might consider using BAPIs, ITS, or the GUI (*Graphical User Interface*) method. An example of a *synchronous connection* is one that has an entry screen, written in Java, with

---

Firewalls and Proxy Servers

Relating to the Internet/intranet, a *firewall* is a combination of hardware and software that enables you to communicate with an outside network, while limiting outside access to your network. The most important part of a firewall is the proxy server. *Proxy servers* make a firewall safely permeable to users behind the secured entrance, while closing entryways in the private network to potential attacks from the outside. The proxy server must act as both a server and client. It acts as a proxy client when it accepts approved requests for external servers, and as a proxy server when it requests services from those servers on behalf of its clients. Other types of firewalls include packet filtering, as well as commercial software that monitors for open ports and other potential illegal entry vehicles.

---

several input fields. After the user finishes entering data on a screen, the program will perform an RFC call to SAP to validate the values. The same example, however, is *asynchronous* if you simply take the values from the screen and send them to SAP without requiring a return validation/confirmation message. If you do not need an immediate response, you can also consider using the full range of protocols, such as RFCs and IDocs, or the transaction method.

What Is the Knowledge Level of the Programming and Support Staff?

The knowledge level of the programming and support staff is a key point that is often overlooked in the application development stage. You must consider the types of technologies with which both the development and the support staff are familiar. If one of your potential technologies is not going to be used elsewhere in the organization and there is another way to set up the application, use the alternate method. For example, if you develop a solution that uses Business Connector and no other solution is using this technology, then you are forcing the support staff to learn about Business Connector just to support your application. A possible alternative in this case is to use RFCs.

GUI-Based Object-Oriented Solutions

With GUI-based solutions, you are basically replacing the SAP GUI with an object-oriented based application. This approach allows you to get away from the standard SAP screens and to develop custom screens with Java, Visual Basic, or C++. This type of solution is quite common when you want to integrate an existing non-SAP application with SAP (to either retrieve or store information).

Pros

The GUI-based solution is a fairly easy way to set up an application that shields people from the standard SAP system. This approach allows you to develop applications that are fairly easy to use and are hardware independent. You can also use GUI-based solutions for specialized situations; for instance, you can develop an application that accepts input from a bar code reader or responds to verbal commands.

Because the GUI solution involves simply feeding data to SAP screens, you don't need technical knowledge of how data is laid out. If your application is written in Visual Basic, the SAP Automation suite has a code generator that will generate code for a set of defined SAP screens.

Cons

The GUI-based solution relies on the sequence of SAP screens, and is therefore vulnerable to changes in the way SAP operates if you upgrade your instance of SAP. Of course, you can develop your own transactions in SAP and then develop GUI interfaces to integrate with the transactions, but this approach requires a significant development effort, along with knowledge of both SAP and the object-oriented language. If you are considering this type of solution, you will also want to look at the DCOM (*Distributed Component Object Model*) connector mentioned later in this chapter.

RFC/BAPI-Based Java

This method of connecting to SAP allows you to use all SAP functionality that is incorporated around business objects through the use of BAPIs. Through SAP, you can generate the stub for either server or client code for an existing RFC. Examples of the languages that can be supported appear in Figures 16.1 and 16.2.

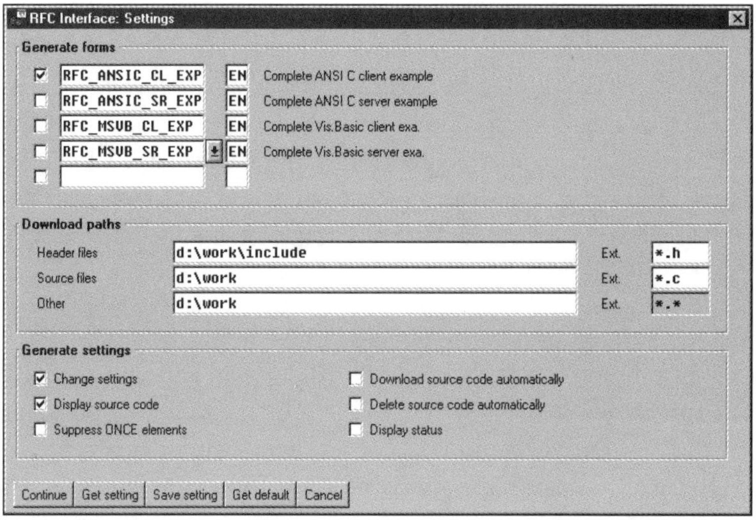

FIGURE 16.1 *The first step in the creation of a stub to an RFC, showing default language choices*

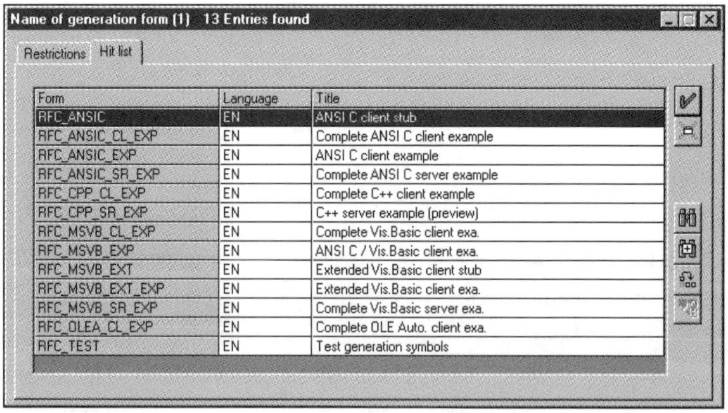

FIGURE 16.2 *Programming languages supported in stub creation*

Pros

This technology provides both synchronous and asynchronous communication to SAP and does not require the programmer to know anything about ABAP. By using BAPIs, you can perform entire business operations with a single function call, such as Create Sales Order.

This approach also shields you from any changes that might occur from an upgrade to the SAP system. BAPIs, by definition, have defined deprecation plans, and must be available for at least two major SAP version upgrades.

Cons

To use RFCs and BAPIs, you need more knowledge of SAP's business logic than if you used a GUI-based solution. In addition, you must still come up with a way to call the RFC. You can accomplish the call with a tool like the Orbix server or with the SAP RFC gateway, but this step still requires some setup.

You can avoid calling up the RFCs directly (even when using the DCOM connector) if you approach the SAP system from outside the corporate firewall.

Internet Transaction Server

ITS enables you to execute SAP transactions, reports, and RFCs through a Web browser.

ITS Advantages

For simple reports, ITS is very easy to use. A standard ABAP report can be accessed through the ITS system in a matter of minutes. By design, ITS is secure and is a scalable solution, so you can set it up to handle any type of demand. Most of the program logic is done in ABAP. If you have a current SAP installation, the support staff can probably support the underlying ABAP in an ITS transaction.

ITS is developed by SAP, and thus is integrated into the SAP development cycle. You can develop a solution that includes ABAP, HTML, graphics, and so forth, and transport all the objects, through SAP, from the development to the consolidation and production systems. Consequently, you reduce the risk of your HTML pages being out of sync with the underlying ABAP code.

ITS Disadvantages

Complicated screens and screen sequences are not handled easily with ITS. Complicated screens require manual coding of HTML, and you must develop an HTML page for every screen that the user can display.

In addition, the amount of time that users can maintain a connection to the SAP system is limited. Though this limit can be set quite high (depending on the hardware installed), it still forces users to complete their transaction in a fixed amount of time.

ITS requires Windows NT servers to handle the intranet/Internet requests. This configuration typically requires a minimum of two systems (one for the Agate and another for the Wgate), along with hardware to support your development environment. For complicated transactions, your development staff will require a knowledge of SAP, ABAP, ITS, and HTML to effectively develop an application.

Other Object-Oriented Languages

Other object-oriented languages can integrate with SAP through a technology called the *DCOM Component Connector*. This tool, written jointly by SAP and Microsoft, allows ABAP objects (BAPIs) to integrate with COM components written in Visual Basic, Java, C++, or any other COM-compliant language, through Microsoft's DCOM. Basically, the SAP DCOM Connector (*DCOMCC*) is an extension to the Remote Function Call Software Development Kit (*RFC SDK*), which is available through SAP's Web site. The connector enables a Windows program to view SAP business objects and BAPIs as native COM components.

 TIP

For more information on the connector, download the RCF SDK from SAP's Web site and unzip the file. Find a subdirectory called CCWWW within the unzipped files and from that subdirectory, point your browser to the file CCTOP.HTM.

ABAP

Organizations often have applications developed via a technology with which a particular individual is comfortable. Although this approach is good for the short term, sometimes it is better to have the application developed within the framework of SAP. Usually an organization that has SAP also has (and will continue to have) the resources to develop and support ABAP languages. As of release 4.0 of SAP, the SAP development library supports graphics, ODBC, and OLE applications. Also, the ABAP language is being enhanced to become more object-oriented. Using ABAP or a combination of ABAP and ITS is usually a long-term, cost-effective way to develop applications.

Integrating SAP with Other Software

Some applications are simply written to act as interfaces, that is, to transfer data from one system to another. SAP has come up with some new technologies that can either reduce the size of or eliminate the need for these types of applications.

Business Connector

The SAP Business Connector provides XML-based secure access to and from SAP applications. Business Connector executes on a server that enables you to receive applications with XML-formatted files; the connector translates these into an intermediate document structure and executes the corresponding SAP transaction. If you send standard SAP IDocs to Business Connector, it will convert the IDocs to an XML-formatted file and send it to the other system.

MySAP.com

MySAP.com is SAP's latest foray into the B2B (*Business to Business*) world, and is a viable way to integrate applications from one system to another (including both to and from an SAP instance). Companies can exchange transaction-related documents through a portal on the Internet (mySAP.com), as if the transactions were taking place on a single instance of SAP. Suppose that your corporation wants to contract out manufacturing of a widget. If both you and your contract manufacturer are set up on mySAP.com, you will be able to transmit purchase orders, sales orders, invoices, and so on through the mySAP.com portal, without having to develop any point-to-point interfaces.

What Is XML?

XML (*Extensible Markup Language*) is a method for putting structured data in a text file. If you look at an XML file with a text editor, you will notice a similarity to HTML. XML has tags and attributes, as shown in the following sample:

```
<?xml version="1.0"?>
<NAMELIST NAME="Prima Publishing"></NAMELIST>
      .
      .
```

Compared to HTML, however, XML is much more strict about data layout. You can get away with a missing end tag in HTML, but this is not accepted in XML; an application cannot and should not make a guess about a data file. HTML is used for presentations, whereas XML is used for storing data. Because XML files are text files, they are platform independent; therefore, users can more readily share data between different applications. You'll find more information on XML at www.w3.org/XML.

Summary

There are many ways to integrate an application with SAP, and the job of an IT developer is to determine the method that makes the most sense for the organization. You need to analyze the application and determine how the data should flow to and from the SAP system. You also need to consider the environment in which the application will run: Is it online, offline, within the corporate firewall, or outside of it? Another consideration is the knowledge level of both the development staff and the people who will support the integration solution after it is installed.

After you have examined the application, you can evaluate the various technologies and determine which is the best for you. This chapter outlined several alternatives, and, even though the thrust of this book is in the use of Java, you should also consider other potential technologies, such as ITS.

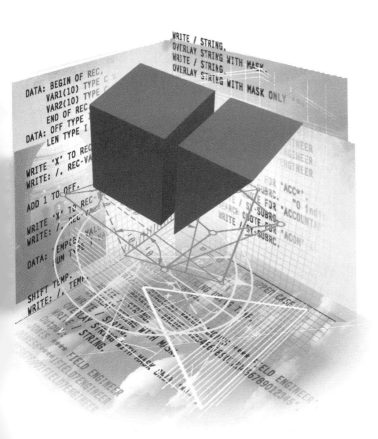

Chapter 17

Design Considerations for HTML/ RFC-Based SAP Interfaces

In This Chapter

◆ Browser Independence

◆ Security

◆ Creating User-Friendly Web Interfaces

◆ Languages, Currency, and Units of Measure

◆ SAP Transaction Concept and Security

Many factors come into play when you are interfacing with an ERP system from an outside source such as ITS, Java (via BAPIs), or even regular RFCs (*Remote Function Calls*). The system with which you are connecting is an integrated system that must have data integrity throughout. You cannot post one side of an accounting transaction and ignore an error that occurs when you post the other side of the same transaction. You must also consider security of the system as a whole, and ensure that users can view or change only data that they are allowed to change.

Interfacing through a Web browser also has its complications, as you must consider not only the flow of the transaction through SAP, but also the browser's behavior in areas such as data caching. In addition, you must consider issues such as what happens when the user presses the Back button on the browser, which is local to the browser and is not communicated to SAP, and make sure that the transaction works for all brands of browsers to which your users have access. This chapter takes you through these and some other common problems so that your interfaces will be user-friendly and work smoothly and securely.

Browser Independence

One of the first things to do when starting to develop an intranet/Internet application is to determine to which brand of browsers the users of your application will have access. If you are working solely with an intranet application, you may have policies within your company that specify which browser the workers should use. However, if your application will be accessible for the Internet, then you can expect multiple browsers to be used.

If you are developing an ITS transaction or an HTML (*Hypertext Markup Language*) page with a Java applet that will be used solely in an intranet and your company only uses one browser, you are free to use browser-specific extensions that are not part of standard HTML. Examples of HTML extensions are shown in Table 17.1.

Table 17.1 HTML Extensions

Vendor	HTML Extension	Explanation
Netscape	<blink>	Makes text blink
Netscape	<q>	Quotation
Netscape	<embed>	Creates a console for a sound player
Microsoft	<Marquee>	Moves text across the screen
Microsoft	<iframe>	Independent frame
Microsoft	<bgsound>	Specifies an audio file

If you are developing HTML pages that need to support multiple browsers, the best course of action is to use the standards posted by the W3C (*World Wide Web Consortium*) HTML validation service. This service will check to ensure that all of the source code at the designated URL is compliant with the latest standards. The URL for this site is http://validator.w3.org, and it appears in Figure 17.1.

Caching and Synchronization of Data

Most Web browsers enable the user to navigate between Web pages by using the Back and Forward buttons or sometimes a History function. The expiration date of the Web page determines whether the page can be taken from the browser cache or must be regenerated by making a request to the Web server.

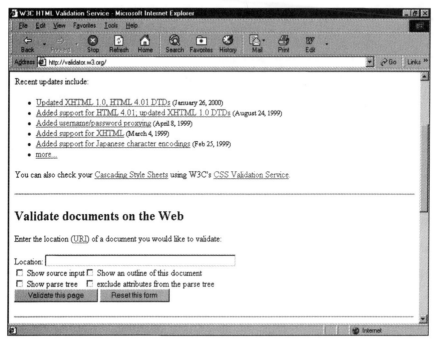

FIGURE 17.1 *HTML validation from the W3C*

NOTE

When a page is displayed in a browser, the browser can hold this page in memory for quick retrieval at the user's request. This process is referred to as *caching*. SAP also uses caching for database, program, and screen access.

An HTML template can request with either of the following operations:

◆ **Post.** Pages generated by an HTTP POST operation are always cached. The Web browser uses POST operations whenever an HTML FORM statement specifies METHOD="POST".

◆ **Get.** Pages generated by GET operations are never cached. The ITS explicitly sets a no-cache option in the HTTP header when the page is sent to the Web browser, regardless of the caching options set in the Web browser. The Web browser uses GET operations for hypertext links and FRAMESET documents.

Because the synchronization of data between the Web page and SAP depends on the type of HTTP (*Hyptertext Transfer Protocol*) operation, you need to be careful when you use hyperlinks in ITS transactions. The user can click on the hyperlink and then press the Back function on the browser. In this scenario, the underlying SAP transaction is not informed about the Back operation. To get around this problem, you should check for the function code AWSS, which ITS sends when it wants to synchronize a Web transaction. In the ABAP program of the screen, you can then call the function module ITS_GET_SYNC_INFO, which returns an internal table containing the assignment of subscreen areas and subscreens for the ITS.

SAP has its own caching as well. Most SAP caching is done for database files and SQL calls to these files. Though SAP does take care of any potential problems, such as multiple people reading and writing to the same record, you can tune this caching to make tools like ITS run faster. The basic approach here is to control the number of rows ahead (from zero rows to all rows) that SAP buffers for a standard SQL call. For optimal performance you usually do not want to turn off the buffering (set the number of read ahead rows to zero), since the communication between the database server and the application server and then to your external application will be slow. By allowing buffering, the data is already up at either the application server or, in the case of Java, the Orbix server, which will make your applications run more quickly.

Security

If you are developing an interface that can be accessed from outside the firewall (an ITS report is a typical example), you must ensure that "company proprietary" documents and data cannot be accessed. This point may sound obvious, but you'd be surprised at the controversy and discussions that it can bring up. Do you want your product's availability and lead times posted for your competitors to view? Are your customers comfortable with having access to their data on the Web, where it might possibly be accessed by a malicious hacker (one example being the hacker who broke into a widely used site and posted thousands of Visa numbers)?

Numerous Web robots regularly search and index many of the publicly available Web servers. The robots provide the data pools that make Web search services like Excite work. If you do not want specific pages on your public server to be available to these search engines, you can create a /robots.txt file in your local URL. This text file contains two basic pieces of data: User-agent, which tells the robot you want to restrict something, and Disallow, which describes what you want to disallow. In the following example, we restrict all Web robots (sometimes called *spiders*) from visiting any URL starting with /myhomepage.

```
User-agent: *
Disallow: /myhomepage
```

If you are developing some Java code to work through the Orbix server, you will probably have to consider restricting who can access the server. This process is done through the Orbix server setup (see Chapter 4, "Setting up the Development and Operating Environments"), and allows you to restrict both who has access to the server and the methods that can be used. In a normal production environment, even if it is for use behind a firewall, you will want to include some restrictions in here. Otherwise, you run the risk of some clever Java programmer in your company gaining access to data that he or she should not have.

Creating User-Friendly Web Interfaces

A significant cost to a corporation is the training of its staff to use the ERP (*Enterprise Resource Planning*) system effectively. Let's face it, SAP and other ERP systems are not the easiest systems to use—even a "simple" sales order transaction can take a user through 10 or more screens. Users of this transaction must be taught not only the significance of all the fields that they view or change, but also the overall sales order process. And these training costs are not one-time expenses; if a person trained to perform a specific transaction changes jobs, a new person will need to be trained for the same transaction.

The high cost of training is one of the driving factors for moving some ERP functions and reports out to the intranet/Internet. Internet transactions must be intuitive enough for users to easily figure out. Thus when you write a Web interface into SAP, regardless of whether the interface is using Java or not, you must ensure that it is intuitive and will require either no training or very limited training.

Multimedia elements help to make Web transactions user-friendly. You should include items like the company's logo, pictures of products, or maps to service locations. Well-designed Web pages also rely heavily on forms and hyperlinks. Instead of asking customers to type in a product number, give them a choice of products with hyperlinks to click on.

Overall, you must keep the design and screen flow as simple as possible and keep in mind that the person using the Internet transaction may not be a trained professional SAP user. Some quick tips for creating your HTML pages follow.

◆ Determine who your likely audience will be and what problem they are trying to solve.

◆ Choose meaningful words or phrases for links.

◆ Keep pages short and avoid long waits for downloads of data or images (30 kilobytes is a good maximum size for a Web page).

◆ Preview your application/Web page on various systems before releasing it for general use.

◆ Graphics with a transparent background tend to look better than big block graphics.

◆ If users are likely to print out your page (for example, if it is some kind of report), give them a link so that they can see the whole report on one page (and hence get the whole printout with one click).

◆ Consider duplicating navigational headers at the bottom of your pages.

◆ Don't publish or display registered or company proprietary information for sites that are outside the firewall.

◆ Spell check your HTML pages.

◆ Date your pages.

◆ Don't put links to someone else's pages without first getting permission. (The page's owner may not want a link to their site.)

◆ Avoid publishing pages that are "under construction."

Languages, Currency, and Units of Measure

Another factor that is sometimes neglected in interface design, especially when it comes to Internet screen design, is that the screen can be viewed from around the world. If you are designing interfaces for a large multinational corporation, you need to allow for factors such as various login languages. Therefore, when you are writing your Java programs, you must get data element descriptions from SAP instead of coding the prompts yourself. One of the major advantages of an ERP system is that the data, including the *metadata* (the data about the data), is centralized, as you can see in Figure 17.2. This example shows the descriptions for the SAP data element EKGRP.

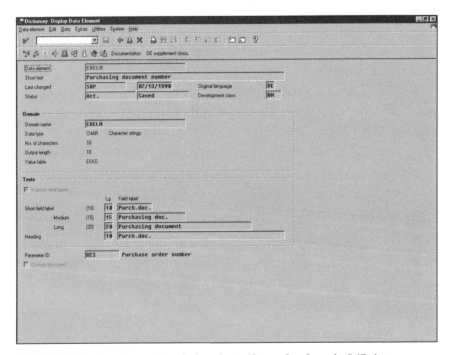

FIGURE 17.2 *Data element descriptions for purchase orders from the SAP data dictionary*

Retrieving field prompts in the login language from SAP means that you have to maintain them in only one place. Unfortunately, SAP does not provide a standard BAPI for retrieving data element definitions. This step, however, is relatively easy, as the following example shows.

```
Function Module BAPI_Z_DATAELEMENT_GETDETAIL
*"——————————————————————————————————————
*"
*"local interface:
*"        IMPORTING
*"                VALUE(DATAELEMENT) LIKE  DD02L-FELDNAME
*"        EXPORTING
*"                VALUE(SHORT_DESC) LIKE   DD02L-TEXT
*"                VALUE(MED_DESC) LIKE   DD02L-TEXT
*"                VALUE(LONG_DESC) LIKE   DD02L-TEXT
*"        TABLES
*"                RETURN STRUCTURE  BAPIRET2
*"——————————————————————————————————————
```

This BAPI will return the three descriptions (if they exist) for the current login language.

```
data: int_dd04T like structure dd04t occurs 10 with header line.
call function 'DD_DTEL_GET'
    exporting
        LANGU           = sy-langu
        ROLL_NAME       = Data_element
    tables
        dd04t_tab_n     = int_dd04t.
    read table int_dd04t index 1.
    if sy-subrc ne 0.
        return-msgno = '001'.
        retrn-message = 'Cannot find Data Element Descriptions'.
        append return.
    endif.
    short_desc      = int_dd04t-scrtext_s.
    med_desc        = int_dd04t-scrtext_m.
    long_desc       = int_dd045-scrtext_l.
ENDFUNCTION.
```

You can make this routine more generic by passing in the language you want the text returned in, but because you are likely to want the same language that you are using for the login to do this call, the language can be derived from the SAP system variables. Therefore, when developing BAPIs, keep the number of variables as low as possible. If you use the standard factories to generate the fields for the BAPI call, the amount of time the factory call takes is proportional to the number of variables.

> **NOTE**
>
> Note that the naming convention for this BAPI is a little different from the SAP standard. According to that standard, a BAPI function module is labeled as BAPI_<OBJECT NAME>_<FUNCTION>. However, the standard does not show how to represent a customer-created BAPI for a standard SAP object (such as this one). Hence I threw the Z_ into the name so that people will realize that this item is a customer BAPI.

The preceding BAPI enables you to use MATNR in your Java code to represent material number and to display the prompts in the user's login language or on reports that your Java application produces. The same type of approach can be used for date format and currency or a preferred unit of measure. These features will not only enhance the overall user experience but also, over the long term, reduce the amount of code that you need to write or maintain.

SAP Transaction Concept and Security

You must also keep in mind the SAP transaction concept when designing any type of outside interface into the SAP system. Even if the interface is a simple Java screen or an ITS transaction, you must ensure that you do not compromise the integrity of the data within SAP.

A *transaction* is a sequence of actions that logically belong together, for example, a finance transaction in which a value is subtracted from one account and added to another. The LUW (*Logical Unit of Work*) here is the posting of both rows in the database. If one row is posted and the other row is not, a data inconsistency will occur. An SAP transaction comprises at least one LUW, but might comprise many. For instance, month-end jobs often process many two-sided financial transactions. Each transaction has its own LUW.

If you are updating any data in the SAP system, your external interface must call only properly constructed BAPIs. By definition, BAPIs must perform a complete LUW and cannot create data inconsistencies (if a problem occurs with any SQL statement, the entire transaction is rolled back at the database level and a return code is generated).

Another thing to consider with regard to SAP transaction data is that multiple users are on the system at one time. For example, suppose that your Java application needs to update a specific field in the customer master for a given set of selection criteria. Even if you call a BAPI to perform this function, you might still cause a data integrity issue if you are not careful, as the following scenario points out.

Suppose you are running a Java application, which reads in a customer master record, allows you to change some values, and then writes the entire record back to SAP via a BAPI call. In principle, this process sounds OK, but what if another user in SAP wants to edit the same record? In this case, your Java program could read in the customer master record; at the same time, the other user could go into the SAP transaction to modify the customer data and quickly save the changes. You then make your changes and write the changes via the BAPI call, but if you write all the fields of the customer master, you will unknowingly overwrite the other person's changes.

If everyone is using standard SAP transactions, this problem won't develop because SAP locks an object if a person is currently editing it. When the first person is finished, another person can go into the transaction, read all of the previous changes, and then make any desired modifications. However, when external interfaces are employed, such as Java through BAPI calls or even things like ALE (*Application Link Enabling*), it is important that you modify only the fields that you intend to, and not write back fields that you have not changed.

Summary

Incorporating all the functions necessary to make your interface both practical and easy to use is relatively simple when you are designing a new external interface to SAP.

You must consider your users, their equipment, and the location from which they will be accessing the SAP system. Making your screens simple and providing options for features like multilanguage support ensures that your transaction will be used. In addition, you must make sure that the connection is secure and that you do not compromise the overall integrity of the data within the SAP system. To provide the necessary integrity, you must always use properly written BAPI calls and ensure that you only write fields that you have modified.

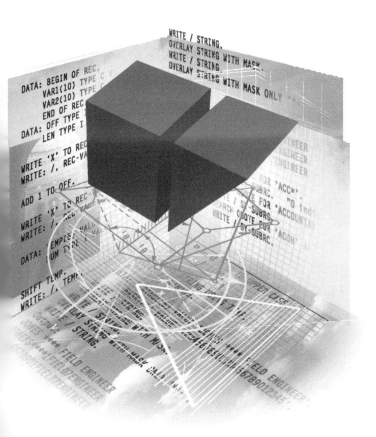

Chapter 18

BAPI
Development

In This Chapter

◆ The Relationship between BAPIs and the BOR

◆ Standards for BAPIs

◆ Design of BAPIs

◆ Connecting the BAPI to the BOR

◆ RFCDES Definition

◆ Outbound BAPIs

Now that you have an idea of how Java programs can be used with SAP through the BOR (*Business Object Repository*), you will probably see the need to write some of your own custom BAPIs. For example, you might want to access a customer-developed package within SAP or set up functions that SAP has not yet created. For this chapter, we assume that the object you want to work with is already in the BOR and that all you need to do is add a method (BAPI) to it. If you have gone through the initial Java chapters, you have a good understanding of the basics of object-oriented programming, and with this knowledge you should find that the creation of objects with the BOR is quite simple.

The Relationship between BAPIs and the BOR

BAPIs are defined as API (*Application Programming Interface*) methods of SAP business objects. These business objects and their BAPIs are described and stored in the BOR (see Chapter 12, "SAP's Business Object Repository"). Currently within SAP, a BAPI is implemented as a function module that is stored and described in the Function Builder.

As of release 4.5A, BAPIs can also describe *interfaces* (definitions of functions) that are implemented outside the R/3 system. This type of BAPI is known as a BAPI for outbound processing. The target system is determined for the BAPI call in the distribution model of ALE (*Application Link Enabling*). BAPIs used for outbound processing are defined in the BOR as API methods of SAP interface types. This approach allows functions to be implemented outside the R/3 system in a standardized fashion.

To define a BAPI to an object in the BOR, the function module must be fully developed. BAPI development is accomplished using a combination of the Function Builder Tool and the Data Dictionary (as required).

One of the nice aspects about BAPIs is that if an underlying change occurs in the BAPI itself, the calling programs do not have to change the way they call the BAPI. However, SAP upgrades may require a change in the way a BAPI is called. If a released BAPI is to be replaced by a different BAPI, the new BAPI should be given a new name and the old BAPI should be marked as obsolete. Thus many SAP BAPIs end with a 2 (for example, AddItem2).

Standards for BAPIs

Before we get into the nuts and bolts of building a BAPI, you should know about the standards and rules that SAP has imposed for BAPIs.

- A BAPI cannot contain the ABAP statement COMMIT WORK. Using a COMMIT WORK in a BAPI may trigger unwanted tasks in the calling program (for example, perform XXX on commit). If a COMMIT WORK is to be performed, it should be done through the BapiService.TransactionCommit call from the program that is calling the BAPI. The BAPI should then perform its updates through the update task, based on the On Commit principle of SAP ABAP.

- BAPIs should be able to function on their own, without the need to call other BAPIs. Also, keep in mind that BAPIs are function modules that are part of function groups. Function groups have shared global memory, and a BAPI should not rely on some prior function module call to the same group to set this shared memory.

- BAPIs cannot call up any dialog boxes or output any type of display (including lists). A BAPI may be called by a system that is external to SAP (for example, a Java program) that will not be able to handle the dialog or list display.

◆ BAPIs should not contain any message statements.

◆ BAPIs also cannot contain the ABAP commands CALL TRANSACTION or SUBMIT REPORT.

◆ BAPI structures cannot use Include structures.

◆ Global memory should not be used to transfer data to or from a BAPI. Along these same lines, you should not use parameter IDs (through set or get) in a BAPI.

Because each BAPI should be able to run on its own without any prior calls to other BAPIs, all pertinent authorization checks should be performed in every BAPI.

Standards for Parameters

The standards for parameters are as follows:

◆ SAP has indicated that all BAPI parameters must be in the English language and be meaningful. You should not have fields like FLAG or RESTRICT because they do not intuitively indicate what the parameter does.

◆ When dealing with numerical values such as quantity or currency, you must also specify a parameter to indicate the unit that the quantity is in or the type of currency you are dealing with.

◆ You must either define all BOR fields in the input and export parameters, or not define the fields at all.

◆ All key fields in GetDetail and GetList BAPIs must be displayed as text fields.

◆ Also, whenever possible, F4 input help for fields in BAPI parameters must be made available. The F4 help documents the parameters and is often the only documentation that is easily available for a programmer to reference.

◆ All BAPIs must have either an export parameter named RETURN or a table named RETURN. This variable tells the calling program whether any problems were encountered during the BAPI call. The standard here is that the RETURN parameter is set to initial if no problems were encountered in the BAPI's execution. The RETURN parameter is modeled after the structure BAPIRET2 and can be filled via the function module BALW_BAPIRETURN_GET2.

The fields of structure BAPIRET2 are shown in Table 18.1.

Table 18.1 Structure for BAPIRET2

Field	Type	Description
TYPE	CHAR 1	S = success message E = error message W = warning message I = information message A = termination message (abort)
ID	CHAR 20	Message ID. The BAPIRET2 structure takes into account the name space extension for the message class as of release 4.0. If you want messages to be compatible with earlier R/3 releases, use only the first two characters of the message ID.
NUMBER	NUMC 3	Message number.
MESSAGE	CHAR 220	Full message text from table T100. All variables (in fields Message_V1 to Message_V4) have been replaced with text.
LOG_NO	CHAR 20	Number of application log. This field is empty if no log is used.
LOG_MSG_NO	NUMC 6	Current number of messages in the application log.
MESSAGE_V1		
MESSAGE_V2		
MESSAGE_V3		
MESSAGE_V4	CHAR 50	Fields for the variable texts of the message specified in ID and NUMBER fields.
PARAMETER	CHAR 32	Identifies the parameter containing the invalid value.
ROW	INT 4	Identifies the line number of the data record containing the invalid value.
FIELD	CHAR 30	Identifies the field containing the invalid value.
SYSTEM	CHAR 10	System (logical system) in which the message was generated.

Standardized BAPIs

Before you start to develop your BAPI, you need to consider whether it falls into a category that SAP calls *Standard BAPIs*. These BAPIs provide basic functionality that can be used on many SAP objects. An example of a standardized BAPI is the GetList BAPI. This BAPI returns a list of the objects of which it is a method. Therefore, if you are going to write a similar BAPI for a customer-built object, you should call the method GetList, not ShowObject or ListEntries. This approach enables other programmers to easily navigate and use your BAPIs.

GetList

The GetList standard BAPI imports the object keys and retrieves the objects that meet the input criteria. The list of fields for each listed object should be extensive enough to allow the user to easily differentiate the objects. Ideally, you should put a user exit in this BAPI that would allow a programmer to modify the list of fields returned for each object.

GetDetail

The GetDetail standard BAPI imports the object keys and returns details from one specific object. Ideally, a user exit should be coded into the BAPI that will allow a programmer to modify which fields are returned.

GetStatus

The GetStatus BAPI is an Instance BAPI that returns the current status of an object (for example, a sales order).

ExistenceCheck

The ExistenceCheck BAPI is an Instance BAPI that checks whether the specified object actually exists. Remember that this BAPI does not return data about the object; it simply determines whether the object exists. Therefore, for performance reasons, when coding the database Select statements, make sure to retrieve as little information as possible.

```
select matnr into loc_matnr from mara where matnr = mara-matnr.
```

Create or CreateFromData

The Create or CreateFromData BAPI creates a single instance of an object.

Change

The Change BAPI changes an existing object.

Delete and UnDelete

The Delete BAPI deletes objects from the database. *Deleting* does not necessarily mean physically deleting the item; it may just mean to mark the object's delete indicator (the record is deleted later by some archiving procedure). The Undelete BAPI resets the delete indicator on a record.

Add(subobject) and Remove(subobject)

Certain objects have subobjects attached to them, for example, a sales order that has line items. In the SalesOrder example, you could set up the AddItem and RemoveItem BAPIs to actually add and remove items from the sales order.

Replicate and SaveReplica

The Replicate and SaveReplica BAPIs are implemented as methods of replicable business objects. These BAPIs enable specific instances of an object type to be copied to one or more systems. Replicate and SaveReplica are used mainly to transfer data between distributed systems within the context of ALE.

Design of BAPIs

The development of a BAPI begins in the design stage, in which you determine the function that needs to be done and which business objects it will affect. BAPIs can be broadly defined into two categories, Instance methods and Class methods. An *Instance method* deals with a single instance of an object, whereas a *Class method* deals with many or all of the objects that have been instantiated from a class. An example of an Instance BAPI is GetDetail, which returns specific information about a sales or purchase order. An example of a Class BAPI is GetList, which lists many sales or purchase orders.

The first part of the design step is to determine how the BAPI will interface with the object in the BOR. This step primarily means the identification of parameters that will be imported and exported, but also means a review of existing BAPIs for that object. You want to make sure that the new BAPI will not affect or repeat functionality that exists in the current BAPIs. The relationship between parameters in the BOR, Function Builder, and Data Dictionary are shown in Figure 18.1.

When determining the import and export parameters, make sure to determine whether the parameters will be mandatory or not. Also, if your BAPI is going to be creating things, return the keys of the newly created objects in separate parameters (not in the RETURN parameter).

Specific naming conventions are used in the development of BAPIs. The name of the function module should be BAPI_<OBJECT_NAME>_<METHOD>. In addition, you should use the prefix BAPI for any objects you create in the Data Dictionary.

When creating a normal function module you do not have to define the input parameter's data structure. If you leave the reference field blank, the parameter takes on

---

Parameter and Table Handling

When you are setting up the call to a BAPI (or any RFC), you must remember that parameters are not passed the same way as they are if you were making a normal function call. Most function modules set up their parameters to be passed by reference. This method is more efficient than passing the values themselves, because only the pointer to the variable needs to be moved around when the function module is called. With RFCs, parameters cannot be passed by reference because two different environments are involved. Therefore, the *value* of the parameter must be passed.

Tables are also dealt with differently when using an RFC versus when a function module is called on the same SAP system. With an RFC call, we are dealing with two different environments; the results in the entire contents of the table are passed during the initial call to the RFC. This action creates a local copy of the table on the server. The original table on the client is not updated until the RFC call is finished.

With this information in mind, make sure to select parameters and tables carefully. You want to pass as little data as possible between SAP and the calling system.

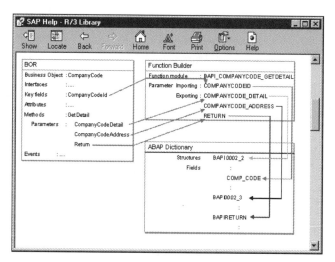

FIGURE 18.1 *The relationship of parameters between BOR, Function Builder, and Data Dictionary*

the characteristics of the variable that the calling program passes. However, this information is not available to your BAPI if it is called remotely, because all that is coming to it is the value of the parameter. Therefore, you must define the characteristics for every parameter for a function module that is used as a BAPI.

NOTE

A parameter's length does not have to exactly match that of the calling variable. If you declare a parameter as 100 characters long and the calling program passes in a 30-character variable, the remaining 70 characters are padded with spaces. You must make sure, however, that your parameters are at least as long as the variables that will be passed to them.

An example of a BAPI function module follows.

```
Function Module BAPI_PO_GETDETAIL
*"- - - - - - - - - - - - - - - - - - - - - - - - - - - - - - - - -
*"
*"local interface:
*"          IMPORTING
*"                VALUE(PURCHASEORDER) LIKE  BAPIEKKO-PO_NUMBER
*"                VALUE(ITEMS) LIKE  BAPIMMPARA-SELECTION DEFAULT 'X'
```

```
*"              VALUE(ACCOUNT_ASSIGNMENT) LIKE  BAPIMMPARA-SELECTION
*"                              DEFAULT SPACE
*"              VALUE(SCHEDULES) LIKE  BAPIMMPARA-SELECTION
*"                              DEFAULT SPACE
*"              VALUE(HISTORY) LIKE  BAPIMMPARA-SELECTION
*"                              DEFAULT SPACE
*"              VALUE(ITEM_TEXTS) LIKE  BAPIMMPARA-SELECTION
*"                              DEFAULT SPACE
*"              VALUE(HEADER_TEXTS) LIKE  BAPIMMPARA-SELECTION
*"                              DEFAULT SPACE
*"              VALUE(SERVICES) LIKE  BAPIMMPARA-SELECTION
*"                              DEFAULT SPACE
*"        EXPORTING
*"              VALUE(PO_HEADER) LIKE  BAPIEKKOL STRUCTURE  BAPIEKKOL
*"              VALUE(PO_ADDRESS) LIKE  BAPIADDRESS
*"                              STRUCTURE  BAPIADDRESS
*"        TABLES
*"              PO_HEADER_TEXTS STRUCTURE  BAPIEKKOTX OPTIONAL
*"              PO_ITEMS STRUCTURE  BAPIEKPO OPTIONAL
*"              PO_ITEM_ACCOUNT_ASSIGNMENT STRUCTURE  BAPIEKKN
*"                              OPTIONAL
*"              PO_ITEM_SCHEDULES STRUCTURE  BAPIEKET OPTIONAL
*"              PO_ITEM_TEXTS STRUCTURE  BAPIEKPOTX OPTIONAL
*"              PO_ITEM_HISTORY STRUCTURE  BAPIEKBE OPTIONAL
*"              PO_ITEM_HISTORY_TOTALS STRUCTURE  BAPIEKBES OPTIONAL
*"              PO_ITEM_LIMITS STRUCTURE  BAPIESUH OPTIONAL
*"              PO_ITEM_CONTRACT_LIMITS STRUCTURE  BAPIESUC OPTIONAL
*"              PO_ITEM_SERVICES STRUCTURE  BAPIESLL OPTIONAL
*"              PO_ITEM_SRV_ACCASS_VALUES STRUCTURE  BAPIESKL
*"                              OPTIONAL
*"              RETURN STRUCTURE  BAPIRETURN OPTIONAL
*"----------------------------------------------------------------

* reset all structures and tables
CLEAR: PO_HEADER, PO_ADDRESS, PO_ITEMS, PO_HEADER_TEXTS,
        PO_ITEM_ACCOUNT_ASSIGNMENT, PO_ITEM_SCHEDULES,
        PO_ITEM_TEXTS, RETURN, EKPOKEY, PO_ITEM_HISTORY,
        PO_ITEM_HISTORY_TOTALS, PO_ITEM_LIMITS, PO_ITEM_SERVICES,
        PO_ITEM_CONTRACT_LIMITS, PO_ITEM_SRV_ACCASS_VALUES,
        CEKKO, CEKPO, CEKKN, CEKET, CEKAN, SEKKO, SEKPO, CADR.
```

```
REFRESH:
        PO_HEADER_TEXTS, PO_ITEM_ACCOUNT_ASSIGNMENT, PO_ITEM_SCHEDULES,
        PO_ITEM_TEXTS, PO_ITEMS, RETURN, EKPOKEY, PO_ITEM_HISTORY,
        PO_ITEM_HISTORY_TOTALS, PO_ITEM_LIMITS, PO_ITEM_SERVICES,
        PO_ITEM_CONTRACT_LIMITS, PO_ITEM_SRV_ACCASS_VALUES,
        CEKKN, CEKET, SEKKO, SEKPO.
* select the header data from database
SELECT SINGLE * FROM EKKO WHERE EBELN EQ PURCHASEORDER.
IF SY-SUBRC NE 0.
    PERFORM FILL_BAPIRETURN TABLES RETURN
                               USING   'E'
                                       'W5'
                                       '107'
                                       PURCHASEORDER
                                       SPACE
                                       SPACE
                                       SPACE.
    EXIT.
ENDIF.
* authority check
PERFORM PO_AUTHORITY_HEADER TABLES RETURN
                               USING   EKKO.
IF NO_AUTHORITY NE SPACE.
    PERFORM FILL_BAPIRETURN TABLES RETURN
                               USING   'E'
                                       'W5'
                                       '033'
                                       SPACE
                                       SPACE
                                       SPACE
                                       SPACE.
    EXIT.
ENDIF.
.......
.......
SORT PO_ITEMS BY PO_NUMBER PO_ITEM.
SORT PO_ITEM_ACCOUNT_ASSIGNMENT BY PO_ITEM SERIAL_NO.
SORT PO_ITEM_SCHEDULES BY PO_ITEM SERIAL_NO.
SORT PO_ITEM_HISTORY BY PO_ITEM SERIAL_NO.
```

```
SORT PO_ITEM_HISTORY_TOTALS BY PO_ITEM SERIAL_NO.
SORT PO_ITEM_LIMITS BY PCKG_NO
SORT PO_ITEM_CONTRACT_LIMITS BY PCKG_NO LINE_NO.
SORT PO_ITEM_SERVICES BY PCKG_NO LINE_NO.
SORT PO_ITEM_SRV_ACCASS_VALUES BY PCKG_NO LINE_NO SERNO_LINE.
ENDFUNCTION.
```

Setting the REMOTE Status and Configuration

To enable a function module to be called as a BAPI, two things must be done in addition to the actual ABAP coding. The first concerns the attributes section of the function module configuration, shown in Figure 18.2. In this screen, make sure to verify that the module can be called via a remote call.

Second, you need to make sure that the system that will be calling your function module is entered in the RFCDES table; the system administrator usually does this. The basics of the RFCDES table are discussed later in this chapter in the section titled "The Purpose of RFCDES."

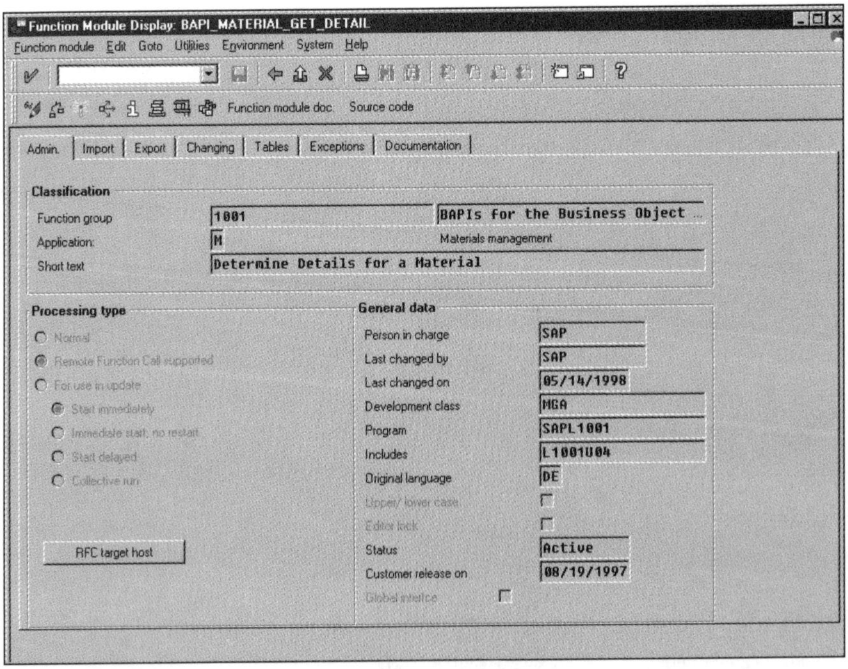

FIGURE 18.2 *Attributes for a function module that can be used as an RFC*

Connecting the BAPI to the BOR

If the function module on which your BAPI is based has been fully implemented or modified, you can define it as a method of an SAP business object in the BOR.

You use the BOR/BAPI Wizard to perform this step by following the menu path TOOLS, Business Framework, BAPI Development, Business Object Builder. Select the business object to which you are going to attach your BAPI and then choose Utilities, API Methods, Add Method.

Now type in the name of your new BAPI. Remember that if you are creating a BAPI named BAPI_MATERIAL_BURN, the method that you want to add is BURN, not BAPI_MATERIAL_BURN.

After the BAPI has been attached to the business object, it is ready for testing. When testing is complete, you will want to release the BAPI. The process of releasing a BAPI, in effect, freezes it. If any future changes are made to the same business object, a check is done to ensure that the change is compatible with existing, released BAPIs. Releasing a BAPI is a two-step process.

1. Go to the Function Builder and select the menu path Function Module, Release, Release.

2. Go to the Business Object Builder, drill down, select your BAPI, and then select Edit, Change Release Status, Object Type Component, In Released.

RFCDES Definition

In a typical SAP installation, the ABAP programmer does not have to be concerned about how the configuration is done for RFCs. This step is typically done either by the people who take care of the SAP environment or by the people who take care of customization in general. At times, however, knowing how the configuration is done is useful, especially when trying to establish a connection to a new system.

The Purpose of RFCDES

The SAP table RFCDES contains the information of the remote destinations and is maintained through transaction SM59. When you make a call to a remote system, as the following example does, the SAP system goes to the RFCDES table to determine the communication parameters, system parameters, and login information required to make the call to the remote system.

```
CALL FUNCTION 'RFC_GET_YTRACK_TOTREC' DESTINATION 'PLUTO'
        EXPORTING
            TABLE = 'YTRACK'
        IMPORTING
            NUMBER = WC_RECS.
```

If you go directly to transaction SM59, you see a screen similar to that shown in Figure 18.3.

This screen shows the possible types of destinations that can be configured. Depending on your system configuration, not all types may be shown; for instance, Figure 18.3 does not have a Type 2 connection, which refers to an R/2 destination. The types of possible connections are listed in Table 18.2.

TIP

Remember that for an RFC function to work for SAP-to-SAP calls, the correct entries need to be in the RFCDES table on both the client and the server.

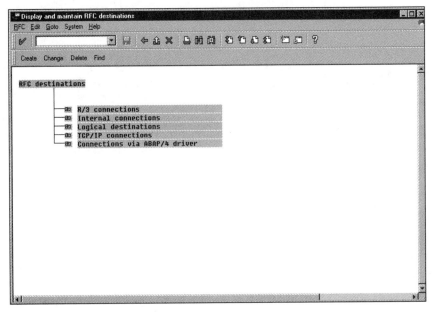

FIGURE 18.3 *RFC overview from transaction SM59*

Table 18.2 RFCDES Destination Types

Type	Description
2	R/2 system.
3	R/3 system.
I	R/3 system connected to the same database as the current system.
L	Logical entries, which can refer to each other and are typically used to define login information. With a type L entry, you can define logical names for another RFCDES's entries and then add other data (such as user ID and password).
X	Systems in which device drivers in ABAP have been specially installed.
S	An R/2 connection with the destination as an SNA (*System Network Architecture*) or APPC (*Advanced Peer to Peer Communications*).
T	Type T destinations are for external programs that use the RFC APIs to receive RFCs.
M	Asynchronous RFC connections to other R/3 systems via CMC (protocol X.400).

Details of the RFCDES Entries

When you drill down through the menu in Figure 18.3 or create a new destination, you come to a screen similar to that in Figure 18.4. The exact fields in this view depend on the RFC type. The one shown here is for an R/3 connection.

Outbound BAPIs

We usually just think of BAPIs as functions within SAP that other systems can use. As of release 4.5A, SAP allows you to have outbound BAPIs. These types of BAPIs are functions that are called on systems outside of the R/3 environment.

The only items that are defined for an outbound BAPI are the parameters for the call, as there is no program on the R/3 system. An example of an outbound BAPI is to save data within a data warehouse that is external to SAP. Each time you process a business event, such as creating a sales order, you would then invoke an outbound BAPI that would trigger an RFC on the warehouse system.

The target system for an output BAPI is usually determined by the distribution model of the ALE.

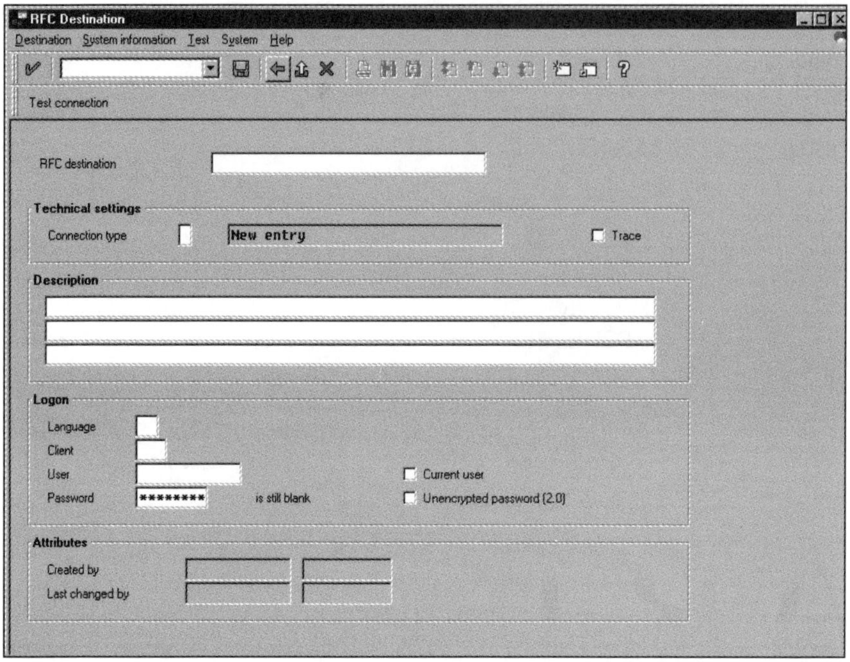

FIGURE 18.4 *Detail view of an RFC destination screen*

Summary

SAP's BOR and its connection with BAPIs provide a standard method for accessing both SAP data and functionality. As you have already seen, this standard connection can be used for systems that are external to SAP, such as Java applications. BAPIs are currently based on RFCs, and the transaction BAPI can be used to determine which BAPIs are available, and their calling parameters. The development of a BAPI is similar to the development of a standard SAP function module. You must include required fields, follow a few rules, and make sure that the BAPI is implemented in a way that is consistent with the way SAP sets up its BAPIs.

Chapter 21, "BAPI Collection," contains an overview of BAPIs that are available as of SAP release 4.5B.

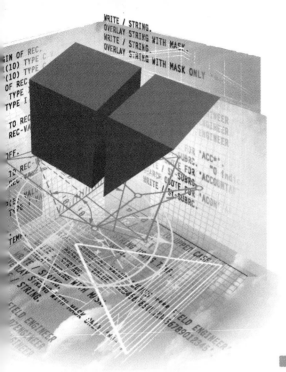

PART III

Details on Java RFC and BAPI Connections

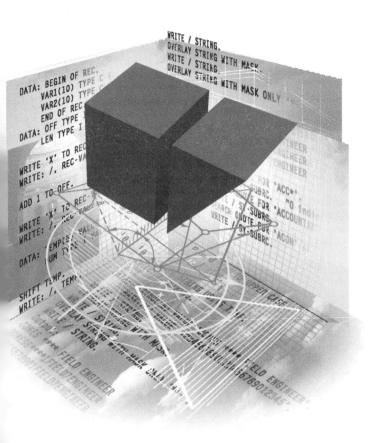

Chapter 19

The COM.SAP.RFC Package

In This Chapter

- ◆ Class Hierarchy
- ◆ Class Descriptions
- ◆ Interface Hierarchy
- ◆ Interface Descriptions

The com.sap.rfc package comprises the working classes used in a Java interface to SAP. Remember that a *package* is simply a collection of classes that share some properties.

Class Hierarchy

Following is the hierarchy of the classes used in a Java interface to SAP.

```
java.lang.Object
    com.sap.rfc.ComplexInfo
    com.sap.rfc.ConnectInfo
    java.util.EventObject
        com.sap.rfc.ConnectionEvent
        com.sap.rfc.MethodEvent
    com.sap.rfc.FactoryManager
    com.sap.rfc.MiddlewareInfo
    com.sap.rfc.SimpleInfo
    com.sap.rfc.SystemInfo
    com.sap.rfc.UserInfo
```

Class Descriptions

The following sections outline the primary functions and useful aspects of the classes contained within the com.sap.rfc package.

com.sap.rfc.ComplexInfo

Every structure or table that is to be used in an RFC from Java must hold one instance of this class. This class stores information about objects, such as field type and length, and passes it to the RFC call. Remember that a ComplexInfo structure can be contained in another ComplexInfo structure.

The most common constructor for this class is

```
ComplexInfo(IfieldInfo[] fieldInfos, java.lang.String fieldname)
```

With this form you pass in an array of information about the fields contained within the structure, along with the name of the ComplexInfo object if it is a field of another ComplexInfo object. For stand-alone ComplexInfo structures, the name can be a null.

The following methods can be used with the structure:

- **clone()**. Creates a copy of the ComplexInfo object.
- **equals(obj)**. Compares one ComplexInfo object to another. If the two objects are the same, the Boolean TRUE is returned.
- **findField(fieldname)**. Returns the index of the desired field. If the field is not found, then this method will throw the JRfcComplex-DataNoSuchFieldException exception.
- **getcount()**. Returns the number of objects in the ComplexInfo object.
- **getFieldInfo(fieldname or index)**. Returns an IFieldInfo object that describes the desired field.
- **getLength()**. Returns the length of the ComplexInfo object.
- **isFilled()**. Checks whether the ComplexInfo object is populated (you can use the constructor ComplexInfo(), which creates an empty object).
- **setComplexInfo(fieldInfos, FieldName)**. Populates the data in the object. This element is not a constructor but works the same way for the data population of the object.

com.sap.rfc.ConnectInfo

This class contains information about the connection to the SAP R/3 system. The constructor for this class, as shown below, has many parameters. Each of these parameters can also be viewed and set through methods.

```
ConnectInfo(Rfcmode, Destination, Hostname, System Number, Gateway Host, Gateway
Service, System Name, Group Name, Message Server)
```

- ◆ **Rfcmode**. The type of RFC connection, set to ConnectInfo.RFC_MODE_VERSION_3 for the current release.
- ◆ **Destination**. The three-character SAP identifier for the system to which you want to connect.
- ◆ **Hostname**. The name of the system that hosts the destination system. This name is usually specified with the full TCP address (or alias to this address).
- ◆ **System Number**. The SAP number that identifies the destination.
- ◆ **Gateway Host**. The name of the gateway host.
- ◆ **Gateway Service**. The gateway service.
- ◆ **System Name**. The SAP system name (used for load balancing only).
- ◆ **Group Name**. The name of the specific group of application servers (again for load balancing only).
- ◆ **Message Server**. The name of the message server (again for load balancing only).

Many methods are associated with the ConnectInfo class, most of which have to do with viewing or setting the variables just described. Each of the following Get methods has an associated Set method, which can be used to set the variables in the object.

- ◆ **addPropertyChangeListener(Listener)**. This method subscribes to changes for any of the ConnectInfo properties. An associated method is removePropertyChangeListener().
- ◆ **getDestination()**. Returns the destination name of the target system.
- ◆ **getGatewayHost()**. Returns the gateway host name.
- ◆ **getGatewayService()**. Returns the gateway service.
- ◆ **getGroupName()**. Returns the name of the specific group of application servers.

- **getHostName( )**. Returns the host machine name of the target system.
- **getLoadBalancing( )**. Returns the Boolean value of TRUE or FALSE, indicating whether load balancing is turned on or off.
- **getMsgServer( )**. Returns the host name of the message server.
- **getRfcMode( )**. Returns the current connection mode.
- **getSystemName( )**. Returns the SAP system name.
- **getSystemNo( )**. Returns the SAP system number.

com.sap.rfc.ConnectionEvent

The ConnectionEvent class supports the ConnectionListener interface and is instantiated when an RFC connection is opened or closed. The current release does not have any methods or variables.

com.sap.rfc.MethodEvent

The MethodEvent class supports the MethodListener interface. The constructor for this event takes on two forms. The first allows you to pass just the object that fires the event, and the other allows you to also pass the RfcModule used to perform the method call.

```
MethodEvent(object) or MethodEvent(object, rfcModule)
```

This class has two methods.

- **getRfcModule( )**. Returns the rfcModule property value.
- **setRfcModule(rfcModule)**. Sets the rfcModule property value.

com.sap.rfc.FactoryManager

This class manages factories for specific middleware. Methods for the com.sap.rfc.FactoryManager class include:

- **getAPIRelease( )**. Returns the release number of the common RFC interface for Java.
- **getMiddlewareInfo( )**. Returns the middlewareInfo property value, which can be used at run time to determine which middleware is being used.
- **getRfcConnectionFactory( )**. Returns a reference to a factory for IRfcConnections.

- ◆ **getRfcModuleFactory( )**. Returns a reference to a factory for IRfcModules.
- ◆ **getSimpleFactory( )** Returns a reference to a factory for ISimples.
- ◆ **getSingleInstance( )**. Returns a single instance of the class FactoryManager.
- ◆ **getStructureFactory( )** Returns a reference to a factory for IStructures.
- ◆ **getTableFactory( )**. Returns a reference to a factory for ITables.
- ◆ **setMiddlewareInfo(middlewareInfo)**. Sets the middlewareInfo property of the FactoryManager.

com.sap.rfc.MiddlewareInfo

The com.sap.rfc.MiddlewareInfo class holds the data for a specific type of middleware and must be instantiated before factories can be retrieved from the factory manager. This class contains constructors and methods that can implement a new middleware. Such development, however, is complicated and beyond the scope of this introductory book.

com.sap.rfc.SimpleInfo

The class implements the IFieldInfo interface and stores information for a simple data type. Each piece of data that will be either imported or exported through an RFC interface must be instantiated by the com.sap.rfc.SimpleInfo class.

The constructor for this class allows you to define the name, type, and length of the variable and the number of decimals (in the case of floating-point data). The format is as follows:

```
SimpleInfo(name, type, length, decimals)
```

Methods that can be used with the com.sap.rfc.SimpleInfo class include:

- ◆ **clone( )**. Creates a copy of an existing SimpleInfo object.
- ◆ **equals(object)**. Allows you to compare to field definitions. Remember that this method does not compare the value of the object, simply the data declaration.
- ◆ **getDecimals( )**. Returns the number of decimals defined.
- ◆ **getFieldName( )**. Returns the name of the variable.

◆ **getLength( )**. Returns the length of the variable.

◆ **getOffset( )**. Returns the offset of the variable.

◆ **getType( )**. Returns the type of variable. This type is the RFC data type and hence is an SAP data type.

◆ **isFilled( )**. Returns a Boolean TRUE or FALSE to indicate whether the object has been populated.

◆ **setOffset(offset)**. Sets the offset of the data field.

◆ **setSimpleInfo(name, type, length, decimals)**. This method is similar to the constructor and allows you to set the meta information for an object in a single call.

com.sap.rfc.SystemInfo

This class holds information related to the R/3 system to which you are connected. The information is returned through the RFC RFC_SYSTEM_INFO. To use this class you must define a list of system variables to be retrieved through the constructor; this list is an array of IField objects.

```
SystemInfo(systemParams[])
```

After the object has been constructed, you can use the method getItem (index or variable name) to retrieve the value of the variables. The method getItemCount() will return the number of variables used in the construction of this object.

com.sap.rfc.UserInfo

This class holds the user logon information. Through the constructor, you pass through the user name, password, and so on, which are then combined with the ConnectInfo class to establish the connection with the R/3 system.

```
UserInfo(User Name, Password, Client, Language)
```

Methods for the com.sap.rfc.UserInfo class include most of the standard methods that you have already seen, for example, clone(), and methods to get and set all the properties in the object. Note that each Get method has a corresponding Set method.

◆ **addPropertyChangeListener(Listener)**. Subscribes the object to any change that may occur in the UserInfo properties.

- ◆ **clone( )**. Creates a duplicate instance of the object.
- ◆ **equals(object)**. Returns a Boolean value to indicate whether two objects are identical.
- ◆ **getClient( )**. Returns the client of the UserInfo object.
- ◆ **getLanguage( )**. Returns the language of the UserInfo object.
- ◆ **getPassword( )**. Returns the password of the UserInfo object.
- ◆ **getUserName( )**. Returns the username of the UserInfo object.

Interface Hierarchy

Below is a high-level overview of the Interface Hierarchy for the com.sap.rfc package showing the relationships between the various interfaces; knowing these relationships is important for determining inheritance properties.

```
java.lang.Cloneable
    com.sap.rfc.IField
com.sap.rfc.IComplexField
    com.sap.rfc.IRow
    com.sap.rfc.IStucture
    com.sap.rfc.ISimpleField
        com.sap.rfc.ISimple
    com.sap.rfc.IFieldInfo
    com.sap.rfc.IParameter
    com.sap.rfc.IComplexParam
        com.sap.rfc.IStructure
        com.sap.rfc.ITable
com.sap.rfc.IImpExpParam
com.sap.rfc.ISimpleParam
    com.sap.rfc.ISimple
com.sap.rfc.IStructure
java.util.EventListener
    com.sap.rfc.ConnectionListener
    com.sap.rfc.MethodListener
com.sap.rfc.ICursor
com.sap.rfc.IRfcConnection
com.sap.rfc.IRfcConnectionFactory
com.sap.rfc.IRfcModule
```

```
com.sap.rfc.IRfcModuleFactory
com.sap.rfc.ISimpleFactory
com.sap.rfc.IStructureFactory
com.sap.rfc.ITableFactory
java.io.Serializable
    com.sap.rfc.IField
    com.sap.rfc.IComplexField
        com.sap.rfc.IRow
        com.sap.rfc.IStructure
com.sap.rfc.ISimpleField
        com.sap.rfc.ISimple
        com.sap.rfc.IFieldInfo
```

Interface Descriptions

The following interfaces are included in the com.sap.rfc package.

com.sap.rfc.IField

This interface is the building block interface for all data interfaces. Commonly used methods are as follows:

- ◆ **clear()**. Clears the content of this field.
- ◆ **clone()**. Clones the field.
- ◆ **getFieldInfo()**. Returns information describing this field. See IFieldInfo in this chapter for more information.
- ◆ **getFieldName()**. Returns the name of the field.

com.sap.rfc.IComplexField

This interface is really just a collection of data fields that implement the IField interface; it holds data about structures and tables. Because fields within structures can be structures themselves, the nesting of field information can go on infinitely.

- ◆ **getComplexField(index or fieldname)**. Returns the complex field at a given field index position from the field list.
- ◆ **getComplexInfo()**. Returns the complex info associated with this parameter.

◆ **getField(index or fieldname)**. Returns an IField structure for the requested field.

◆ **getFieldCount( )** Returns the number of fields in the field list.

◆ **getSimpleField(index or fieldname)**. Returns the simple field that matches the given name from the field list.

◆ **isEmpty( )**. Checks whether the field list is empty.

◆ **setField(index, field)**. Sets the field at the given field index position in the field list.

com.sap.rfc.IRow

This interface contains a group of data fields that represent a single table row. The only direct (*noninherited*) method in this interface is getTable(); this method returns the ITable object associated with the row.

Methods in the com.sap.rfc.IRow interface include the following:

◆ **getCurrentRow( )**. Returns the current row.

◆ **getFirstRow( )**. Returns the first row of the table.

◆ **getLastRow( )**. Returns the last row of the table.

◆ **getNextRow( )**. Returns the next row of the table. The fetch direction of the table determines the reading direction (see ITable in this chapter for more details).

◆ **getPosition( )**. Returns the current row index.

◆ **getPreviousRow( )**. Returns the previous row of the table. The fetch direction of the table determines the reading direction (see *ITable* in this chapter for more details).

com.sap.rfc.ISimpleField

This interface is used for classes which implement fields of various types; the various data types are listed next. Two methods can be used with all of these data types. The first is Get, for example, getBigDecimal(); this method returns the value of the field. If the data type of the field is not the same as the corresponding Get call, then the value is cast to the same type as the call. The other method is Set, for example, setBigDecimal(value). The Set method actually sets the value of the variable. The value that you send should be the same as the type of call; that is, you should not send an object of type BigDecimal through the call setByte(). If possible, the Set methods will do a type conversion, but they will throw the exception JRfcSimpleDataAbapConversionException if the conversion cannot be made. Also, the type property of the variable is set to match the value of the last Set call.

Types of Variables

The following types of variables are used: BigDecimal, BigInteger, Boolean, Byte, ByteArray, Char, Date, Double, Float, Int, Long, Short, SimpleInfo, String, Time, and Timestamp. You can also get a variable through the method getTypedValue. This method takes a parameter that indicates the type of variable you want to have returned. A similar method, called setTypedValue, allows you to set both the variable and data type.

There are also the methods getTypedValue(type) and setTypedValue(type, value), where *type* can be any of the following values:

```
SF_STRING, SF_CHAR, SF_BYTEARRAY, SF_BOOLEAN, SF_BYTE, SF_SHORT, SF_INTEGER,
SF_LONG, SF_FLOAT, SF_DOUBLE, SF_BIGINTEGER, SF_LONG, SF_FLOAT, SF_DOUBLE, SF_BIG-
INTEGER, SF_BIGDECIMAL, SF_DATE, SF_TIME, SF_TIMESTAMP.
```

com.sap.rfc.ISimple

This interface is implemented by classes that contain data such as ISimpleField and ISimpleParam, as can be seen in the interface hierarchy shown earlier in this chapter. The com.sap.rfc.ISimple interface does not have any new methods.

com.sap.rfc.IFieldInfo

This interface is used to get the *metadata* (data about data definitions) for a field.

Methods for this interface include:

- ◆ **clone()**. Makes a copy of an existing IFieldInfo object.
- ◆ **getFieldName()**. Returns the name of the field.
- ◆ **getLength()**. Returns the length of the field/structure in bytes.
- ◆ **getType()**. Returns the RFC data type.
- ◆ **isFilled()**. Returns the Boolean value of TRUE or FALSE to indicate whether the IFieldInfo contains data.

com.sap.rfc.IParameter

The com.sap.rfc.IParameter interface is used for classes that work with parameters in RFC functions. Methods associated with this interface include the following:

- ◆ **clone( )**. Creates an exact copy of the object.
- ◆ **getFieldInfo( )**. Returns the field info object of this parameter.
- ◆ **getParameterName( )**. Returns the name of this parameter used during an RFC call.
- ◆ **setFieldInfo(fieldInfo)**. Sets the field info for this parameter.
- ◆ **setParameterName(name)**. Sets the parameter name for this parameter.

com.sap.rfc.IComplexParam

This interface is used for complex parameters of RFC functions, such as structures and tables. Only two methods are directly related to this interface: getComplex-Info() and setComplexInfo(complexInfo). Both methods are simply used to get or set the objects related to the parameter interface. The sections on IStructure and ITable in this chapter specify additional methods that can be used for accessing more detailed information on the structure or table.

com.sap.rfc.IStructure

This interface manages a list of data fields for remote function calls. The IStructure interface is implemented by classes that require a series of fields to be associated together. The important methods for this interface are inherited from the interface IComplexField(); see IComplexField for a list of methods.

com.sap.rfc.ITable

The ITable interface is implemented by classes that require an array of structures (remember that these structures may be as simple as a single field). The methods for this interface are as follows:

- ◆ **acceptUpdates( )**. Performs the middleware's acceptUpdates method.
- ◆ **appendRow(row)**. Appends a row to the bottom of the current table object.
- ◆ **copyFrom(table)**. Copies the contents of one table to another, completely overwriting the contents of the destination table.

◆ **createCursor(index)**. Creates a new cursor for this table at the specified row number. A *cursor* is a kind of pointer that indicates the position of the current read operation. When you start reading from a table, the cursor is set to 1 to indicate that the first row to be read is row 1. After that row is read, the cursor is set to 2.

◆ **createEmptyRow( )**. Returns a structure that is the same as the table object. The contents of the table are not affected. Typically, you perform this call to get the exact table structure; then you fill up the fields of the structure and append or insert the row into the table.

◆ **deleteAllRows( )**. Deletes all rows from the table.

◆ **deleteRow(index)**. Deletes a specific row from the table.

◆ **getDefaultCursor( )**. Returns a reference to the default cursor for the table. The default cursor is created when the table is created.

◆ **getReadBufferSize( )**. Returns the number of bytes in the table fetch cache.

◆ **getResultSet(readOnly)**. Returns an object like the standard java.sql.ResultSet interface, which is used in SQL queries. Because we are not really going against a real database but an array of data, several of the properties and methods of this object have no meaning and will return a NULL or FALSE value. More details on this interface can be found on Sun's Java Web page (see Appendix A, "Other Web Resources," for this and other useful URLs).

◆ **getRow(index)**. Returns the specified row, or next row as indicated by the cursor if no index is passed.

◆ **getRowCount( )**. Returns the total number of rows in the table.

◆ **getRowLength( )**. Returns the length (in bytes) of a row of a table. Note that in SAP all rows in a table have the same length.

◆ **getTableName( )**. Returns the name of the table.

◆ **getUpdatePolicy( )**. Returns the update policy of the table.

◆ **insertRow(index, row)**. Inserts a row into the table. Following the insertion, the new row will have the index number passed as a calling parameter.

◆ **isEmpty( )**. Returns a Boolean TRUE or FALSE to indicate whether the table contains any data.

◆ **isFetchForward( )**. Returns a TRUE if the direction of the fetch for the table is forward.

◆ **moveFrom(table)**. Moves the contents of the passed table into the current table object.

◆ **setFetchForward(isFetchForward)**. Sets the fetching direction of the table (TRUE for forward, FALSE for backward).

◆ **setReadBufferSize(number of rows)**. Sets the number of rows of the table to read into the buffer.

◆ **setUpdatePolicy(updatePolicy)**. Sets whether the table is allowed to be updated (TRUE indicates that it can be updated).

◆ **updateRow(index, row)**. Updates a specific row in the table.

com.sap.rfc.IImpExpParam

This interface is for classes that import and export parameters in RFC functions. Refer to interface/class ISimpleParam and IStructure for details on methods.

com.sap.rfc.ISimpleParam

This interface is also for classes and interfaces that import and export parameters for RFC functions. The two main methods associated with this interface are

◆ **getSimpleInfo( )**. Returns an object of type SimpleInfo.

◆ **setSimpleInfo( )**. Sets the SimpleInfo information for this object.

Refer to SimpleInfo for more details on methods.

com.sap.rfc.ConnectionListener

The interface ConnectionListener sets events based on the communication status between your Java program and the middleware. Events that can be raised include:

◆ **connected(event)**. Is raised when a new SAP connection is established.

◆ **disconnected(event)**. Is raised when an existing SAP connection is closed.

◆ **failed(event)**. Is raised when a new SAP connection cannot be established.

com.sap.rfc.MethodListener

The MethodListener interface defines events that are related to the execution of RFCs in SAP.

- ◆ **executed(event)**. A synchronous SAP function call that finishes successfully.
- ◆ **failed(event)**. A synchronous SAP function call that fails.

com.sap.rfc.ICursor

The ICursor interface is used with the ITable object. This interface merely serves as a tool for table handling. ICursor offers no functionality that cannot be solved by using the methods of ITable (and the associated IRow objects).

com.sap.rfc.IRfcConnection

This interface is the main interface for the SAP RFC connection. IRfcConnection is responsible for managing all R/3 connection information. The methods associated with this interface follow.

- ◆ **abort(string)**. Actively shuts down the connection to R/3 with the associated string as an error message.
- ◆ **addConnectionListener(Listener)**. Adds a new connection listener.
- ◆ **addPropertyChangeListener(Listener)**. Adds a new PropertyChangeListener.
- ◆ **clear()**. Clears the user and connection info in this connection.
- ◆ **close()**. Closes the connection to the SAP R/3 system.
- ◆ **getConnectInfo()**. Returns the ConnectInfo object used in the connection to the SAP R/3 system.
- ◆ **getR3Release()**. Returns the actual R/3 Release property. This property is part of the information retrieved by the method getSystemInfo().
- ◆ **getRFCTraceLevel()**. Returns the RFC trace level on the server side.
- ◆ **getSystemInfo()**. Returns the system information from the SAP R/3 system. The function module RFC_SYSTEM_INFO retrieves the information.

◆ **getUserInfo( )**. Returns the UserInfo object used in the connection to the SAP system.

◆ **isValid( )**. Returns a Boolean value to indicate whether the connection to the SAP system is still valid.

◆ **open( )**. Opens a connection to an SAP R/3 system. This connection is established by using the information in ConnectionInfo and UserInfo.

◆ **removeConnectionListener(listener)**. Removes a connection listener.

◆ **removePropertyChangeListener(listener)**. Removes a Property-ChangeListener.

◆ **setConnectInfo(connectInfo)**. Sets the connectInfo object to be used in opening a connection.

◆ **setRFCTraceLevel(newTraceLevel)**. Sets the trace level (at the server side).

◆ **setUserInfo(userInfo)**. Sets the userInfo object to be used in opening a connection to SAP.

com.sap.rfc.IRfcConnectionFactory

This interface is used by all of the factories that create instances of classes by implementing the IRfcConnection interface. The only method associated with this interface is createRfcConnection(ConnectInfo, UserInfo). This method creates the IRfcConnection object; that is why it is called the IRfcConnection "factory."

com.sap.rfc.IRfcModule

This interface deals with SAP RFC function calls and the related parameters used in the function module calls. Methods for this interface are as follows (note that when referencing import and export parameters by index, index numbers start at 0):

◆ **addExportParam(param)**. Adds an export parameter to the RFC module (the parameter is returned from the function module). You can associate a parameter with only one function module; attempting to associate a parameter with more than one function module will throw an exception.

- **addImportParam(param)**. Adds an import parameter to the RFC module (the parameter is sent to the function module). You can associate a parameter with only one function module; attempting to associate a parameter with more than one function module will throw an exception.

- **addTableParam(table)**. Adds a table parameter to the RFC module. As with import and export parameters, a table can only be associated with one RFC function at a time. Unlike import and export parameters, however, data in tables is passed both ways (both to and from the RFC function module).

- **call()**. Invokes a one-way call to the SAP system by passing import parameters and table data.

- **callReceive()**. Invokes a two-way call to the SAP system by sending the import parameters and table data to the RFC and then receiving the export parameters and table data. This one method is equivalent to performing a call() and a receive(). This method can return one of three values:

  RFC_OK. Signifies that the call was successful.

  RFC_CLOSED. Signifies that the connection was closed by the other end.

  RFC_CALL. Signifies that the SAP system is issuing an RFC call to the original object that performed the initial call.

- **createTransID()**. Returns a transaction ID from the SAP system. The transaction ID is stored inside an object on the server side and can be used for subsequent calls for the same logical unit of work. This method allows you to perform many related calls and to keep a common thread among them.

- **getConnection()**. Returns the RFC connection referenced by the RFC module object.

- **getExportParam(index or name)**. Returns an export parameter referenced either by index or name.

- **getExportParamCount()**. Returns the total number of export parameters that are associated with an RFC function.

- **getFunctionName()**. Returns the name of the function module.

- **getImportParam(index or name)**. Returns an import referenced either by index or by name.

♦ **getImportParamCount( )**. Returns the total number of import parameters that are associated with an RFC function.

♦ **getSimpleExportParam(index or name)**. Returns a Simple export parameter.

♦ **getSimpleImportParam(index or name)**. Returns a Simple import parameter.

♦ **getStructExportParam(index or name)**. Returns an export parameter that is a structure.

♦ **getStructImportParam(index or name)**. Returns an import parameter that is a structure.

♦ **getTableParam(index or name)**. Returns a table referenced either by index or by name.

♦ **getTableParamCount( )**. Returns the total number of tables that may be used in the RFC function.

♦ **getTransID( )**. Returns a previously created transaction ID.

♦ **indirectCall( )**. Makes a one-way transactional call to the R/3 system. Ensures that a transaction ID has been obtained either through create-TransID() or getTransID().

♦ **listen( )**. Checks whether an RFC request is available. Returns RFC_OK if an RFC event is pending, RFC_RETRY if nothing has arrived, and RFC_FAILURE if an error has occurred.

♦ **receive()**. Makes a one-way call to R/3 receiving both export parameters and table data. This method can be called only after a call() is issued.

♦ **removeExportParam(param index or name)**. Removes a previously assigned Export parameter. After this method is called, you can assign the parameter to another RFC.

♦ **removeImportParam(param index or name)**. Removes a previously assigned Import parameter. After this method is called, you can assign the parameter to another RFC.

♦ **removeTableParam(table index or name)**. Removes a previously assigned table from an RFC. After this method is called, you can assign the table to another RFC.

♦ **replaceExportParam(newparam)**. Replaces one export parameter with another.

- **replaceImportParam(newparam).** Replaces one import parameter with another.

- **replaceTableParam(newtable).** Replaces one table parameter with another.

- **setConnection(value).** Sets the RFC connection referenced by this function object.

- **setFunctionName(name).** Sets the name of the function module represented by this RFC module object.

- **setTransID(id).** Sets the transaction ID stored in this RFC module.

com.sap.rfc.IRfcModuleFactory

This interface is a factory in which to create IRfcModule interfaces. Following are the two ways in which these interfaces can be created.

- **autoCreateRfcModule(connection, rfcModuleName).** Creates an IRfcModule instance with the name specified and a connection to an SAP R/3 system.

- **createRfcModule(connection, rfcModuleName, importParams, exportParams, tableParams).** Creates an IRfcModule instance with the connection, the name, and all import, export, and table parameters.

com.sap.rfc.ISimpleFactory

This interface is a factory for the creation of ISimple interfaces. It has one basic method, createSimple(simpleInfo, paramName), which creates a simple field with the specified name and field information.

com.sap.rfc.IStructureFactory

This interface is a factory for the creation of IStructure interfaces. Two basic methods are associated with this interface:

- **autoCreateStructure(paramName, connection, structureName).** Creates a structure parameter retrieving the meta information for the R/3 system.

- **createStructure(complexInfo, paramName).** Creates a structure parameter after all meta data has been given.

com.sap.rfc.ITableFactory

This interface is a factory for creating ITable interfaces. Like IStructureFactory, ITableFactory has two methods:

◆ **autoCreateTable(paramName, connection, tableName)**. Creates an object with the ITable interface using the specified information.

◆ **createTable(complexInfo, paramName)**. Creates an object with the ITable interface using the specified meta data.

Summary

The com.sap.rfc package offers numerous classes and interfaces; start with the basic ones, such as ISimpleField, and read through the examples in earlier chapters. Then start writing simple Java programs until you get used to the conventions for sending and returning data, as well as for handling exceptions. The key difference between good and great code is that great code cleanly handles all exceptions.

You can find more documentation for the classes shown in this chapter through the HTML pages that are installed on your system when you install the SAP Automation Suite. The location of this documentation seems to change after each new release, so look for a Docs directory somewhere under the high-level installation directory. You can also use the Windows Explorer Find File command to locate HTML pages such as index.html or IField.html.

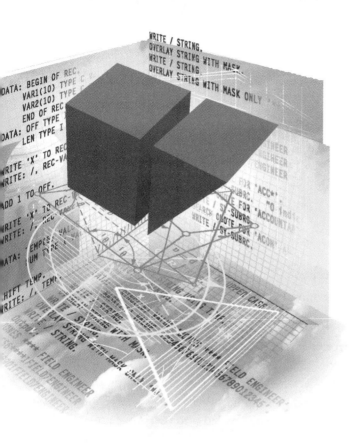

Chapter 20

The COM.SAP.
RFC.EXCEPTION
Package

In This Chapter

- ◆ Class Hierarchy
- ◆ JRfcBaseException
- ◆ JRfcBaseRuntimeException
- ◆ JRfcRemoteOutOfMemoryError

When an exceptional circumstance arises in a Java method, the method *throws* an error or exception. This error or exception is an object that is instantiated from the Java class Throwable. Throwable has two subclasses, Error and Exception. Instances of Error are internal errors in the Java run-time environment that you usually cannot control from a program. The other subclass, Exception, can be handled in your Java programs and can be divided into two broad areas, run-time exceptions and non–run-time exceptions. Of these, run-time exceptions are usually caused by code that is not robust.

Class Hierarchy

The following diagram shows the class hierarchy of the COM.SAP.RFC EXCEPTION package. Remember that in a class hierarchy, subclasses inherit methods and variables from superior classes.

```
java.lang.Object
    java.lang.Throwable (implements java.io.Serializable)
        java.lang.Exception
            com.sap.rfc.exception.JRfcBaseException
                com.sap.rfc.exception.JRfcIOException
                    com.sap.rfc.exception.JRfcRemoteException
                        com.sap.rfc.exception.JRfcRemoteAutoCreateException
                        com.sap.rfc.exception.JRfcRemoteServerException
                        com.sap.rfc.exception.JRfcRfcBaseException
                            com.sap.rfc.exception.JRfcRfcAbapException
                            com.sap.rfc.exception.JRfcRfcConnectionException
```

```
                    com.sap.rfc.exception.JRfcRfcParameterException
        java.lang.RuntimeException
            com.sap.rfc.exception.JRfcBaseRuntimeException
                com.sap.rfc.exception.JRfcClassCastException
                com.sap.rfc.exception.JRfcComplexDataException
                    com.sap.rfc.exception.JRfcComplexDataNoSuchFieldException
                com.sap.rfc.exception.JRfcIllegalArgumentException
                com.sap.rfc.exception.JRfcIllegalStateException
                com.sap.rfc.exception.JRfcIndexOutOfBoundsException
                com.sap.rfc.exception.JRfcMiddlewareException
                com.sap.rfc.exception.JRfcNoSuchParameterException
                com.sap.rfc.exception.JRfcNullPointerException
                com.sap.rfc.exception.JRfcSimpleDataException
                    com.sap.rfc.exception.JRfcSimpleDataAbapConversionException
                    com.sap.rfc.exception.JRfcSimpleDataCastException
                    com.sap.rfc.exception.JRfcSimpleDataDateTimeFormatException
                    com.sap.rfc.exception.JRfcSimpleDataNumberFormatException
                    com.sap.rfc.exception.JRfcSimpleDataUnknownTypeException
        class java.lang.Error
            com.sap.rfc.exception.JRfcRemoteOutOfMemoryError
```

JRfcBaseException

The JRfcBaseException class provides common methods for some of the other exception classes. These common methods are described next, and can be used in any exception class that is under JRfcBaseException in the class hierarchy.

- ◆ **getCausingException()**. Returns the last exception raised.
- ◆ **getClassname()**. Returns the class name of this exception.
- ◆ **toString()**. Converts the exception message to a string.

JRfcIOException

This class is a subclass of JRfcBaseException and, in broad terms, is a class within the hierarchy that contains subclasses to deal with input/output errors. Of course, this class inherits all of the methods of JRfcBaseException. Currently, all I/O errors that are thrown have to do with a remote system, such as the Java server or the SAP system itself.

JRfcRemoteException

This class is a subclass of JRfcIOException. JRfcRemoteException is used if an exception occurs with a remote object, such as the SAP system.

JRfcRemoteAutoCreateException

Finally, a real exception! This class is nested under the JRfcRemoteException class, and is thrown to indicate that the automatic creation of an IRfcModule, an IStructure, or an ITable has failed.

JRfcRemoteServerException

This exception is thrown to indicate that an error has occurred in the remote server of certain middleware.

JRfcRfcBaseException

This class is the base class for exceptions thrown when an attempt to communicate with an R/3 system fails. See the inherited exception classes for the various reasons why an attempt to communicate can fail.

JRfcRfcAbapException

This class is raised if an exception occurs in the execution of a program on the SAP system. In addition to the methods inherited by superior classes, this class has the following methods:

- **getAbapMessage()**. Returns the ABAP exception message.
- **getMessage()**. Returns the ABAP exception message.

JRfcRfcConnectionException

This exception is thrown when a communication problem, including all problems concerning unreachable or unavailable servers (message server, application server, router, or ORB server), occurs with the R/3 system.

The following fields are defined within this class:

- **strIntstat**. Internal description of the RFC connection.
- **strKey**. RFC error code.

◆ **strMessage**. Text describing the error.

◆ **strStatus**. State of the RFC connection.

The getMessage() method, which returns RFC messages, is also defined for this class.

JRfcRfcParameterException

This exception is thrown if the interface of a remotely called function module does not fit the parameters provided. This situation includes missing obligatory parameters, parameters of the wrong type, or names of function modules that do not exist.

JRfcBaseRuntimeException

This class and the classes below it are exceptions that can occur during regular operation of an application. The JRfcBaseRuntimeException is similar to JRfcBaseException. This class has three primary methods that are inherited by the lower classes in the hierarchy.

◆ **getCausingException()**. Returns the originating exception.

◆ **getClassname()**. Returns the class that raised the exception.

◆ **toString()**. Returns the exception as a string.

JRfcClassCastException

This exception is thrown when you attempt to cast a class to a subclass type that is not in the hierarchy.

JRfcComplexDataException

This class contains subclasses that deal with problems related to complex data, such as structures or tables.

JRfcComplexDataNoSuchFieldException

This exception is raised if the Java program tries to access a field in a structure or table that does not exist.

JRfcIllegalArgumentException

This exception is raised when an illegal value is passed back to the method.

JRfcIllegalStateException

This exception class may be thrown to indicate that an object's state does not allow the desired operation.

JRfcIndexOutOfBoundsException

This exception class is thrown to indicate that an index of some kind (such as to an array, a string, or a vector) is out of range. The index is either negative or greater than or equal to the number of indexed elements.

JRfcMiddlewareException

This exception class is thrown to indicate that what went wrong is specific to the middleware implementing the Java access to RFC.

JRfcNoSuchParameterException

This exception is thrown if a parameter with a certain name cannot be found.

JRfcNullPointerException

This exception class is thrown when an application attempts to use a null pointer in a case where an object is required.

JRfcSimpleDataException

This exception class is used as the base class for all exceptions related to simple data items.

JRfcSimpleDataAbapConversionException

This exception class is thrown to indicate that an instance of type ISimple is not able to convert its data into the corresponding ABAP data type. For example, a

Simple is mapped to an ABAP field of type CHAR with a length of 30. Any attempt to store a java.lang.String with a length greater than 30 would result in this exception class being thrown.

JRfcSimpleDataCastException

This exception class is thrown when the internal data cannot be cast to a desired type. For example, SimpleDataCastException is thrown if the getByte() method is invoked on an object of a class implementing ISimpleField, and the object contains data that cannot be interpreted as a byte (for example, 12345, "longstring", 1.2345, "19971216").

JRfcSimpleDataDateTimeFormatException

This exception is thrown to indicate that an attempt was made to convert a string to a date or time object, but the string did not have the correct format.

JRfcSimpleDataNumberFormatException

This exception is thrown to indicate that an attempt was made to convert a string to one of the numeric types, but the string did not have the correct format.

JRfcSimpleDataUnknownTypeException

This exception is thrown to indicate that an attempt was made to set a simple data item to an unknown type.

JRfcRemoteOutOfMemoryError

This class is an extension of java.lang.Error and indicates that the remote Java Server has run out of memory. All your program can do at this point is to alert the user to contact the system administrator. The usual reason that the Java Server runs out of memory is that too many threads have been opened on the system. If this situation occurs in a production environment, some type of load balancing may be required.

Thus, another good reason to use BAPIs when accessing SAP through Java is that BAPIs, by definition, are complete business units of work. Each call that you make will be either successful or unsuccessful. Partial database updates are not allowed because they may leave corrupt data on the system.

Summary

The straightforward package COM.SAP.RFC.EXCEPTION contains only a few methods. The class hierarchy diagram at the beginning of this chapter laid out the interdependence of the various exceptions. Java code cannot do too much with respect to errors that occur on the Java server or with SAP, except to end gracefully or perhaps to let the user try the operation again. Run-time errors should not occur very often if you have clean code. Let the Java classes build the complex data types; hard-coding values for field names in structures might later cause an exception if the structure or data definition changes in SAP. Use BAPIs all of the time; by definition, they perform an entire unit of work and will not corrupt the SAP database.

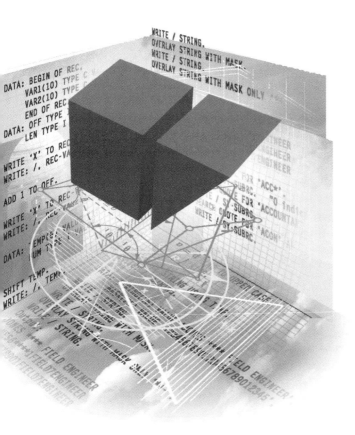

Chapter 21

BAPI Collection

In This Chapter

◆ CCMS

◆ Financial Accounting

◆ Human Resources

◆ Logistics

◆ Basis/CA

This chapter briefly describes many of the BAPIs that are available in version 4.5B. The listing is broken down into five major categories: CCMS (*Computer Center Management System*), logistics, financial accounting, human resources, and Basis/CA (*Cross Application*).

CCMS

Following is a list of the CCMS BAPIs.

SystemMngmtSession

◆ **CheckVersion**. Checks whether a particular version of an interface is supported.

◆ **DescribeInterface**. Queries the long name of an interface.

◆ **EnterLogmsg**. Enters an external message in the XMI log.

◆ **GetVersions**. Gets query-supported versions of the XMI interface.

◆ **Logoff**. Logs the user off an external management tool.

◆ **Logon**. Logs the user on to an external management tool.

◆ **SelectLog**. Retrieves a selection of translated entries in the XMI log.

◆ **SetAuditlevel**. Sets the audit level of an XMI session.

◆ **UploadMsgFormats**. Transfers external message formats.

SystemServiceInfo

- **GetBackgroundResourcesOnDate**. Determines all background resources available on a particular date.

- **GetBgrdResourcesOnDateOnServer**. Determines the background resources of the server on a particular date.

- **GetCurrentBackgroundResources**. Determines the background resources currently available in the system.

- **BackgroundJob**. Controls background job execution.

- **Abort**. Cancels job.

- **AddABAPStep**. Appends a job step with an ABAP program to a job.

- **AddExternalStep**. Assigns an external program to a job step.

- **CheckStatus**. Reconciles job status with actual status, according to the database.

- **Close**. Completes the job definition.

- **CountByName**. Counts how many jobs have a particular name.

- **Delete**. Deletes a job in the R/3 system.

- **GetDefinition**. Reads a job definition.

- **GetStatus**. Determines job status.

- **GetVariantListForReportname**. Determines all defined variants of an ABAP program.

- **ModifyABAPStep**. Assigns an ABAP program to a particular job step.

- **ModifyExternalStep**. Assigns an external program to a particular job step.

- **Open**. Creates a job.

- **ReadJobLog**. Reads the job log.

- **ReadSpoolList**. Reads the spool list of the ABAP job step.

- **Select**. Selects jobs according to various criteria.

- **StartAsSoonAsPossible**. Starts a job as soon as possible.

- **StartImmediately**. Starts a job immediately.

User

- ◆ **ActgroupsAssign**. Changes the entire activity group assignment.
- ◆ **ActgroupsDelete**. Deletes the entire activity group assignment.
- ◆ **Change**. Changes the user.
- ◆ **Clone**. Creates a user clone using templates from another system.
- ◆ **Create**. Creates a user.
- ◆ **Delete**. Deletes a user.
- ◆ **Display**. Displays an object.
- ◆ **GetDetail.** Reads the user detail data.
- ◆ **Lock**. Locks the user.
- ◆ **ProfilesAssign**. Assigns profiles.
- ◆ **ProfilesDelete**. Deletes all profile assignments.
- ◆ **Unlock**. Unlocks the user.

UserCompany

The Clone BAPI clones the user company.

Financial Accounting

Following is a list of the financial accounting BAPIs.

APAccount

- ◆ **GetBalancedItems**. Lists the clearing transactions carried out for a vendor account in a given period.
- ◆ **GetCurrentBalance**. Displays a vendor's balance for the current fiscal year.
- ◆ **GetKeyDateBalance**. Displays a vendor's total balance on a given key date.
- ◆ **GetOpenItems**. Lists a vendor's open items at a given key date.
- ◆ **GetPeriodBalances**. Displays a vendor's current balance for the current fiscal year, along with the transactions and purchases per period.
- ◆ **GetStatement**. Lists the postings made to a vendor account in a given period.

ARAccount

◆ **GetBalancedItems**. Lists the clearing transactions carried out for a customer account in a given period.

◆ **GetCurrentBalance**. Provides a customer's balance for the current fiscal year.

◆ **GetKeyDateBalance**. Supplies a customer's total balance at a given key date.

◆ **GetOpenItems**. Lists a customer's open items at a given key date.

◆ **GetPeriodBalances**. Lists a customer's current balance for the current fiscal year, together with the transactions and sales per period.

◆ **GetStatement**. Lists the postings made to a customer's account in a given period.

AcctngActivityAlloc

◆ **Check**. Checks an activity allocation document.

◆ **Post**. Posts the entered activity allocation document.

AcctngBilling

◆ **Check**. Ascertains whether a billing document can be posted in accounting.

◆ **Post**. Posts the billing document in accounting.

AcctngEmplyeeExpnses

◆ **Check**. Checks whether results from human resources payroll and trip costs accounting can be posted in accounting.

◆ **Post**. Posts in accounting results from payroll and trip costs accounting.

AcctngEmplyeePaybles

◆ **Check**. Checks whether results from payroll and trip costs accounting from human resources can be posted in accounting.

◆ **Post**. Posts the results from payroll accounting and trip costs accounting in human resources to accounting.

AcctngEmplyeeRcvbles

- ◆ **Check**. Checks receivable postings resulting from payroll accounting.
- ◆ **Post**. Posts receivable postings resulting from payroll accounting.

AcctngGLPosting

- ◆ **Check**. Verifies general ledger postings.
- ◆ **Post**. Posts a transaction to the general ledger account.

AcctngGoodsMovement

- ◆ **Check**. Checks whether the material posting can be made in accounting.
- ◆ **Post**. Carries out the material posting in accounting.

AcctngInvoiceReceipt

- ◆ **Check**. Checks whether an invoice receipt can be posted in accounting.
- ◆ **Post**. Posts the invoice receipt in accounting.

AcctngPurchaseOrder

- ◆ **Check**. Checks whether the data from a purchase order (relevant to accounting) can be posted.
- ◆ **Post**. Posts data from a purchase order to accounting.

AcctngPurchaseReq

- ◆ **Check**. Checks whether the data from a purchase requisition can be posted.
- ◆ **Post**. Posts the purchase order requisition data to accounting.

AcctngRepostRevenues

- ◆ **Check**. Checks a document with revenues.
- ◆ **Post**. Posts a document with revenues.

AcctngRepstPrimCosts

◆ **Check**. Checks a document with primary costs.

◆ **Post**. Posts a document with primary costs.

AcctngSalesOrder

◆ **Check**. Checks a sales order.

◆ **Post**. Posts a sales order.

AcctngSalesQuotation

◆ **Check**. Checks a customer quotation.

◆ **Post**. Posts a customer quotation.

AcctngSenderActivity

◆ **Check**. Checks a document with sender activities.

◆ **Post**. Posts a document with sender activities.

AcctngServices

◆ **CheckAccountAssignment**. Validates characteristics from the coding block in posting transactions in human resources and logistics.

◆ **PreCheckPayrollAccountAssign**. Checks account assignments at different levels of detail.

AcctngStatKeyFigures

◆ **Check**. Checks a document with statistical key figures.

◆ **Post**. Posts a document with statistical key figures.

AcctngTravelExpenses

◆ **Check**. Checks trip expenses.

◆ **Post**. Posts trip expenses.

ActivityType

◆ **GetList**. Lists all activity types by selection requirements.

◆ **GetPrices**. Lists activity type prices for a key date.

AssetAcquisition

◆ **Check**. Checks asset acquisition.

◆ **Post**. Posts asset acquisition.

AssetPostCapitaliztn

◆ **Check**. Simulates a postcapitalization in asset accounting.

◆ **Post**. Posts a postcapitalization in asset accounting.

AssetRetirement

◆ **Check**. Checks asset retirement.

◆ **Post**. Posts asset retirement.

BusProcStructureCO

◆ **Create**. Creates fixed process structures for CO (*Controlling*) business processes.

BusinessArea

◆ **ExistenceCheck**. Checks whether an object exists.

◆ **GetDetail**. Gets business area details.

◆ **GetList**. Gets a business area list.

BusinessProcessCO

◆ **CreateMultiple**. Creates one or more business processes.

◆ **GetDetail**. Details information for a business process on a given date.

◆ **GetList**. Determines a list of business processes using selection criteria.

◆ **SetStructure**. Enters a process template in business process master data.

Company

- ◆ **ExistenceCheck**. Checks the existence of an object.
- ◆ **GetDetail**. Obtains detailed entries for a company.
- ◆ **GetList**. Gets a list of companies.

CompanyCode

- ◆ **ExistenceCheck**. Checks whether an object exists.
- ◆ **GetDetail**. Obtains company code details.
- ◆ **GetList**. Gets a list of company codes.
- ◆ **GetPeriod**. Returns a corresponding fiscal year and posting period.

ControllingArea

- ◆ **Find**. Derives a controlling area from the company code.
- ◆ **GetDetail**. Retrieves details about the controlling area.
- ◆ **GetList**. Reads a cost accounting area.
- ◆ **GetPeriod**. For a controlling area, returns both the fiscal period and fiscal year for a specific posting date.
- ◆ **GetPeriodLimits**. For a controlling area, returns the first and last day of a period.
- ◆ **GetRelatedCompCodes**. Determines the company codes assigned to one controlling area.

ControllingDocument

The FindDetails BAPI reads CO (Controlling) documents: manual actual postings.

CostActivityPlanning

- ◆ **CheckActivityInput**. Checks activity input.
- ◆ **CheckActivityOutput**. Checks activity output, including quantities and prices.
- ◆ **PostActivityInput**. Posts activity input.

◆ **PostActivityOutput**. Posts activity output, including quantities and prices.

CostCenter

◆ **GetActivityPrices**. Reads prices for cost center/activity type.

◆ **GetActivityQuantities**. Reads plan activity.

◆ **GetActivityTypes**. Lists cost centers/activity types.

◆ **GetDetail**. Provides detailed information about a cost center for a key date.

◆ **GetList**. Lists all cost centers, according to selection criteria.

CostEstimate

◆ **GetDetail**. Determines detailed information for a cost estimate.

◆ **GetExplosion**. Determines quantity structure for a cost estimate.

◆ **GetItemization**. Determines itemization for a cost estimate.

◆ **GetList**. Determines cost estimate lists.

CostObject

◆ **GetDetail**. Determines details for a general cost object.

◆ **GetList**. Determines general cost objects for a controlling area.

CostObjectNode

◆ **GetDetail**. Determines details for a cost object node.

◆ **GetHierarchy**. Determines cost object hierarchy.

◆ **GetList**. Determines a cost object node in a controlling area.

CostType

◆ **GetFixAccount**. Reads the fixed account assignment for a company code, business area, or cost element.

◆ **GetFixAccountList**. Reads fixed account assignments (from TKA30).

Creditor

- **ChangePassword**. Enables the user to change a vendor password.
- **CheckPassword**. Enables a password for a vendor to be checked.
- **CreatePasswordRegistry**. Creates an entry for a vendor in password management.
- **DeletePasswordRegistry**. Deletes an entry for a vendor in password management.
- **ExistenceCheck**. Checks on the existence of a vendor.
- **Find**. Finds vendors matching a query.
- **GetDetail**. Calls up a vendor's detailed data.
- **GetPasswordRegistry**. Reads status information concerning password management for a vendor.
- **InitPassword**. Initializes a vendor password.

Customer

- **ChangeFromData1**. Changes a customer data record.
- **CreateFromData1**. Creates a customer data record.
- **GetContactList**. Retrieves a list of customer contact persons.
- **GetDetail1**. Provides customer details.
- **GetInternalNumber**. Provides internal customer numbers.
- **GetList**. Retrieves a list of addresses.
- **Search1**. Searches for a customer data record.

Debtor

- **ChangePassword**. Changes a customer's password.
- **CheckPassword**. Checks a customer's password.
- **CreatePasswordRegistry**. Creates a customer entry in password management.
- **DeletePasswordRegistry**. Deletes a customer's entry in password management.
- **ExistenceCheck**. Checks on the existence of a customer.
- **Find**. Finds customers matching a query.

- **GetDetail**. Calls up detailed information about a customer.
- **GetPasswordRegistry**. Reads status information relating to password management for a customer.
- **InitPassword**. Initializes a customer's password.

FunctionalArea

- **ExistenceCheck**. Verifies whether a functional area exists.
- **GetDetail**. Retrieves details about a functional area.
- **GetList**. Lists functional areas.

DebtorCreditAccount

- **GetDetail**. Returns data from the master record of a customer account in a credit control area.
- **GetHighestDunningLevel**. Returns data for the highest dunning level of a credit account in a credit control area.
- **GetOldestOpenItem**. Returns data on the oldest open item in a credit account.
- **GetOpenItemsStructure**. Returns data on the open item structure of a credit account.
- **GetStatus**. Returns accounts receivable summary data.

EmployeeTrip

- **Approve**. Approves an individual employee trip.
- **Cancel**. Cancels an individual employee trip.
- **CollectMileage**. Returns the miles or kilometers traveled by an employee within a time interval.
- **CreateFromData**. Creates employee trips from data.
- **CreateFromDataWeekly**. Creates simplified weekly reports for trip costs recording.
- **Delete**. Deletes individual employee trips.
- **ExistenceCheck**. Checks for the existence of a trip.
- **GetDetails**. Returns detailed data about an employee trip.

◆ **GetDetailsWeekly**. Returns detailed data belonging to a trip costs weekly report.

◆ **GetExpenseForm**. Returns a standard form for trip costs accounting.

◆ **GetExpenseForm**. Returns an HTML standard form for trip costs accounting as HTML tables.

◆ **GetList**. Returns a list of trips for an employee.

◆ **GetOptions**. Lists all tables and parameters that could be required to create a trip.

◆ **GetOptionsWeekly**. Lists all tables and default values needed to create a simple weekly report.

◆ **GetStatus**. Establishes the status of a trip.

◆ **SetOnHold**. Sets trip to wait status.

FinancialProduct

◆ **Change**. Changes security.

◆ **CreateFromData**. Creates security.

◆ **GetDetail**. Reads security detailed data.

◆ **GetList**. Reads a security list.

FinancialTransaction

◆ **Change**. Changes a transaction.

◆ **CreateFromData**. Creates a transaction.

◆ **GetDetail**. Displays transactions.

◆ **GetList**. Retrieves a list of transactions.

FixedAsset

◆ **Change**. Changes an asset.

◆ **CreateFromData**. Creates an asset.

◆ **GetDetail**. Details information for an asset.

◆ **GetList**. Returns information on selected assets.

GeneralLedger

- **GetDocumentItems**. Determines document items in a general ledger.
- **GetGLAccountBalance**. Provides the closing balance of a general ledger account for a chosen year.
- **GetGLAccountCurrentBalance**. Returns the closing balance of a general ledger account for the current year.
- **GetGLAccountPeriodBalances**. Posts period balances for each general ledger account.

GeneralLedgerAccount

- **ExistenceCheck**. Checks for the existence of an object.
- **GetBalance**. Returns the final balance for a general ledger account for a specified fiscal year.
- **GetCurrentBalance**. Returns the closing balance for a general ledger account for the current fiscal year.
- **GetDetail**. Provides further information about a general ledger account.
- **GetList**. Provides a list of general ledger accounts for a company code.
- **GetPeriodBalances**. Returns the general ledger account balances per posting period for a given fiscal year.

InternalOrder

- **Create**. Creates an internal order from transferred data.
- **GetDetail**. Delivers master data, statuses, and allowed transactions for internal orders.
- **GetList**. Delivers lists of internal orders according to various criteria.

InvestmentProgram

- **ExistenceCheck**. Checks for the existence of the investment program.
- **GetLeaves**. Outputs end nodes of the investment program.
- **GetRequestsAndLeaves**. Outputs appropriation requests and end nodes of the investment program.
- **SaveEntityReplicas**. Saves assigned entities in a summarization database.

♦ **SaveValueReplicas**. Saves summarized values in a summarization database.

OpenInfoWarehouse

♦ **GetCatalog**. Gets the OpenInfoWarehouse catalog.

♦ **GetData**. Executes the OpenInfoWarehouse query.

ProfitCenter

♦ **GetDetail**. EC-PCA (*Profit Center Accounting*): Returns detail information about a profit center.

♦ **GetList**. EC-PCA: Returns a list of profit centers meeting a given selection criteria.

ProfitCenterDocument

♦ **Delete**. Deletes profit center documents.

♦ **PlanSaveReplica**. Saves a copy of a document.

♦ **Reverse**. Reverses existing document line items.

♦ **SaveReplica**. Replicates PCA line items.

♦ **SaveReplicaPlanData**. Replicates profit center plan documents.

ResourceCO

The SaveReplica BAPI replicates individual CO resources.

Vendor

The GetInternalNumber BAPI supplies new internal vendor numbers.

Human Resources

Following is a listing of human resources BAPIs.

Applicant

♦ **ChangePassword**. Changes a password.

♦ **CheckPassword**. Checks a password.

- ◆ **CreateFromData**. Creates an applicant record.
- ◆ **CreatePassword**. Creates a password.
- ◆ **DeletePassword**. Deletes a password.
- ◆ **ExistenceCheck**. Performs an existence check.
- ◆ **GetPassword**. Retrieves a password.
- ◆ **GetStatus**. Retrieves the status of an applicant.
- ◆ **InitPassword**. Initializes a password to a given value.

Attendee

- ◆ **ChangePassword**. Changes an attendee's password.
- ◆ **CheckExistence**. Checks the existence of an attendee.
- ◆ **CheckPassword**. Checks an attendee's password.
- ◆ **GetBookList**. Retrieves attendee bookings.
- ◆ **GetCompanyBookList**. Retrieves bookings of a group attendee.
- ◆ **GetCompanyPrebookList**. Retrieves a group attendee's prebookings.
- ◆ **GetPrebookList**. Lists attendee prebookings.
- ◆ **GetTypeList**. Lists Internet attendee types.

BusinessEvent

- ◆ **GetInfo**. Retrieves business event information.
- ◆ **GetLanguage**. Returns business event languages.
- ◆ **GetSchedule**. Retrieves the time schedule of a business event.
- ◆ **Init**. Returns default values for standard parameters.

BusinessEventGroup

- ◆ **GetEventTypeList**. Lists business event types in a business event group.
- ◆ **GetList**. Reads the business event group hierarchy.

BusinessEventType

- ◆ **GetEventList**. Returns dates of business event type.
- ◆ **GetInfo**. Retrieves information on business event type.

◆ **GetListFromQualification**. Returns business event types for a specified qualification.

◆ **GetListFromTarget**. Retrieves business event types for a specified target group.

◆ **GetListFromName**. Returns business event types for specified object text.

◆ **GetListFromDescription**. Retrieves business event types for a specified description.

◆ **SubtypesForDescription**. Returns subobjects of Description infotype.

EmpBenefitHealthPlan

◆ **GetDependents**. Returns a list of the dependents an employee has included in benefit plan enrollments.

◆ **GetPossDependents**. Returns a list of the dependents an employee may include in health plan enrollments.

EmpBenefitInsurePlan

◆ **GetBeneficiaries**. Returns a list of the beneficiaries an employee has included in benefit plan enrollments.

◆ **GetPossBeneficiaries**. Returns a list of the beneficiaries an employee may include in benefit plan enrollments.

EmpBenefitMiscelPlan

◆ **GetBeneficiaries**. Lists the beneficiaries an employee has included in benefit plan enrollments.

◆ **GetDependents**. Lists the dependents an employee has included in benefit plan enrollments.

◆ **GetInvestments**. Lists the investments an employee has selected in benefit plan enrollments.

◆ **GetPossBeneficiaries**. Lists the beneficiaries an employee may include in miscellaneous plan enrollments.

◆ **GetPossDependents**. Lists the dependents an employee may include in miscellaneous plan enrollments.

◆ **GetPossInvestments**. Lists the investments an employee may select in miscellaneous plan enrollments.

EmpBenefitSavingPlan

◆ **GetBeneficiaries**. Returns beneficiaries for savings plans.

◆ **GetInvestments**. Returns investments for savings plans.

◆ **GetPossBeneficiaries**. Returns possible beneficiaries for savings plans.

◆ **GetPossInvestments**. Returns possible investments for savings plans.

EmpBenefitStockpPlan

◆ **GetBeneficiaries**. Lists beneficiaries for stock purchase plans.

◆ **GetPossBeneficiaries**. Lists possible beneficiaries for stock purchase plans.

Employee

◆ **ChangePassword**. Changes an employee's password.

◆ **CheckPassword**. Checks an employee's password.

◆ **CreatePassword**. Creates a password entry.

◆ **DeletePassword**. Deletes a password entry.

◆ **Dequeue**. Unlocks an employee.

◆ **Enqueue**. Locks an employee.

◆ **GetList**. Returns a list of employees matching a query.

◆ **GetPassword**. Reads a password entry.

◆ **InitPassword**. Initializes a password entry.

EmployeeAbsence

◆ **Approve**. Unlocks an Absences infotype record.

◆ **Change**. Changes an Absences infotype record.

◆ **Create**. Creates an Absences infotype record.

◆ **Delete**. Deletes an Absences infotype record.

◆ **GetDetail**. Reads an Absences infotype record.

- **GetList**. Retrieves a list of Absences infotype records.
- **GetDetailedList**. Reads instances with data.
- **Request**. Creates a locked absence.
- **SimulateCreation**. Simulates the creation of an Absences infotype record.

EmployeeAbstract

- **ChangePassword**. Changes a password.
- **CheckPassword**. Checks a password.
- **CreatePassword**. Creates a password.
- **DeletePassword**. Deletes a password.
- **Dequeue**. Unlocks employees.
- **Enqueue**. Locks employees.
- **ExistenceCheck**. Checks whether a personnel number exists.
- **GetList**. Finds personnel numbers for specified search criteria.
- **GetPassword**. Gets a password.
- **InitPassword**. Retrieves an initial password.

EmployeeAttAbs

- **GetDetail**. Retrieves original derived absence/attendance data.
- **GetList**. Returns a list of existing absences/attendances according to selection criteria.

EmployeeBankDetail

- **Approve**. Unlocks a Bank Details record that was created via the Request method.
- **Change**. Changes a Bank Details record.
- **Create**. Creates a Bank Details record.
- **CreateSuccessor**. Creates a subsequent Bank Details record.
- **Delete**. Deletes a Bank Details record.
- **GetDetail**. Reads a Bank Details record.

- **GetList**. Returns a Bank Details record matching certain criteria.
- **GetDetailedList**. Reads instances with data.
- **Request**. Creates a locked Bank Details record.
- **SimulateCreation**. Simulates the creation of a Bank Details record.

EmployeeBasicpay

- **Approve**. Unlocks a Basic Pay record that was created via the Request method.
- **Change**. Changes a Basic Pay record.
- **Create**. Creates a Basic Pay record.
- **CreateSuccessor**. Creates a subsequent Basic Pay record.
- **Delete**. Deletes a Basic Pay record.
- **GetDetail**. Reads a Basic Pay record.
- **GetList**. Returns a Basic Pay record matching certain criteria.
- **Request**. Creates a locked Basic Pay record.
- **SimulateCreation**. Simulates the creation of a Basic Pay record.

EmployeeBenAdjReason

The GetList BAPI defines adjustment reasons that are currently valid for an employee.

EmployeeBenefit

- **CheckSelection**. Performs a consistency check with company rules.
- **CreateOffer**. Defines a benefits offer.
- **CreatePlans**. Writes the employee's elections to the database.
- **DeletePlans**. Deletes a plan for a specified period.
- **GetCorequisitePlans**. Delivers corequisite plans.
- **GetParticipation**. Returns details of an employee's enrollments.

EmployeeDateSpecific

The GetDetailedList BAPI reads instances with data.

EmployeeFamilyMember

- **Approve**. Unlocks a Family/Related Person record that was created via the Request method.
- **Change**. Changes a Family/Related Person record.
- **Create**. Creates a Family/Related Person record.
- **CreateSuccessor**. Creates a subsequent Family/Related Person record.
- **Delete**. Deletes a Family/Related Person record.
- **GetDetail**. Reads a Family/Related Person record.
- **GetList**. Returns a Family/Related Person record matching certain criteria.
- **GetDetailedList**. Reads instances with data.
- **Request**. Creates a locked Family/Related Person record.
- **SimulateCreation**. Simulates the creation of a Family/Related Person record.

EmployeeFamMemberUs

- **Approve**. Unlocks a family.
- **Change**. Changes a family.
- **Create**. Creates a family.
- **Delete**. Deletes a family.
- **GetDetail**. Displays a family.
- **GetDetailedList**. Reads instances with data.
- **GetList**. Reads instances.
- **Request**. Creates a locked family.
- **SimulateCreation**. Simulates the creation of a family.

EmployeeFiscalDataCA

- **GetDetailedList**. Reads instances with data.

EmployeeGenBenInfo

- **GetOpenEnrollmentPeriod**. Checks whether an open enrollment period exists and whether the period is indicated.

EmployeeIntControl

◆ **Approve**. Unlocks an Internal Control record that was created by the Request method.

◆ **Change**. Changes an Internal Control record.

◆ **Create**. Creates an Internal Control record.

◆ **CreateSuccessor**. Creates a subsequent Internal Control record.

◆ **Delete**. Deletes an Internal Control record.

◆ **GetDetail**. Reads an Internal Control record.

◆ **GetList**. Returns an Internal Control record matching criteria.

◆ **Request**. Creates a locked Internal Control record.

◆ **SimulateCreation**. Simulates the creation of an Internal Control record.

EmployeePersonalData

◆ **Change**. Changes a Personal Data record.

◆ **Create**. Creates a Personal Data record.

◆ **CreateSuccessor**. Creates a subsequent Personal Data record.

◆ **Delete**. Deletes a Personal Data record.

◆ **GetDetail**. Reads a Personal Data record.

◆ **GetList**. Returns a Personal Data record matching criteria.

◆ **GetDetailedList**. Reads instances with data.

◆ **SimulateCreation**. Simulates the creation of a Personal Data record.

EmployeePayrollAcc

◆ **GetDetail**. Returns a remuneration statement for one personnel number.

◆ **GetDetailHtml**. Retrieves a payroll form for employees, in HTML format.

◆ **GetResultList**. Returns a directory of payroll results for one personnel number.

EmployeePrivAddress

◆ **Approve**. Unlocks an Addresses record that was created by the Request method.

- ◆ **Change**. Changes an Addresses record.
- ◆ **Create**. Creates an Addresses record.
- ◆ **CreateSuccessor**. Creates a subsequent Addresses record.
- ◆ **Delete**. Deletes an Addresses record.
- ◆ **GetDetail**. Reads an Addresses record.
- ◆ **GetDetailedList**. Returns an Addresses record matching criteria.
- ◆ **GetList**. Reads instances with data.
- ◆ **Request**. Creates a locked Addresses record.
- ◆ **SimulateCreation**. Simulates the creation of an Addresses record.

EmployeePrivateAdrUS

- ◆ **Change**. Changes an employee's address.
- ◆ **Create**. Creates an address.
- ◆ **CreateSuccessor**. Creates a subsequent employee address.
- ◆ **GetDetail**. Reads an employee address.
- ◆ **GetDetailedList**. Reads instances with data.
- ◆ **Request**. Creates a locked employee address.
- ◆ **SimulateCreation**. Simulates the creation of an employee address.

EmployeeTimeQuota

The GetDetailedList BAPI determines the quota data for a personnel number.

EmployeeTimeValSpec

- ◆ **Check**. Checks different payments.
- ◆ **CheckBonus**. Checks a bonus.
- ◆ **CheckCurrency**. Checks currency.
- ◆ **CheckPosition**. Checks an item.
- ◆ **CheckWageGroupLevel**. Checks a pay scale/level.
- ◆ **GetCurrency**. Determines a currency.

EmployeeUser

The GetEmployee BAPI determines an employee from an SAP user.

EmployeeW4W5InfoUS

- ◆ **Approve**. Unlocks an employee W4/W5 information record.
- ◆ **Change**. Changes an employee W4/W5 information record.
- ◆ **Create**. Creates an employee W4/W5 information record.
- ◆ **Delete**. Deletes an employee W4/W5 information record.
- ◆ **GetDetail**. Reads an employee W4/W5 information record.
- ◆ **GetDetailedList**. Reads employee W4/W5 details of information instances.
- ◆ **GetList**. Reads employee W4/W5 information instances.
- ◆ **Request**. Creates a locked employee W4/W5 information record.
- ◆ **SimulateCreation**. Simulates the creation of a W4/W5 information record.

JobRequirement

The GetList BAPI reads a requirement profile.

Location

The GetListAll BAPI lists business event locations.

PayrollAccDocument

- ◆ **Display_Acc**. Displays a document (from AC).
- ◆ **GetList**. Reads a requirement profile.

PTimeOverview

- ◆ **SaveReplica**. Distributes an employee's time overview.
- ◆ **Get**. Determines an employee's time overview.
- ◆ **Replicate**. Triggers the distribution of an employee's time overview.
- ◆ **DeleteReplica**. Deletes the distribution of an employee's time overview.

PTManagerAttAbsence

- ◆ **ManageChange**. Starts and controls the Change att./absences process.
- ◆ **ManageCreation**. Starts and controls the Create att./absences process.
- ◆ **ManageDelete**. Starts and controls the Delete att./absences process.

PTManagerExtAttAbs

- ◆ **Check**. Checks attendance/absence without account assignment.
- ◆ **CheckCollision**. Checks collision.
- ◆ **CheckQuota**. Checks a quota deduction.
- ◆ **CheckWithActivityAllocation**. Checks attendance/absence with activity allocation.
- ◆ **CheckWithCostAssignment**. Checks attendance/absence with cost allocation.
- ◆ **Insert**. Inserts attendance/absence without account assignment.
- ◆ **InsertWithActivityAllocation**. Inserts attendance/absence with activity allocation.
- ◆ **GetDetailedList**. Reads the details of objects.

PTManagerExtPEvent

The Insert BAPI uploads time events.

PTMgrExtPExpenses

The Insert BAPI uploads employee expenditures.

PTManagerExtTimeSpec

- ◆ **Display**. Displays external data in infotype.
- ◆ **GetStatus**. Defines the status of a record in an interface table.

PTManagerExtRemunSpec

- ◆ **Check**. Checks external remuneration information (without account assignment).

- ◆ **CheckWithActivityAllocation.** Checks external remuneration information (with activity allocation).
- ◆ **CheckWithCostAsignment.** Checks external remuneration information (with cost allocation).
- ◆ **Insert.** Inserts external remuneration information in a table (without account assignment).
- ◆ **InsertWithActivityAllocation.** Inserts remuneration information in a table (with activity allocation).
- ◆ **InsertWithCostAsignment.** Inserts external remuneration information in a table (with cost assignment).

Qualification

The GetList BAPI reads a qualifications profile.

QualificationType

- ◆ **GetDetail.** Reads detailed information.
- ◆ **GetList.** Returns a list of qualifications that meet given selection criteria.

TimeAvailSchedule

The Build BAPI determines employees' availability.

TimeMgtConfirmation

The Post BAPI transfers confirmations from logistics to human resources.

WorkflowObject

- ◆ **BapiPrebookAttendance.** Prebooks attendance.
- ◆ **DeleteAttendance.** Deletes attendance.
- ◆ **BookAttendance.** Books attendance.

Logistics

Following is a listing of logistics BAPIs.

Batch

- ◆ **Change**. Changes a batch.
- ◆ **Create**. Creates a batch.
- ◆ **GetDetail**. Batches detailed information.
- ◆ **GetLevel**. Determines batch level.
- ◆ **Replicate**. Distributes a batch.
- ◆ **SaveReplica**. Replicates a batch.

ControlRecipe

- ◆ **GetList**. Reads control recipe lists.
- ◆ **Request**. Requests and transfers a control recipe.

CustomerInquiry

- ◆ **Change**. Changes a customer inquiry.
- ◆ **CreateFromData**. Creates a customer inquiry.
- ◆ **CreateFromData2**. Creates a customer inquiry.

CustomerQuotation

- ◆ **Change**. Changes a customer quotation.
- ◆ **CreateFromData**. Creates a customer quotation.
- ◆ **CreateFromData2**. Creates a customer quotation.

DangerousGood

- ◆ **Replicate**. Requests dangerous–goods instances.
- ◆ **SaveReplicaMultiple**. Saves replicated dangerous goods instances.

GoodsMovement

- ◆ **CreateFromData**. Creates a BAPI posting of goods movements with MB_CREATE_GOODS_MOVEMENT.
- ◆ **GetItems**. Lists goods movement items plus header data.
- ◆ **Cancel**. Reverses goods movement.
- ◆ **GetDetail**. Displays details of goods movement.

InboundDelivery

◆ **ConfirmDecentral**. Verifies replaced inbound deliveries from a decentralized system.

◆ **SaveReplica**. Duplicates inbound deliveries.

ItCustBillingDoc

◆ **CreateFromData**. Creates a customer billing document using an external document.

◆ **Simulate**. Simulates a customer billing without posting data.

◆ **IsCancelled**. Determines whether the billing document has been canceled.

◆ **CancelFromData**. Cancels a specific customer billing document.

Kanban

◆ **GetListForSupplie1**. Provides Kanban (production and material flow) data for vendors.

◆ **GetListForSupplier**. Provides Kanban data for vendors.

◆ **SetInProcess**. Sets status to In Process.

MatAllocationTable

◆ **GetDetailedList**. Creates a list of allocated tables and items for a store.

◆ **ConfirmRequest**. Reports requested quantities for items and delivery phases.

Material

◆ **Availability**. Provides ATP (*Available to Promise*) information.

◆ **ExistenceCheck**. Checks the existence of an object.

◆ **GetBatchCertificate**. Retrieves a quality certificate for a batch in PDF (*Portable Document Format*) format.

◆ **GetBatches**. Returns batches for material.

◆ **GetDetail**. Determines detailed data about material.

◆ **GetInternalNumber**. Retrieves the internal number of a material.

◆ **GetList**. Retrieves a list of materials.

MaterialPhysInv

◆ **ChangeCount**. Changes the count for particular items of a physical inventory document.

◆ **Count**. Enters the count for particular items of a physical inventory document.

◆ **Create**. Creates a physical inventory document.

◆ **GetDetail**. Reads the header and items of a physical inventory document.

◆ **GetItems**. Lists physical inventory documents with headers and items.

◆ **GetList**. Lists physical inventory document header records.

◆ **PostDifferences**. Posts differences.

MaterialReservation

◆ **CreateFromData**. Creates a reservation.

◆ **GetDetail**. Gets detail for material reservation.

◆ **GetItems**. Lists reservations.

Network

◆ **ExistenceCheck**. Checks the existence of an object.

◆ **GetDetail**. Reads detailed information for a network (including all objects).

◆ **GetInfo**. Reads detailed information about networks (including all objects).

◆ **Maintain**. Edits networks (including all objects).

OutboundDelivery

◆ **ConfirmDecentral**. Delivers confirmation from a decentralized system.

◆ **SaveReplica**. Replicates deliveries.

PaymentCardServices

- **Check**. Validates a credit card.
- **CheckNumber**. Verifies a credit card number.

PieceOfEquipment

- **CreateFromData**. Creates equipment.
- **DismantleAtFuncloc**. Dismantles equipment at a functional location.
- **DismantleFromHierarchy**. Dismantles from the equipment hierarchy.
- **GetCatalogProfile**. Determines the catalog profile for equipment.
- **GetDetail**. Reads equipment details.
- **GetListForCustomer**. Lists all equipment for a customer.
- **InstallAtFuncloc**. Installs equipment at a functional location.
- **InstallInHierarchy**. Installs equipment in an equipment hierarchy.
- **Update**. Changes equipment.

PlannedIndepReqmt

- **Change**. Changes planned independent requirements.
- **CreateFromData**. Creates independent requirements.
- **GetDetail**. Gets details on independent requirements.

PlannedOrder

- **Change**. Changes PlannedOrder.
- **Create**. Creates PlannedOrder.
- **Delete**. Deletes PlannedOrder.
- **ExistenceCheck**. Checks the existence of a PlannedOrder.
- **GetDetail**. Gets header, components, and capacity data of a PlannedOrder.
- **GetDetailedList**. Gets details about a PlannedOrder.

ProcessCharactrstcPI

- **GetHelpValues**. Gets allowed values for a process characteristic.
- **GetList**. Gets a list of process characteristics.

ProcessMessagePI

◆ **Create**. Creates a processing message.

◆ **ExistenceCheck**. Checks process message existence.

ProdOrdConfirmation

◆ **Cancel**. Cancels production order confirmation.

◆ **CreateActConfMultiple**. Enters activity confirmation.

◆ **CreateAtHeaderLevelMultiple**. Enters order confirmation.

◆ **CreateTimeEventMultiple**. Enters time event confirmation.

◆ **CreateTimeTicketMultiple**. Enters time ticket confirmation.

◆ **ExistenceCheck**. Checks the existence of an object.

◆ **GetAtHeaderLevelProposal**. Recommends data for order confirmation.

◆ **GetDetail**. Provides detailed data for production order confirmation.

◆ **GetList**. Retrieves confirmation lists.

◆ **GetTimeEventProposal**. Recommends data for time event confirmation.

◆ **GetTimeTicketProposal**. Recommends data for time ticket confirmation.

ProcurementOperation

◆ **GetCatalogs**. Lists the allowed catalogs.

◆ **GetInfo**. Provides information on objects that are to be generated for purchasing.

ProductCatalog

◆ **GetDetail**. Reads header data.

◆ **GetItem**. Reads an individual product catalog item.

◆ **GetItems**. Reads items.

◆ **GetLayout**. Reads layout.

◆ **GetLayoutDescription**. Reads text for layout area/products/gif area items.

◆ **GetLayoutDocuments**. Reads documents for layout area/layout area items.

◆ **GetList**. Reads a catalog list.

◆ **GetPrices**. Reads prices.

◆ **GetSalesArea**. Reads a sales area.

◆ **GetVariants**. Reads variants.

ProjectDefinition

◆ **CreateFromData**. Creates a project definition.

◆ **ExistenceCheck**. Checks the existence of an object.

◆ **GetDetail**. Reads the details about a project definition.

◆ **Update**. Changes a project definition.

PurchaseOrder

◆ **CreateFromData**. Creates a new purchase order.

◆ **GetDetail**. Gets detail on a purchase order.

◆ **GetItems**. Gets items from a purchase order.

◆ **GetItemsForRelease**. Lists items that are released.

◆ **GetList**. Gets purchase orders.

◆ **GetReleaseInfo**. Gets release information.

◆ **Release**. Releases a purchase order.

◆ **ResetRelease**. Resets the release of a purchase order.

PurchaseReqItem

◆ **CreateFromData**. Creates a requirement coverage request.

◆ **GetList**. Reads a requirement coverage request.

◆ **Release**. Releases a purchase requisition.

◆ **ResetRelease**. Cancels the release of purchase requisitions.

◆ **SingleReleaseNoDialg**. Releases a purchase requisition.

PurchaseRequisition

◆ **Change**. Changes a purchase requisition.

◆ **CreateFromData**. Creates a new purchase requisition.

◆ **Delete**. Deletes a purchase requisition.

◆ **GetDetail**. Gets details of a purchase requisition.

◆ **GetItems**. Lists items on a purchase requisition.

◆ **GetItemsForRelease**. Gets items available for release.

◆ **GetReleaseInfo**. Gets release information for a requisition.

◆ **Release**. Releases a purchase requisition.

◆ **ResetRelease**. Cancels the release of a purchase requisition.

PurchasingInfo

The GetList BAPI gets a list of purchasing information records.

QualityNotification

◆ **CreateFromData**. Creates a quality notification.

◆ **GetCatalogProfile**. Determines a catalog profile.

◆ **GetKeyFigures**. Determines related quality notifications.

◆ **GetListForCustomer**. Selects quality notifications for a customer.

◆ **GetMaterialListFCust**. Gets a materials list for a customer.

RetailMaterial

◆ **Availability**. Reports on availability of retail material.

◆ **Clone**. Creates and changes a new retail material.

◆ **ExistenceCheck**. Checks on the existence of a retail material.

◆ **GetBatchCertificate**. Gets quality certification.

◆ **GetBatch**. Gets a list of batches for a material.

◆ **GetCharacsMerchandiseHierachy**. Gets characteristics.

◆ **GetComponents**. Gets the components of a material.

◆ **GetDetail**. Gets detail information on retail material.

◆ **GetInternalNumber**. Gets the internal number of the material.

◆ **GetVariantNumbers**. Gets the variations of the material.

SalesOrder

◆ **ChangeFromData**. Changes an existing sales order.

◆ **CreateFromDat1**. Creates a sales order.

◆ **CreateFromDat2**. Creates a sales order.

◆ **CreateFromData**. Creates a sales order.

◆ **GetList**. Gets sales orders.

◆ **GetStatus**. Gets sales order status.

◆ **Simulate**. Simulates a sales order.

Service

◆ **GetDetail**. Gets details of Service Master records.

◆ **GetList**. Gets a listing of Service Master records.

ServiceEntrySheet

◆ **Create**. Creates an entry sheet.

◆ **Delete**. Deletes an entry sheet.

◆ **GetDetail**. Gets detailed data on an entry sheet.

◆ **GetList**. Gets a list of entry sheets.

◆ **GetReleaseInfo**. Gets release information for an entry sheet.

◆ **Release**. Releases an entry sheet.

◆ **ResetRelease**. Cancels a release on an entry sheet.

ServiceNotification

◆ **CreateFromData**. Creates a service notification.

◆ **GetList**. Selects service notifications according to customer or contact person.

SettlementRequstList

The Create BAPI creates a settlement request list.

SiteLayoutModule

◆ **Change**. Changes items of a layout module.

◆ **GetItem**. Retrieves material data for a layout module.

SingleSettlementReqs

The CreateMultiple BAPI creates multiple settlement requests.

SourceOfSupplyDeterm

The GetSourcesOfSupply BAPI retrieves material/material group.

WorkBreakdownStruct

◆ **GetInfo**. Reads detailed information about a WBS (*Work Breakdown Section*).

◆ **Maintain**. Projects maintenance.

◆ **SaveReplica**. Creates a copy of a WBS.

Basis/CA

Following is a listing of Basis/CA BAPIs.

BackgroundJob

◆ **Abort**. Cancels a job.

◆ **AddABAPStep**. Appends a job step (an APAP program with a variant) to a background job.

◆ **AddExternalStep**. Assigns an external program to a job step.

◆ **CheckStatus**. Reconciles job status (according to the database) with actual status.

◆ **Close**. Completes a job definition.

◆ **CountByName**. Counts how many jobs have a particular name.

◆ **Delete**. Deletes a job in the R/3 system.

◆ **GetDefinition**. Reads a job definition.

◆ **GetStatus**. Gets the status of a job.

◆ **ModifyABABStep**. Assigns an ABAP program to a particular job step.

◆ **ModifyExternalStep**. Assigns an external program to a particular job step.

◆ **Open**. Creates a job.

◆ **ReadJobLog**. Reads the job log.

◆ **ReadSpoollist**. Reads the spool list of ABAP job steps.

◆ **Select**. Selects jobs according to various criteria.

◆ **AsSoonAsPossible**. Starts a job as soon as possible.

◆ **StartImmediately**. Starts a job immediately.

Barcode

The SendList BAPI receives bar code confirmation from an external archive.

BusPartnerEmployee

◆ **ChangePassword**. Changes an existing password.

◆ **CheckPassword**. Verifies a password.

◆ **CreatePassword**. Creates/changes a password.

◆ **DeletePassword**. Deletes a password.

◆ **GetInternalNumber**. Retrieves new internal contact person numbers.

◆ **GetList**. Lists addresses.

◆ **GetPassword**. Gets an entry for a contact person password.

◆ **InitPassword**. Initializes a password.

Document

◆ **Change**. Changes a document.

◆ **CheckIn**. Checks in a document.

◆ **CheckOutModify**. Checks out a document to be modified.

◆ **CheckOutView**. Checks out a document to be viewed.

◆ **CreateFromData**. Creates a document.

◆ **CreateFromSource**. Creates a new document by referencing an existing document.

◆ **CreateNewVersion**. Creates a new version of an existing document.

◆ **Delete**. Deletes a document.

◆ **Dequeue**. Unlocks a document.

◆ **Enqueue**. Locks a document.

◆ **ExistenceCheck1**. Verifies the existence of a document.

◆ **GetActualVersion**. Gets the current version of a document.

◆ **GetApplication**. Gets an application for a document.

◆ **GetDataCarrierDetail**. Gets data carrier details.

◆ **GetDataCarrierList**. Gets a list of all data carriers.

◆ **GetDetail**. Gets details on a document.

◆ **GetDocumentTypeDetail**. Gets details on the document type.

◆ **GetFrontendType**. Gets the appropriate front-end type.

◆ **GetList**. Retrieves a list of all documents.

◆ **GetObjectDocuments**. Gets objects that are linked to a document.

◆ **GetStatus**. Gets the status of a document.

◆ **GetStatusList**. Gets a status list of several documents.

◆ **GetStructure**. Gets the structure associated with documents.

◆ **SetFrontendType**. Sets the front-end type.

◆ **SetStatus**. Sets the status of the document.

Class

◆ **GetCharacteristics**. Reads characteristics allocated to class.

◆ **GetClassifications**. Reads characteristic values assigned to objects in a class.

◆ **SelectObjects**. Finds objects in a class.

Currency

◆ **GetDecimals**. Gets the number of decimals for currency.

◆ **GetList**. Gets a list of several currencies.

ExchangeRate

◆ **Create**. Inserts an entry in a table of exchange rate.

◆ **CreateMultiple**. Inserts one or more exchange rates in SAP tables.

◆ **GetCurrentRates**. Lists exchange rates per exch.rate type and date.

◆ **GetDetail**. Retrieves the exchange rate stored for exch.rate type, currency pair, value, and date.

◆ **GetFactors**. Displays relevant factors for the exchange rate.

◆ **GetListRateTypes**. Lists all exchange rate types used for conversion.

◆ **SaveReplica**. Replicates currency rates.

AddressContPart

◆ **Change**. Changes the address of a person in a company.

◆ **GetDetail**. Gets details on the address.

◆ **SaveReplica**. Saves a copy of the original address.

AddressOrg

◆ **Change**. Changes the address of an organization.

◆ **GetDetail**. Gets details on the address.

◆ **SaveReplica**. Saves a copy of the original address.

AddressPers

◆ **Change**. Changes the address of a person.

◆ **GetDetail**. Gets details on the address.

◆ **SaveReplica**. Saves a copy of the original address.

FlightBooking

◆ **Cancel**. Cancels a booking.

◆ **CreateFromData**. Creates a booking.

◆ **GetDetail**. Lists booking details.

◆ **GetList**. Lists bookings.

FlightConnection

- ◆ **GetDetail**. Lists flight details.
- ◆ **GetList**. Lists flights.

FlightCustomer

- ◆ **ChangePassword**. Changes an Internet password.
- ◆ **CheckPassword**. Checks an Internet password.
- ◆ **CreateFromData**. Generates an Internet password.

HRMasterDataReplica

The SaveReplicaMultiple BAPI replicates human resources master data and human resources organizational data.

OrgMasterDataReplica

The SaveReplicaMultiple BAPI replicates human resources organizational data.

PDobjecttypes

The GetDetailedList BAPI retrieves an object list with detailed information.

SystemMngmtSession

- ◆ **CheckVersion**. Checks whether a particular version of an interface is supported.
- ◆ **DescribeInterface**. Queries the long name of an interface.
- ◆ **EnterLogMsg**. Enters an external message in the XMI log.
- ◆ **GetVersions**. Queries supported versions of XMI interfaces.
- ◆ **Logoff**. Logs off an external management tool.
- ◆ **Logon**. Logs on to an external management tool.
- ◆ **SelectLog**. Selects translated entries in an XMI log.
- ◆ **SetAuditLevel**. Sets the audit level of an XMI session.
- ◆ **UploadMsgFormats**. Transfers external message formats.

SystemServiceInfo

- ◆ **GetBackgroundResourcesOnDate**. Determines all background resources available on a particular date.

- ◆ **GetBgrdResourcesOnDateOnServer**. Determines the background resources of a server on a particular date.

- ◆ **GetCurrentBackgroundResources**. Determines the background resources currently available in a system.

User

- ◆ **ActgroupsAssign**. Changes a whole activity group assignment.
- ◆ **ActgroupsDelete**. Deletes a whole activity group assignment.
- ◆ **Change**. Changes a user.
- ◆ **Clone**. Creates a user clone by using templates from another system.
- ◆ **Create**. Creates a user.
- ◆ **Delete**. Deletes a user.
- ◆ **Display**. Displays an object.
- ◆ **GetDetail**. Reads user detail data.
- ◆ **Lock**. Locks a user.
- ◆ **ProfilesAssign**. Assigns profiles.
- ◆ **ProfilesDelete**. Deletes all profile assignments.
- ◆ **Unlock**. Unlocks a user.

UserCompany

The Clone BAPI clones a user company (especially the address).

PART IV

Appendixes

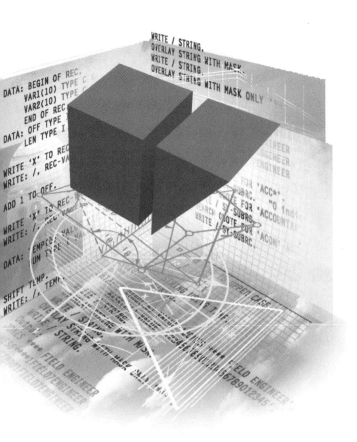

Appendix A

Other Web Resources

Following are some of the best resources for more information on SAP, BAPIs, or Java.

More Information on BAPIs and SAP

The world of BAPIs is changing very quickly, and SAP, along with third-party vendors, is changing the BAPI landscape nearly every day. One of the best ways to keep up with the latest information is through the Internet and technical magazines.

SAP's BAPI Network Home Page

www.sap.com/products/techno/bapis/bapi.htm

This site contains many documents related to BAPIs, including introductory and advanced material on writing and using BAPIs. While here, sign up for the OPEN BAPI network. This network will put you on a mailing list that focuses on events occuring in the SAP BAPI world.

SAP Tech Journal

www.saptechjournal.com

This quarterly magazine from SAP Labs and Miller Freeman Inc. contains a great deal of high-quality technical information on both SAP and BAPIs.

SAP Labs

www.saplabs.com

The SAP Labs site contains many useful utilities, along with the current version of ITS (*Internet Transaction Server*) and Web Studio.

SAP FAQ

www.sapfaq.com

Here you will find very good overall information on SAP and links to many other sites. Topics covered include basic information on SAP, information on R/2 and R/3, book reviews, user groups, and training.

ERPSuperSite

www.erpsupersite.com

Although not specifically for SAP, the ERP SuperSite has information on ERP (*Engineering Resource Planning*) software, its latest features, and loads of links to related articles.

SAP Info

www.sapinfo.com

This Web site provides plenty of information on SAP, both in the way of forums and mailing lists. It also contains basic information on SAP and book reviews.

Resources for Java/HTML/XML

The following are resources for Java, HTML, XML, and other Internet-related resources.

WWW Consortium

www.w3.org

The home page for the WWW consortium contains many useful links, including references to the current and proposed HTML standards.

www.w3.org/XML

The WWW consortium defines the standards for XML. This URL points to the page where you will find the current standards, proposals for new standards, and examples.

Sun

www.sun.com

Sun Corporation is where Java started, and here you will find compilers and loads of documentation and examples.

IBM

www.IBM.com

Here you can find useful documents and free Java applications such as VisualAge for Java, IBM WebSphere Application Server. This software can be deployed across the e-business application framework and turns ordinary Web sites into Java-enabled application servers.

Microsoft

www.microsoft.com

Microsoft is a major player in the Internet as well as Java development, and its Web site has many good resources.

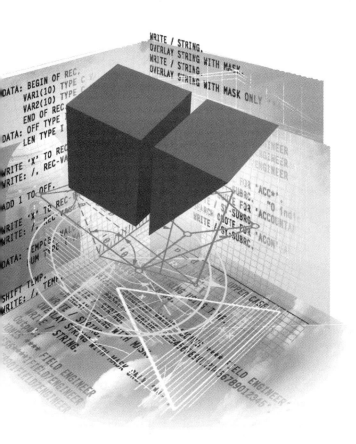

Appendix B

Basic HTML Reference

HTML (*Hypertext Markup Language*) is the text-formatting language of the Web. This appendix explains to the beginning HTML user how the language works, and provides the basic syntax for the most commonly used commands as of version 4.0. HTML and the Web are evolving at a rapid rate, so a good way to get the latest information on them is from the WWW Consortium, which can be found at www.w3.org.

The quick evolution of this language as well as small differences in the way various browsers handle HTML commands can pose a problem for HTML page developers. This appendix attempts to be browser neutral. When developing your HTML pages, you should understand what kind of browser your audience will be using. If your Web page is going to be accessed inside a company that only uses brand XYZ browser, then you can safely use HTML commands specifically for that browser. If, however, your page will be accessed on the Internet, you must try to keep your HTML as generic as possible. You can test your HTML screens for compliance to the HTML standards by going to the W3C HTML Validation Service Web site at validator.w3.org.

Basics

The HTML language comprises elements and attributes to these elements. Some elements require both a start and an end tag, whereas others require only one tag.

 NOTE

This appendix assumes that anything enclosed in angle brackets in HTML is a *tag* and that an *element* is all the tags associated with a command.

An example of a typical HTML element follows.

```
<ELEMENT Attribute1="value" Attribute2="value">
text or other elements
</ELEMENT>
```

HTML elements may be contained within each other, but the closing tags must appear in the reverse order from the starting tags. Thus <A><B> . . . </B></A> is valid, but <A><B> . . . </A></B> would result in a syntax error.

Spaces are important in the HTML language. In general, HTML condenses all consecutive white spaces into a single white space. Also, in starting tags for elements, the element name must immediately follow the opening angle bracket (<). HTML is not case sensitive.

 NOTE

Many HTML programmers and even some HTML authoring tools leave off the closing tag on some elements. They assume, for instance, that when the browser finds a <P> (for *new paragraph*), it will know that the preceding paragraph has come to an end. But with the HTML language becoming more verbose, some browsers are becoming sensitive to the closing tag; therefore, it is a good idea to use closing tags regularly.

HTML Document Structure

The general structure of an HTML document is as follows:

```
<html>
<head>
Head elements
</head>
<body>
Body Elements
</body>
</html>
```

Head Elements

Head elements define characteristics for the entire document. The order of the elements does not matter because information contained in the head is not displayed as part of the document itself.

Base Element

The <BASE> element sets the base URL for the document. Partial URLs in the document are resolved by using this base address. The attribute is HREF and is used in the following fashion:

```
<base href=http://www.myworld.com/dir/>
```

Title Element

Each HTML document must have a title element. The text between the start and end tags is usually displayed in the browser's window header.

```
<title>Test HTML Title</title>
```

Style Element

The <STYLE> element provides style information, such as font, alignment, and color, and controls the presentation of documents. Style information can be specified for individual elements or groups of elements, and can be defined in the HTML document or in an external style sheet. Prior to version 4.0 of HTML, attributes associated with different objects controlled presentation style. Because some Internet users may not have upgraded their browsers to take advantage of HTML 4.0, many HTML documents still do not use the <STYLE> element. The attributes for this element are as follows:

- ◆ **Type**. The language of the style sheet. The style sheet language is specified as a content type (for example, text/css). Authors must supply a value for this attribute; there is no default value for this attribute.
- ◆ **Media**. This attribute defines the intended destination medium for the style information. The default value is "screen".

This appendix does not cover the Style scripting language, which is independent of the HTML language. The following example shows how to force a border around every <H1> element in the document and center it on the page. For more information on this subject, please refer to www.w3.org or to one of the many HTML/CGI/Scripting books that are available.

```
<head>
<style type="text/css">
```

```
H1 {border-width: 1 border: solid; text-align: center}
</style>
</head>
```

META Element

The <META> element allows the definition of data about the HTML document. Some things that can be defined include author, keywords, and expiration date. More than one <META> element is allowed in an HTML document. The attributes of the <META> element are as follows:

- **Name.** The name of the property to be assigned (sometimes the attribute http-equiv is used in place of Name). One common name is "Author."

- **Content.** The value to be assigned to the name specified in the same element declaration.

```
<meta name="Expires" content="Sun, 05 Jun 1999 15:00:00 GMT">
<meta name="keywords" content="Java, SAP, HTML">
```

Body Element Attributes

The general format for the Body element is as follows:

```
<body background="URL" bgcolor="color" link="color" vlink="color"
text="color"> . . . </body>
```

The background URL displays an image as a background for the HTML page. The other attributes define the color (see the "Color Attributes" section later in this appendix). bgcolor is the background color, link is the color of an unvisited link, vlink is the color of a visited link, and text is the default color for the text within the document.

Body Elements

Body elements define and format the contents of the document, including text formatting, links, and importing graphics into the document.

Anchor Element

Links on Web pages are called *anchors* and enable the reader to move from one page to another. The general format for the anchor element is

```
<a HREF="URL" NAME="NAME1" TARGET="TARGET1"> text </a>
```

If the HREF attribute is used, the "URL" can be any valid URL, including images, other HTML documents, telnet, or FTP sites. If the NAME attribute is used, then "NAME1" allows this anchor to be the target of a link. For example, if the element

```
<a NAME="CHAPTER1">The First Chapter</a>
```

is located in a file labeled document.html, it can be accessed from an anchor (in or out of this document) as follows:

```
< HREF="document.html#CHAPTER1">Go to Chapter 1</a>
```

The target attribute indicates where the new data is to be displayed. If it is not defined, then the current browser window is overwritten. Other values can be

- **_blank**. Displays the new document in a new window.
- **_name**. Displays the new document in a frame (with the matching name attribute).
- **_self**. Overwrites the contents of the current window.
- **_parent**. Displays the new document in the parent window (if no parent, this value is the same as _self).
- **_top**. Displays the new document in the entire window (disregards frames).

General Text-Formatting Elements

The following elements are used for text formatting. Note that different browsers may display these elements with slight variations.

...	Use bold font.
<big>...</big>	Use big font.
<i>...</i>	Display text in italics.
<strike>...</strike>	Strikethrough text.
_{...}	Subscript text.

^{. . .}	Superscript text.
<u>. . .</u>	Underline text.
. . .	Emphasize text.
<font color="color" size="size"> . . . </font>	Color and size of font (color is detailed in the next section); size "1" for small through "7" for large.
<blockquote>. . .</blockquote>	Format extended quotations. Typically, browsers provide extra indentation on both sides and highlight the text.
<center> . . . </center>	Center text.
<code> . . . </code>	Separate a computer listing from the rest of the document. Typically monospaced.

Color Attribute

Color in HTML pages can be achieved using either an RGB value or a standard English color name as an attribute for various elements. Examples of elements where color can be specified are <body bkcolor="color"> and <font color="color">. The RGB value is represented as #XXYYZZ, where XX, YY, and ZZ represent a hexadecimal value for red, green, and blue, respectively. A value of 00 indicates none of the color, whereas FF indicates full intensity of the color.

The standard English colors, along with their equivalent RGB values, are as follows:

Red	#FF0000
Orange	#FFA500
Yellow	#FFFF00
Green	#00FF00
Blue	#0000FF
Indigo	#8A2BE2
Violet	#EE82EE
Brown	#A52A2A
Black	#000001
White	#FFFFFF

Hierarchy Header Elements

HTML contains six elements with which you can create a hierarchy within a document. The elements are named <h1> through <h6> and have ending tags (that is, <h1> . . . </h1>). The top level is <h1>.

 NOTE

These header elements should not be used for general text sizing. For that, use the font element mentioned in the "General Text-Formatting Elements" section.

Image Element

To add any kind of graphical content to a page, you need to use the <IMG> element. The following is the general form of the <IMG> element:

```
<img src="URL" align="POS" border="size" height="size" width="size" alt="text" >
```

The src attribute points to the URL of the graphic image to be displayed. The graphic image can be anything that the browser supports. Typical formats include .gif, .jpg, and .avi. The align attribute can have the value of top, middle, bottom, right, or left. The border, height, and width attributes can be assigned values, which are measured in pixels. The last attribute, alt, is used for browsers that do not display graphics; instead, the text string is shown.

Separators

The basic elements that HTML provides to separate sections of text are as follows:

◆ **
** New line.

◆ **<hr>** New line plus place a horizontal line on the document. Attributes that can be used with the <hr> element are align, color, width, and size.

◆ **<p> ... </p>** Starts a new paragraph. Usually the browser inserts a blank line between paragraphs.

Lists

HTML enables you to display several types of lists, including ordered, unordered, menu, and definition.

- **<hl> ... </hl>** Displays the list header text.
- **<li> ... </li>** Displays an item within an ordered, unordered, or menu list.
- **<ol> ... </ol>** Displays ordered lists. Basic attributes for this element are start and type. Type values for the <ol> element are A (uppercase), a (lowercase), I (large Roman numerals), i (small Roman numerals), and 1 (numbers).

```
<ol start="5" type="1">
<li>Item 5</li>
<li>Item 6</li>
</ol>
```

- **<ul> ... </ul>** Displays unordered lists such as bulleted lists. The <ul> element has the attribute type, which can have the values circle, disc, and square.
- **<dl> ... </dl>** Displays definitions. Elements that are used with <dl> are <dt></dt> and <dd></dd>, which contain the definition term and the definition itself, as shown here:

```
<hl>Definitions</hl>
<dl>
<dt>term1</dt><dd>Definition 1</dd>
<dt>term2</dt><dd>Definition 2</dd>
</dl>
```

Tables

The <TABLE> element is very useful for organizing data within a page in a grid pattern. Other elements, <TR>, <TD>, <TH>, and <CAPTION>, are used with the <TABLE> element to define the headers, rows, and data portions of the table.

```
<table>
<caption> . . . </caption>
<tr><th> . . .</th> . . . </tr>
```

```
<tr><td> . . .</td> . . . </tr>
</table>
```

The attributes of the <TABLE> element are shown in the following list. See the end of this appendix for an example of how the <TABLE> element is used.

- ◆ **ALIGN**. Controls the alignment of the entire table on the HTML page. Valid values include left, center, and right.
- ◆ **BGCOLOR**. Controls the background color for the entire table.
- ◆ **BORDER**. Controls the width of the border around the table. If this value is 0 or the attribute is missing, the table will have no borders.

Caption Element

The <CAPTION> element labels a table. Its align attribute can have the values of left, right, top, or bottom.

Table Row Elements

The <TR> element indicates to the browser that a new row in the table has started. The attributes of the <TR> element apply as defaults for the whole table row; they are align and valign.

- ◆ **Align**. Controls the alignment of data within each cell in the row. Valid values include left, center, right, and decimal.
- ◆ **Valign**. Controls the vertical alignment of material within the cell. Valid values include top, middle, and bottom.

Table Header and Table Data Elements

The <TH> element provides column headings. Browsers typically make the font for the column headings a bit bigger and put them in a bold typeface. The <TD> element populates the data in a single cell in the table.

Both of these elements have the same basic attributes:

- ◆ **Align**. Controls the alignment of data within each cell in the row. Valid values include left, center, right, and decimal.
- ◆ **Valign**. Controls the vertical alignment of material within the cell. Valid values include top, middle, and bottom.

◆ **Colspan**. Specifies the number of columns the cell spans.

◆ **Rowspan**. Specifies the number of rows the cell spans.

◆ **Nowrap**. Indicates to the browser not to wrap the text in the cell.

Form Element

The <FORM> element is basically used to coordinate the retrieval of input data and send it to the appropriate place, such as a server, through a CGI (*Common Gateway Interface*). A Web page can contain many <FORM> elements, but you cannot nest them. A generic <FORM> element can look like this:

```
<form action="url" method="method" enctype="XX">

. . .

Data Input elements

. . .

</form>
```

The attributes for the <FORM> element are as follows:

◆ **Action**. Specifies the destination of the input. This attribute can be as simple as a mail address, but usually points to a server-based script.

◆ **Method**. Has two possible values: Get and Post. Get builds up a URL with the contents of the input fields that have values (and *all* hidden input fields) and sends it to the destination specified by the action attribute. Post sends the data directly to the URL specified in the action attribute.

◆ **Enctype**. Defines the encoding method for the data; the default is URLENCODED (that is, the data is embedded in the URL).

Input Element

The <INPUT> element represents a field that the user can edit. The major attributes for this element are listed below, and most of these attributes are used in the example at the end of this appendix.

◆ **Type**. Defines the type of input area desired. Possible values are Button, Checkbox, Text, Radio, Submit, Reset, Hidden, Password, Image, and Textarea.

- **Align**. Used with images to define the location of the image. Possible values are top, bottom, middle, right, left.
- **Checked**. Applies to radio buttons and check boxes and indicates that the field is selected.
- **Maxlength**. Defines the maximum amount of data for text fields.
- **Name**. Specifies the name of the input field. Used when the data is transferred from the page, such as ITS (*Internet Transaction Server*) with SAP.
- **Size**. Specifies the visible size of the text input field.
- **SRC**. Contains the URL of the image if the input field is of type IMAGE.
- **Value**. Specifies the default value of the <INPUT> element.

Select Element

The <SELECT> element allows the user to select from a list of text choices. This element has the following attributes:

- **Multiple**. Allows the user to select more than one choice.
- **Name**. Specifies the name of the field, and is used when the data is transferred from the page to an application like ITS.
- **Size**. Specifies the number of visible choices.

Option Element

The <OPTION> element is used only within the <SELECT> element, and specifies one of the possible values to be selected. This element has the following attributes:

- **Selected**. Indicates that this value is a default value.
- **Value**. Specifies the value to be sent to the CGI script when the page is submitted.

The following example uses both the <SELECT> and <OPTION> elements.

```
<select name="fieldname">
<option value="1">First</option>
<option value="2" selected>Second</option>
<option value="3">Third</option>
</select>
```

Textarea Element

A <TEXTAREA> element is a multiline input text area. This element has the following attributes:

- **Rows**. Specifies the number of visible rows on the page.
- **Cols**. Specifies the number of visible columns on the page.
- **Wrap**. Determines how text wrapping is handled. A value of "OFF" indicates no wrapping. "Virtual" indicates that the long lines are wrapped on the page but are sent as one long line when the data is transferred to the CGI script. "Physical" indicates that long lines are wrapped and are also sent this way to the CGI script.

Java Applets

Java applets can be included within HTML by using the <APPLET> element. The attributes for this element are as follows:

- **Codebase**. Contains the URL that is the base for the code directory.
- **Code**. Contains the URL for the location of the applet code.
- **Alt**. If a browser does not support applets, the text assigned to this attribute is displayed.
- **Name**. Specifies the name of the applet.
- **Align**. Specifies the text alignment of the applet. Valid values include left, right, top, middle, and bottom.
- **Vspace, Hspace**. Allow for offsets of the initial applet area.
- **Width, Height**. Give the initial size (in pixels) of the applet display area, not counting any windows or dialog boxes that the applet brings up.
- **<Parm> Element**. Provides the means to pass parameters to the applet. The attributes for this element are simply NAME and VALUE, which correspond to the name of the parameter and the value to be passed in.

Frames

Frames are a way to break the Web page into areas that can be separately updated. The frame feature requires the elements <FRAMESET>, <FRAME>, and <NOFRAMES>. The concept of frames is a little more difficult to grasp than the rest of HTML, and functions like refreshing of screens or printing can prove troublesome for the user.

Frameset Element

Basically the <FRAMESET> element replaces the <BODY> element in the standard <HTML> file. This element has two main attributes, Rows and Cols, and they are mutually exclusive (you cannot define both attributes for the same <FRAMESET> element).

The values of the Rows or Cols attributes are separated by commas and can be in pixels or percentage of the total browser window space. For example, rows="100,150,80" defines three frames with heights of 100, 150, and 80 pixels, respectively, within the browser window. If the browser's window has more or fewer pixels, it will figure out the ratios to provide the specified appearance. Percentage of window is indicated by simply adding a percent sign (%) behind each number (rows="70%,30%").

Framesets can be nested within one other; thus if we want two rows of three frames each (a total of six separately updateable areas on the browser), the HTML for the main file would look something like this:

```
<!-File: main.html ‡
<html>
<title>MAIN.HTML</title>
<frameset rows="50%,50%"> <!-two rows ‡
    <frameset cols="33%,33%,33%"> <!-3 cols, top row ‡
        <frame src="green.html" name="green">
        <frame src="red.html" name="red">
        <frame src="blue.html" name="blue">
    </frameset>
    <frameset cols="33%,33%,33%"> <!-3 cols, bottom row ‡
        <frame src="yellow.html" name="yellow">
        <frame src="white.html" name="white">
        <frame src="orange.html" name="orange">
    </frameset>
</frameset>
</html>
```

The preceding example would create a browser window with the following frames:

Green	Red	Blue
Yellow	White	Orange

The rules for figuring out which frame is going to appear where are fairly simple. Frames cannot overlap, and they are calculated from the top down and from left to right. We start from the top of the HTML code, and when we have filled up a portion of the screen, we proceed to the next.

Frame Element

The <FRAME> element defines the basic characteristics of one section of the browser window that was defined with the <FRAMESET> element. The attributes that can be applied to the <FRAME> element include the following:

- ◆ **Name**. Specifies the name of the frame, and must be unique within one HTML page. The target attribute of the anchor elements uses the name to update the data in this frame.
- ◆ **SRC**. Specifies a URL pointing to an HTML page that contains the initial contents of the frame.
- ◆ **Marginheight**. Specifies the number of pixels between frames (vertically).
- ◆ **MarginWidth**. Specifies the number of pixels between frames (horizontally).
- ◆ **Noresize**. Has no value assigned to it. If this attribute is in the <FRAME> definition, then the user will not be able to resize this frame (which can effectively stop resizing on many adjacent frames).
- ◆ **Scrolling**. Has either the value of yes (default) or no.

Noframes Element

The <NOFRAMES> element displays a screen if the browser does not support the <FRAME> element. The body statement can be used within the <NOFRAMES> element.

```
<noframes>
<body>
```

```
<p>This screen has frames which are not supported/enabled by your current brows-
er.</p>
</body>
</noframes>
```

URLS

A URL (*Uniform Resource Locator*) is an address that identifies a resource on the Internet. The general format for a URL is

```
method://server:port/path
```

Method refers to one of the rules or protocols used to retrieve or send information. Examples include http, ftp, mailto, and news.

The *server* refers to the computer on which the resource resides. The optional port parameter is used if the port number is different from that of the default for the method.

Path defines the location on the computer of the resource to which the URL is pointing.

TIP

A URL must not contain a space. If a space is required (that is, the document being accessed is My Document.txt), then a %20 (hex ASCII value for space) can be placed in the URL as shown here:

```
http://www.test.com/My%20Document.txt
```

Special Characters

You can use various special characters in an HTML document to print special character strings.

For example, the string <HTML> would print <HTML> on the HTML page. A selection of special HTML characters follows.

Special HTML Characters

Character	Meaning
&lt;	<
&gt;	>
&amp;	&
&quot;	"
	nonbreaking space
&reg;	®, registered symbol
&copy;	©, copyright symbol

International Aspects of HTML

One of the major enhancements in HTML 4.0 versus 3.2 is the improved ability to make documents valid in different languages. The two attributes that can be used are lang and dir. The lang attribute defines the language, and dir defines the direction of the text flow. These attributes are on all relevant elements. More information, including a complete list of language and direction codes, is available at www.w3.org.

```
<!—U.S. English keywords —>
<meta name="keywords" lang="en-us" content="color">
<!—Canadian English keywords —>
<meta name="keywords" lang="en" content="colour">
```

Comments

Comments are text that you want to include in the HTML document but that you do not display on the page. You can add a comment to any HTML document by using the following format:

```
<!—your comment here—>
```

Comments should not be nested and should not span multiple lines.

Sample HTML Document

The following sample outlines many of the features discussed in this appendix. This example consists of three files; the first (main.htm) contains a <FRAMESET> element that points to the two other files (form1.htm) and (form2.htm). The output of this example can be seen in Figure B.1.

MAIN.HTM

```
<!— Main HTML page. Simply contains two frames —>
<html>
<head>
<title>Example HTML page</title>
</head>
<frameset rows=40%,60%> <!— 2 rows —>
    <frame src="form1.htm" name="form1">
    <frame src="form2.htm" name="form2">
</frameset>
<!— Put in a NOFRAMES element just in case —>
<noframes>
<body>
<p>This screen has frames that are not supported/enabled by your current brows-
er.</p>
</body>
</noframes>
</html>
```

FORM1.HTM

```
<html>
<body>
<h1>This is frame #1</h1>
<table> <!— use of table just to format data, no borders, 1 row —>
<tr><td>
<i>An example of an order list</i>
<br><ol start="1" type="1">
<li>Item 1</li>
<li>Item 2</li>
```

```
</ol>
</td>
<td align="right">
<form method="post" action="mailto://kenkroes@bigfoot.com">
Textarea input box
<br><textarea rows="3" cols="30">Default text for text area</textarea>
</form>
</td>
</table>
</body>
</html>
```

FORM2.HTM

```
<html>
<body>
<h1>This is frame #2 </h1>
<table border>
<caption align="top">Table 1 Caption</caption>
<tr> <!— 1st row wil be a header —>
<th align="center">Column 1 from Table 1</th>
<th align="center">Column 2 from Table 2</th>
</tr>
<tr> <!— 2nd row of table —>
<td> <!— 1st column of table —>
<Ul type="circle">
<li>1st bullet</li>
<li>2nd bullet</li>
</ul>

</td>
<td> <!— 2nd column of table —>
<form method="post" action="mailto://kenkroes@bigfoot.com">
Text Input <input type="text" name="textinput1" value="default text" size="20">
<br>Sample Select Box
<select name="selectinput1">
<option value="1">First Option
<option value="2">Second Option
```

```
<option value="D" selected>Default
</select>
<p><input type="submit" value="Submit">
<input type="reset"value="Reset"></p>
</form>
</td></tr>
</table>
</body>
</html>
```

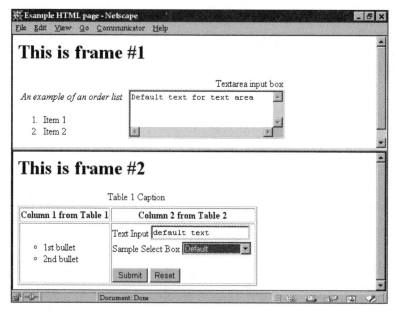

FIGURE B.1 *A sample HTML page*

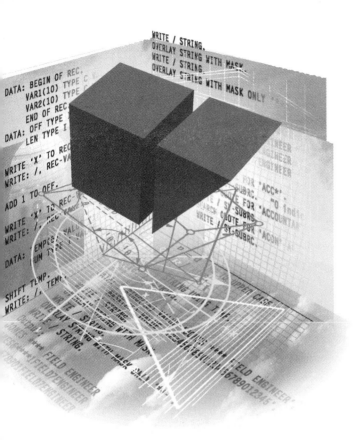

Appendix C

ABAP/4 Data Types to Java Cross-Reference

Data Types

When working with BAPIs or RFCs from an SAP environment, you must be able to both interpret the various types of data that can be returned and convert your variables into these types (for example, numeric, packed, or character). The following table shows the mapping between ABAP and Java data types.

ABAP Data Type	Java Equivalent
CHAR	java.lang.String
INT4	java.math.BigInteger
INT2	java.math.BigInteger
INT1	java.math.BigInteger
NUMC	java.math.BigInteger
PACK	java.math.BigDecimal
LANG	java.lang.String
CURR	java.math.BigDecimal
CUKY	java.lang.String
DATS	java.lang.String
UNIT	java.lang.String
TIMS	java.lang.String
DEC	java.math.BigDecimal
QUAN	java.math.BigDecimal
ACCP	java.lang.String
CLNT	java.lang.String
FLTP	java.math.BigDecimal
RAW	byte[]

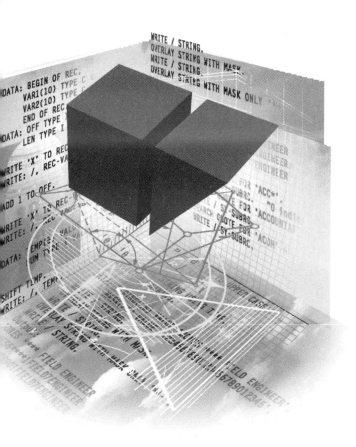

Appendix D

**Using Sun's
Java Compiler**

The Java examples in the body of this book are compiled using Microsoft's Java compiler. Another popular Java compiler, Java 2 SDK (*Software Development Kit*), is available from Sun Microsystems. This appendix explains how to obtain, install, and use the Java 2 SDK compiler, and it also demonstrates some of the other Java resources that are available from Sun. If you are going to use the Java SDK, you may also want to install a DOS command line replacement. There are several shareware and freeware versions available that have features (for example, a vertical scroll bar) that make running the Java SDK commands easier.

Sun's Java History

In the beginning of this book we talked briefly about the history of the Java language, but we did not cover how it was conceptualized and some of the interesting history of the language, before it was named Java. Sun released the Java language on May 23, 1995. The real development of the language started back in 1991, when Sun instructed a group of developers to create the next wave in computing. The team, nicknamed the "Green Project," developed a hand-held device called the *7 (Star Seven), which controlled a wide range of entertainment platforms and appliances. During the development of the *7, the design team came up with a processor-independent programming language, which they initially named Oak.

The design team first envisioned the *7 as a prototype for interactive television, but the television market was not yet ready for this technology. At the same time, the new concept of a public internet was starting to gain popularity, and the two technologies were a perfect match. The first Web browser was called Mosaic (developed by the National Center of Supercomputing Applications at the University of Illinois), and it allowed easy use of graphics for Internet sites. The Sun development team started to work on a Java clone of Mosaic, which they named WebRunner (see Figure D.1). WebRunner was later renamed HotJava Browser (see Figure D.2).

Amazingly, WebRunner was still being developed in 1994, and by the spring of 1995, Java was being incorporated into Netscape, which was the most popular

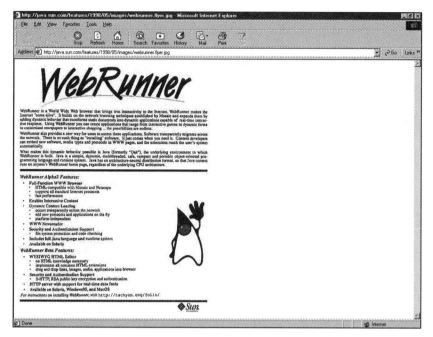

FIGURE D.1 *A flier for WebRunner*

Web browser at that time. The Java language is still less than 10 years old, and it is one of the dominant languages in the marketplace. One of the reasons for the success of this language is that the source code is free. Providing the programming language documentation, compiler, run-time environment, and so on for free allowed people to try out the software and find most of the critical bugs quickly.

Sun's Java division now employs more than 1000 people, and downloads of the JDK from Sun's Web site number over 10,000 a day. More than 15,000 developers attended the JavaOne programming conference, the largest turnout ever for a single programming development conference.

Installing the Java 2 SDK

The latest version of the Java development package is available through Sun's Java Web site at java.sun.com (see Figure D.3).

FIGURE D.2 *A Java headline in the San Jose Mercury News (March 23, 1995)*

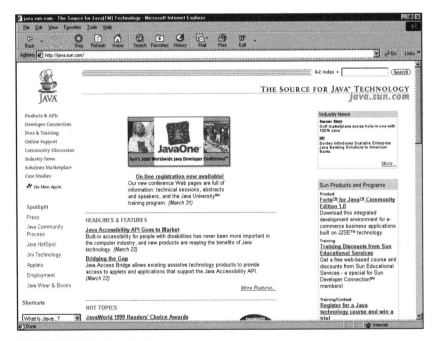

FIGURE D.3 *Sun's main Java page*

Though the content and format of this Web page change regularly, there are always several links to the Developer Connection page. To enter this page, you must register with your name and address, along with a few other pieces of information. Membership is free and provides you with a wide range of services to help you develop your Java skills. These services include access to the JDK, developer and discussion forums, technical support information, and training. Once you have registered, you should see a screen similar to the one shown in Figure D.4.

On the Developer Connection page, you can click on the Products & APIs link, which will take you to a listing of products that Sun offers. From there, you can click on a link to the latest version of the Java SDK (see Figure D.5).

Once you have selected the Java SDK link, you can choose the version and your preferred download method, then download the software to your computer. The current version of the SDK is about 30 megabytes (MB) in size for the download file (this is just the download file size, not the required installation size). The minimum system requirements for the PC version of the Java 2 SDK are a 166 megahertz (MHz) Pentium processor, 48MB of RAM, and 65MB of free disk space.

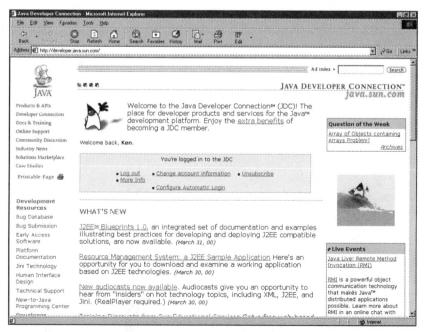

FIGURE D.4 *The Java Developer Connection page from Sun*

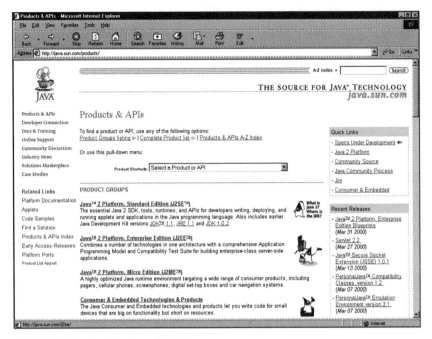

FIGURE D.5 *Sun's Products & APIs page*

TIP

You'll need 185MB of free disk space if you plan to install the separate documentation bundle in addition to the Java 2 SDK. I highly recommend downloading and installing the documentation bundle.

After the file(s) have been downloaded, you will want to print out the installation instructions specific to the version of SDK that you are installing. See Figure D.6 for an example of the installation instructions for the Java 2 SDK.

The file that you download to your computer is executable. When you are ready to install the package, close down all other Windows-based programs and start the executable file (see Figure D.7). You will then be prompted for the installation directory and given a choice of general components to install (see Figure D.8).

After the installation of the program files is complete, you can delete the initial downloaded file; doing so saves space on your hard drive. The next step is to set up your path variable. This process depends on your operating system; Windows

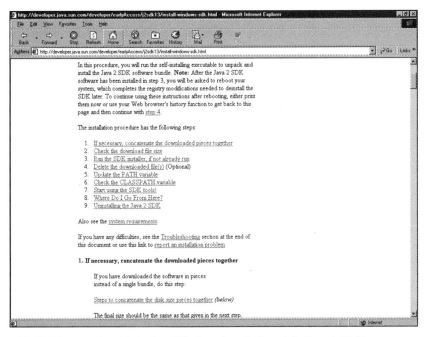

FIGURE D.6 *A list of links for a Windows installation of the Java 2 SDK*

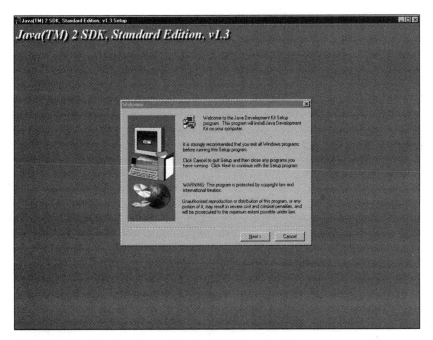

FIGURE D.7 *The first screen of the Java SDK installation process*

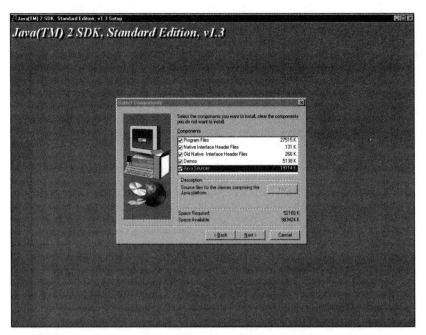

FIGURE D.8 *The component selection during the installation process*

2000 differs from Windows 95/98. Setting the path is optional, but if you want the ability to easily use the compiler and run-time environment from any directory, it is a good idea to set the path. The CLASSPATH system variable should also be set at this time. When you install the SAP Java RFC package, it will set the CLASSPATH environment variable. You should change this so that your CLASSPATH variable also points to your current directory, as shown in Figure D.9. The best way to set your CLASSPATH variable is through the classpath switch, which you can set when you run your Java programs. You will find more information on this later, in the "'Hello World' Example" section.

The installation of the documentation bundle is quite simple. The file that you download from the Sun Web site is a zipped file. There are several products on the market that you can use to extract the files; one of these is Winzip, which is available at www.winzip.com. Extract the files from the zipped file and place them in a newly created subdirectory under the directory where you installed the Java SDK. Call this subdirectory *docs*, or something similar. If you have not changed the default path during the installation of the Java SDK, you should have a directory something like c:\jdk1.3\. When you extract the documentation bundle, its default

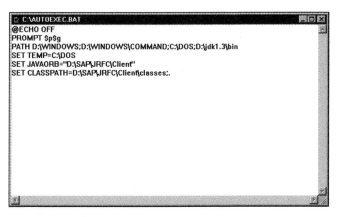

FIGURE D.9 *The autoexec.bat file from the Windows 98 operating system, using the sysedit tool*

path will be c:\jdk1.3\docs. The final directory structure for both the Java SDK and the documentation bundle should look similar to the one in Figure D.10.

 TIP

When you are finished with the installation of the Java SDK and documentation bundle, you must make sure that the directory structure looks like the one in Figure D.10. If you do not set it up this way, the hyperlinks in the documentation will not work correctly.

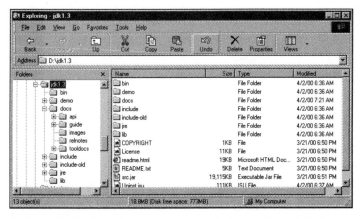

FIGURE D.10 *The directory structure of the Java SDK and the documentation bundle*

You can delete the documentation bundle's zipped file when you are finished. You can view the documentation by opening the HTML page jdk1.3/docs/index.html.

The final step of the installation process is to reboot your computer. This will set up the paths and classpaths correctly if you modified them.

This should complete the installation process for both the Java SDK and the documentation bundle. It is a very simple procedure, but it's a bit time-consuming, because of the need to download very large files from Sun's Web site. Even with a DSL connection, the download process takes about 20 minutes, and the rest of the installation should take about 15 minutes.

The next section will take you through a couple of simple examples, so that you can test out both the compiler and the run-time environment. The documentation bundle also contains many examples and a great deal of other helpful information.

"Hello World" Example

To test the Java SDK compiler, you can develop a small stand-alone application that will simply print a character string to the screen. Traditionally, the "Hello World" string is used for this simple test; the sample code for this test follows. Enter it using any standard text editor, and save it under the file name jsape1.java.

```
/**
 * This class implements an application that simply displays
 * "Hello World!" to the screen
 */
public class jsape1
{
public static void main(String[] args)
        {
          System.out.println("Hello World!");
          }
}
```

To compile this program, open up a DOS window and type in the following command.

```
javac jsape1.java
```

You can then run your program by typing in:

```
java jsape1
```

The compilation and execution of this example is shown in Figure D.11.

If you encounter a problem with the compilation step, carefully review the code and ensure that you typed it in exactly as it is shown. If you get a "Command not found" error, then you probably do not have your path set up correctly; check the "Installing the Java 2 SDK" section earlier in this chapter to make sure that it is set correctly.

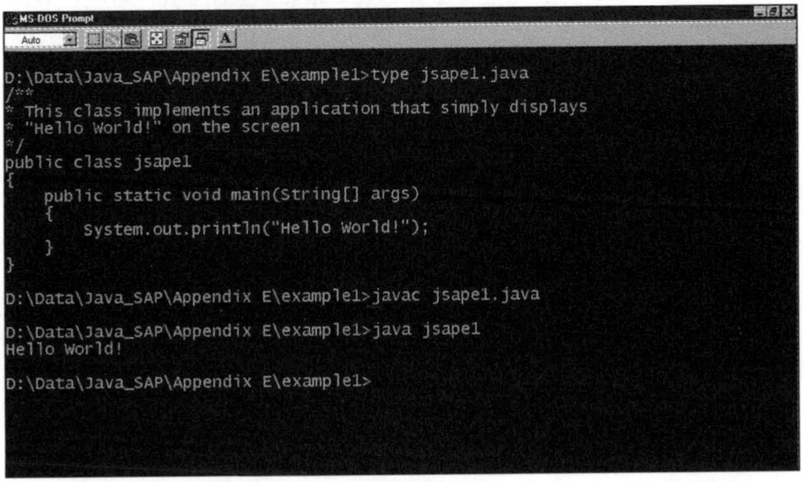

FIGURE D.11 *The compilation of the jsape1.java "Hello World" example*

Components of the Java 2 SDK

The Java 2 SDK comes with a robust set of tools and utilities to help you quickly write and test your Java applications. This section contains a brief summary of each of these tools; more details on each of them can be found in the documentation bundle.

java

This is the launcher or virtual machine for programs written in Java. This tool reads in the pseudo-code defined in the class, translates it to machine and operating-specific instructions, and then executes these instructions. The general format for the command is as follows:

```
java [options] class [arguments]
java [options] -jar file.jar [arguments]
```

The –jar option executes a program from a jar archive. The most commonly used option is the –cp (or classpath) option, which defines the path that is used to search for classes when the program is executing. Classpaths can contain many different search directories, all separated by semicolons. Classpaths can also contain directories of class files and the location of jar and zip files that contain supporting classes for your program.

A short help list can be obtained at any time by typing **java -?**.

NOTE

javaw is a command that works the same as the java command, with the exception that no console window appears unless there is a problem in the program's execution.

javac

This command is used to compile Java programs from text files containing Java commands into the pseudo-code contained in class files. The general format for the command is as follows:

```
javac [options] [source files] [@filelist]
```

If you only have a few files to compile, you can list them directly in the javac command as source files. If you have a large number of files to compile, you can create a list of them in a separate file and pass this single file name to javac with a preceding @ character.

The most commonly used option is the classpath option, which overrides the environment CLASSPATH variable.

javadoc

This command reads in Java source files and produces output in the format of HTML. This output contains the comments and general information about the class, including public and protected classes, methods, and fields. The general format for the command is:

```
javadoc [options] [list of java packages] [list of source files] [@file containing
a list of file names]
```

The options for this command are numerous and can be viewed in the documentation bundle; in general, they control the content and format of HTML pages.

An example of the javadoc command can be performed on the simple "Hello World" program that we tested earlier. The command can be as simple as javadoc jsape1.java. The javadoc output and an example of the main index HTML are shown in Figures D.12 and D.13.

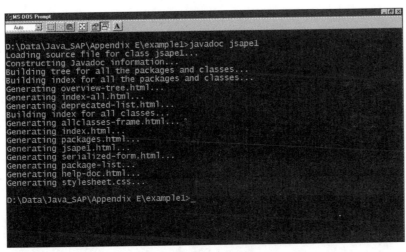

FIGURE D.12 *The output of the javadoc command, showing the list of generated HTML files*

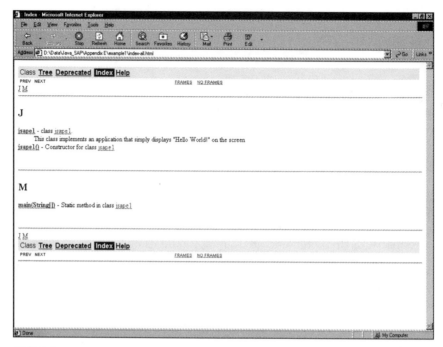

FIGURE D.13 *An example of the index-all.html page generated for the jsape1 example*

jar

This command works much like the popular Windows zip command, taking multiple source files and compressing them into a single jar file. In fact, jar actually uses the zip compression format.

 NOTE

You may be wondering why Java uses a separate compression tool instead of using zipped files. The reason is that an applet can download a single jar file, which can contain many classes, in a single HTTP command. Generally, this is not done with zipped files. Also, having all of the classes brought over in a single HTTP command reduces the overhead dramatically, when compared to retrieving each class on its own. Lastly, using this compression tool also speeds up the execution of the applet.

The general format for the jar command is as follows:

```
jar [options] [manifest] destination input-files
```

The two most commonly used options are the c option (for creating a jar) and the u option (for updating an existing jar). An example of a typical jar command follows:

```
jar cmf testjar *.class
```

The optional manifest parameter is the place in which we hold information about the jar file (metadata). This information includes both data control and version data.

javah

The javah command generates both the C header and C source files from a Java class. You can use this command to tie together Java and C applications.

The general format of the javah command is as follows:

```
javah [options] class
```

The location of the class must be fully qualified. A common option to use is the –stubs option, which triggers the creation of the source files (without it, only the header files are created). To generate C source code stubs, you must also use the –old option to disable the default –jni option (*Java Native Interface*). A complete list of options can be found in the documentation bundle.

javap

The javap command is used to disassemble a class file into a listing of packages, fields, and methods. The general format for the command is:

```
javap [options] class
```

The options generally control the level of output desired, and are discussed in the documentation bundle. An example of the javap command for our "Hello World" example is shown in Figure D.14.

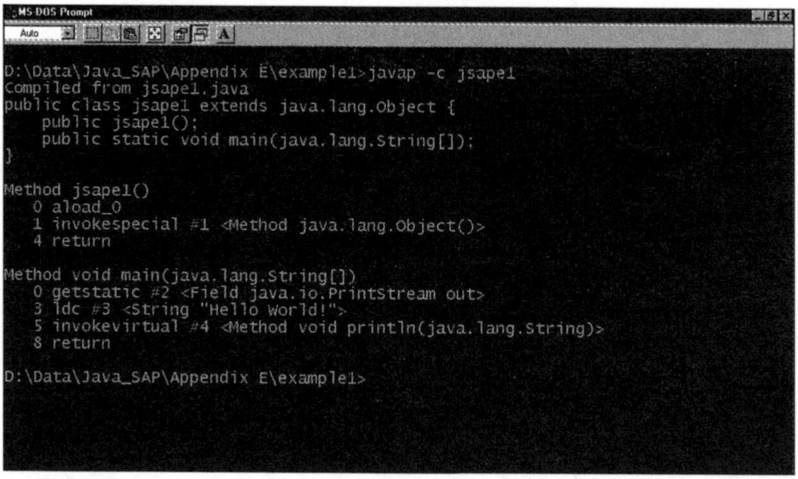

FIGURE D.14 *An example of the javap command for the jsape1 example*

appletviewer

The appletviewer command allows you to view and debug applets without using a browser. The format for the command is simply:

```
appletviewer [options] url
```

The URL of the command points to an HTML page, which will contain the applet tag. One window is brought up for each applet tag in the HTML page. Basically, the appletviewer command will ignore all HTML in the document, except for OBJECT, EMBED, or APPLET tags.

Options that are available for this command are limited to –debug, -encoding, and –J (for passing options to the Java Interpreter).

This command can be demonstrated by using an example from Chapter 10, "JavaBeans, ActiveX, Applets, and the Internet." In Chapter 10, we developed an HTML page that contained two applets. The brief HTML is reproduced here for the sake of convenience, and the result from the appletviewer command is shown in Figure D.15.

```
<!-Test HTML page for Applet communications —>
<html>
<head>
<title>Test Page for AWT Applets</title>
```

```
</head>
<body>
<applet name="Jsap1007" code="Jsap1007.class" width=400 height=200>
Java not supported with this browser
</applet>
<applet name="Jsap1008" code="Jsap1008.class" width=400 height=200>
</applet>
</body>
</html>
```

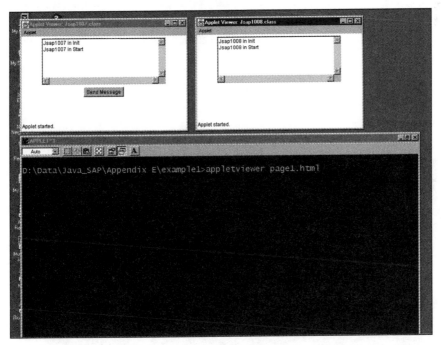

FIGURE D.15 *An example of the appletviewer command for an HTML page with two applets*

extcheck

The extcheck command checks a specified jar file for conflicts to any extensions in the Java SDK. It does so by comparing the version number in the manifest file to that of the currently installed jar files.

jdb

The jdb command allows you to debug your Java programs so you can find out exactly what your programs are doing. This is usually related to finding bugs in programs, but sometimes you simply want to see if there are ways to enhance program efficiency. You can use jdb as you would a java command, along with most of the options that are associated with it. The format for the jdb command is:

```
jdb [options] class [arguments]
```

Options that can be used (in addition to the options supported by the java command) are outlined in the documentation bundle. A commonly used option is the −launch option, which immediately launches the application upon startup of the jdb command. An example session with the -launch option is shown in Figure D.16.

The jdb command can also be used without the −launch option. When the command is used in this form, you are switched from your command window prompt to the debugger prompt. From this prompt you can execute several commands,

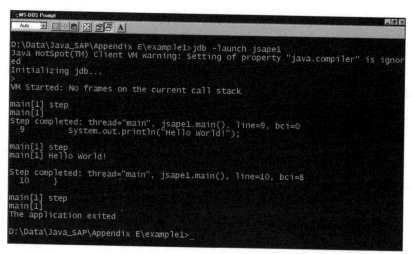

FIGURE D.16 *An example of the jdb command using the −launch option for the "Hello World" example program*

such as the step command shown in Figure D.16. Other common commands that you can enter at the debugging prompt are as follows:

- ◆ **run [class]**. Starts execution of a class.
- ◆ **help**. Displays a quick list of all commands.
- ◆ **print [expression]**. Prints the value of an expression.
- ◆ **set [lvalue] = [value]**. Sets lvalue to value.
- ◆ **stop at class:line**. Sets the breakpoint at a specific line of a source file.
- ◆ **step**. Executes the current line.
- ◆ **cont**. Continues execution.
- ◆ **exit**. Quits the debugging session.

Overall, the Java SDK provided by Sun is a very versatile product. It provides all of the tools necessary to create large Java implementations, yet is easy enough for the novice programmer to understand. Sun also provides excellent documentation, which contains many examples, as well as a helpful set of hyperlinks for easy navigation.

Glossary

Abstract Window Toolkit (AWT). A set of classes that can be used for writing GUI programs.

ActiveX. A set of technologies that enable software components to interact with one another in a networked environment, regardless of the language in which they were created. ActiveX is built on the Component Object Model (COM).

Applet. A Java program that is executed through an interpreter in a browser.

Application Programming Interfaces (APIs). The interfaces and variables that are used by a distinct unit of code. APIs can also be used to access distinct units of code.

Bean. A software object that interacts with other objects, according to a strict set of guidelines.

Business Application Programming Interface (BAPI). A standardized interface that allows both internal and external programs to access business processes and data within SAP.

Business Object Repository (BOR). A hierarchical collection of all the business functions contained within SAP.

Class. The blueprint of an object in object-oriented programming. A class contains the definition of the variables and interfaces that each object should have, along with the variables and interfaces that the class alone will have.

Client. The computer or instance that initiates communication with another computer or instance of software.

Component Object Model (COM). Codeveloped by Microsoft and Digital Equipment Corporation, COM is based on the object-oriented programming concepts. A COM object must support the IUnknown interface.

Data Encapsulation. Combining data and the functions that operate on that data into one composite type. In other words, the data and functions are packaged together in a superior and well-organized bundle (Class).

Enterprise Resource Planning (ERP). A software collection that usually encompasses the main transactions that a business performs. SAP, BAAN, Oracle, and PeopleSoft are examples of ERP software packages.

Firewall. Using a firewall is a method of restricting access both into and out of a software system.

Graphical User Interface (GUI). Software that displays and accepts input from a user.

Hypertext Markup Language (HTML). A language that is used to develop Web pages for the Internet, and for intranets.

Implementation Guide (IMG). A set of configuration steps that must be completed to implement an area of SAP functionality.

Inheritance. A method that allows one object to be created based on the properties and methods of another object.

Instantiate. To create an object from a class.

Interface. A collection of method definitions (without implementations) and constant values.

Intermediate Documents (IDoc). Structured data packets that are sent back and forth between two systems via RFCs.

Internet. A global collection of Web sites.

Internet Transaction Server (ITS). A technology developed by SAP that allows users to execute standard SAP transactions through HTML pages.

Intranet. A collection of Web sites behind a firewall, usually within one corporation.

Metadata. Data that describes how other data is defined.

Method. A piece of software that accesses and manipulates the variables of an object.

Object Linking and Embedding (OLE). Microsoft's object-based technology for sharing information and services across process and machine boundaries.

Object-Oriented Programming (OOP). A programming method that breaks down programs into sets of interacting objects. Examples of programming languages that are centered on this concept are Java and C++.

Polymorphism. The ability to decide which overload member function to invoke based on the real-time type of the object rather than the declared type of the object.

Proxy. A piece of software that acts as a go-between for two applications.

Remote Function Call (RFC). An interface or function module that can be executed on one system from a remote system.

Remote Procedure Call (RPC). A protocol for accessing procedures residing in other computers from C program environments. RPC is related to Remote Function Call (RFC).

Server. The computer or instance that receives the first communication from a client computer or instance.

Structured Query Language (SQL). Microsoft's language for defining and manipulating data.

Thread. The path that a program takes during execution. Threads include not only the program statements, but also the memory stack and register values of the program as it executes.

Transaction. A group of business steps that perform one logical business unit of work.

Uniform Resource Locator (URL). A unique string of characters that define the location of a specific document or Web site on the Internet.

Index

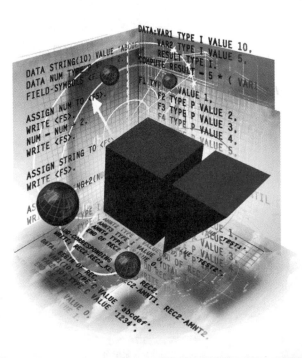